Born in Guangzhou, China, Karen Zhang is a freelance writer, columnist, translator, and blogger. Her work has appeared in various publications, including *Crazy English Speaker* and *Crazy English Teens* magazines, *Coal Hill Review*, *The Loyalhanna Review*, NolaVie of *The Times-Picayune* and *The Pittsburgh Post-Gazette*.

She received her MFA in non-fiction from Chatham University in Pittsburgh, PA. She lives in northern Virginia, USA.

Dedication

For my parents

Endorsements

"If you are simply curious about "real China", read Karen Zhang's Golden Orchid: The True Story of An Only Child in Contemporary China, the honest memoir about life and death and the cultural clash of tradition and modernity in an ordinary family in rapidly changing China…Rarely do Chinese express feelings as directly—and bravely—as Zhang does."
— Lynne Joiner, award-winning author of *Honorable Survivor: Mao's China, McCarthy's America, and the Persecution of John S. Service*

"Does anyone know the responsibility an only child must bear? Karen Zhang asks and paints a poignant and vivid picture of her life in contemporary China."
— Bapsi Sidhwa, bestselling author of *Ice Candy Man* and other novels

"A heart-felt and vivid account of growing up in China's one-child generation, with all the pain and privilege entailed."
— Mei Fong, bestselling author of *One Child: The Story of China's Most Radical Experiment*

Karen Zhang

GOLDEN ORCHID

The True Story of an Only Child in
Contemporary China

AUSTIN MACAULEY PUBLISHERS™

LONDON • CAMBRIDGE • NEW YORK • SHARJAH

A CIP catalogue record for this title is available from the British Library.

ISBN 9781787106772 (Paperback)
ISBN 9781787106789 (E-Book)

www.austinmacauley.com

First Published (2018)
Austin Macauley Publishers Ltd.
25 Canada Square
Canary Wharf
London
E14 5LQ

Acknowledgments

Writing a book is a daunting task. Writing a book in my second language is even more so. I am grateful to everyone who has given me support and guidance along the way. My thanks goes to the MFA in Creative Writing program at Chatham University, including but not limited to, Sandy Sterner for her keen observation and encouragement to extend my thesis into a book; to Marc Nieson for his expertise and inspiration; to Karen Williams for her global perspective; to Sheryl St. Germain for her vision to accept me as the first Chinese international student in the MFA program; and to the other faculty members and fellow students in the MFA community.

I am indebted to Larry Moffi, whose thoughtful reading of my manuscript helped me resolve editing issues with the book. Myrna and Howard Asher gave genuine suggestions to improve the manuscript. I also want to thank Ivy, Yin, and Connie for their sister-like friendship and love since childhood.

I appreciate Lynne Joiner for sharing a writer's woe in publishing and inspiration to defend my work as a writer. Thanks to the two hundred plus agents and publishers in the past years that have turned down my enquiry for their encouragement. David Baldacci once said, "Rejection is a badge of honor for a writer." I certainly have received a big badge which propels me to keep writing. I also want to thank Bob Balaban and Jim Laurie for providing insights on alternative publishing. Many thanks to the editors at Austin Macauley and their staff who have made my book publishing dream come true.

My greatest debt is to my parents who taught me to believe in myself and also let me understand that everybody has something that they were born to be good at. My father patiently endured many rounds of questions for my research of this book. My gratitude also goes to our family friend Mr. Liang who provided invaluable knowledge about Chinese medicine and traditional Chinese culture.

And finally, as always, to Frank and Arnold, the first and last readers.

Prologue

Chinese people often say the country is changing too quickly to adapt. The central government gives birth to all kinds of new regulations almost daily. It is exaggeration but true to its core, that a policy enacted one day, its amendments or retraction are likely to follow the next. More than thirty-five years ago, China implemented the one-child policy in an effort to curb population growth and cut family size. Every married couple, in particular in the urban areas, would have to strictly abide by the "national policy" which allowed each family to have only one child regardless of the baby's gender. Violators would face heavy punishment such as loss of employment, a hefty fine, forced sterilization or abortion, and their unlawful children would be rejected from all social welfare programs and free mandatory education.

Growing concerns about China's ageing population and shrinking labor force finally led to pressure for change. In October 2015, China ended its three decades long one-child policy, allowing married couples to have two children. The news arrived when tens of thousands of young Chinese married couples, many of whom were only children born in the post-1980s, were beginning parenthood. With the new two-child family planning policy in place, I realized the aching fact that I am one of China's first and also last one-child generation.

Just like our parents who found it difficult to talk about those tumultuous years in Red China when they starved, toiled, punished, attempted escape and survived, it would not be easy for us to explain to our children and grandchildren who may grow up with a sibling, what an only-child childhood and adulthood was like, and nor would any policy maker who set up the history-making one-child policy in 1979, have foreseen the filial burden on the one-child generation to care for their elderly parents. The controversial one-child policy is estimated to have prevented about four hundred million births over the course of three decades. And yet this figure also suggests a reason why China now faces an irreversible shortage of labor over the next thirty years.

I remember that my mother's co-workers in the timber factory in Guangzhou, China used to joke with me, hinting it would be joyous for our family if I could persuade my mother to have a little brother. At the age of four, I did not know the tough consequences adults had to face should they have more than one child. All I could grasp from my mother's stern look on her face when this question was posed was that she really needed her job. Mother would work even harder at her job without saying a word. Years later, as a grown woman, I learned from my father in private that before I was born, my mother had a miscarriage when she was pregnant with my big brother. I was saddened. My father seemed to have read my mind. He comforted me and said, "Without that episode, we wouldn't have you. You're the greatest joy in your mother's life." I fell into graver grief for my mother who had just passed on. There was no way for me to find out if my mother's silence to my question about having a little brother was solely because of her painful loss of a child, or the consequential punishment for having a second child.

Neither would matter anymore. The truth is in my parents' day, they were deprived of making choices. Their involuntary silence and submissiveness to the top-down mandates was in fact their key to survival. I am thankful to my father for not letting this pre-history of me be buried together with my mother. In the same vein, as one of China's first and last one-child generation, I shall not let my one-child story flow away with the fast-moving currents of Chinese history.

Chapter 1

The Alarming Call

It was a breezy afternoon in Guangzhou, China. The Beatles' "Yesterday" broke the silence of the editorial office. *Yesterday, all my troubles seemed so far away*...It was my cell phone's ringtone. I usually would not answer the phone until my favorite tune completed its first cycle. But that day—I remember clearly it was in October 2006—the music was unsettling, a harbinger of something I must face. I picked up the phone immediately as if my ringtone was about to become noise pollution. Off I ran to an empty conference room.

"*Wei?*" Hello? I said.

"Can you come to the First Municipal Hospital after work?" came a familiar, low male voice. He was my father.

"*Mama* is in the gastrointestinal ward on the fifth floor of the Internal Medicine Building. It's the second building on the left in the in-patient center."

"What's the matter?" My heart fluttered.

"I accompanied her to the hospital for a checkup today. The doctor suggested she stay for a thorough examination."

"Is her condition serious?" I asked, pressing the phone with my clammy hand against my ear.

"She's OK now. We'll talk about it after you get here."

Father finished the call quickly to cease my bullet-like questioning. He had always been like that. His style was to shorten every phone call or text message with me, examples of his principle of succinct speech.

Disturbed, I walked back to my desk. I glanced at my watch. It was only mid-afternoon, two more hours before getting off work. My mind raced. *What's going on with Mom? Is she in pain? How come she didn't tell me she was going to the hospital today? Can Baba manage till I see them?*

The editorial office was as quiet as a hospital. I knew I could no longer concentrate on my work after the phone call. I paid more attention to my surroundings than I normally would; the sounds of the fans humming in the computer cases, of the electric current passing through the fluorescent light, of the leaves fluttering in the breeze outside the window which became disturbingly loud.

I looked around. Most of my colleagues were women. Only three men in their twenties worked in the office. The gender composition of the staff in the editorial office overly reflected Chairman Mao's famous dictum, *"Women hold up half the sky."* That originally meant that the participation of half the society—its women—played a significant role in the emancipation of humanity. Contemporary Chinese give the maxim a further meaning—women are just as independent and important as men. My colleagues somehow were not chatty. Their lips were sealed, eyes fixed on computer screens. They worked like mute automatons in an upright sedentary position. They worked like *me*. No. I should work like them after I finished the phone call. But Father's words pulled me away from the computer screen.

* * * * * *

I am an only child born of Chinese parents. Like millions of only children who were born in the 1980s and after, I also carry an English name, Karen. The phenomenon has become so popular that many young Chinese prefer addressing one another by their English names. From Laura, Adam and Tracy to the quirky ones like Duckling, Stone, Gates and Einstein, the Chinese Echo Boomers spread their wings of imagination when it comes to their unique English names.

I did not have an English name until the fifth grade when I first studied English. I guessed my English teacher, Nancy (I forget her Chinese name), wanted us to closely experience English culture. She gave all her students English names, including me. I was named Helen, which I later changed to Karen after learning *Helen* was a common name for older women.

Every once in a while, I wondered how much English had transformed me. Since that day in elementary school, when I studied the English word: M-U-M, Mum (I learned British English as a beginner), I addressed Mother in English.

"From now on, I'm going to call you Mum. OK?" I asked when I ran into the kitchen after school.

"Umm—what is it?" Mother said immediately. She was hesitant to be called something fancy and unknown to her, especially since the pronunciation of "Mum" is similar to the Cantonese word for "muddle head."

"*Mum, mum?* You're the *m-u-m*," the muddle head, she said.

"No—it doesn't mean that. It's the English word for *Mama*."

"*Ng ho.* Mum is no good," said Mother while scooping rice from a red plastic rice pail. "*Mama* is just fine. Why bother to change?"

"Pleeease? It's unique. Nobody would call their mothers Mum except *me*. It's special!"

"Let me think about it. Now go, don't be in my way while I'm making dinner."

I did not give up my lobbying. Every day I would say, "Good morning, Mom," or, "Bye, Mom" when leaving for school, "Mom, this dish is delicious." "Mom, can we go shopping this weekend?" "Mom, do you need help in the kitchen?" "Mom—mom—you're wanted on the phone!" I could not remember how long it took, but eventually Mother agreed; or I should say after I had called her "Mom" on all occasions, she had no chance to protest anymore.

* * * * * *

But Mom is sick now. Is she all right? My eyes could not help glancing at the clock at the right bottom corner of the computer screen. Every minute passed as tensely as a countdown clock of a soccer game. I was so anxious to see her that I became annoyed by everything on my desk: the manuscript layout, the reference books, the used magazines and the stationery. Staring at a pile of open letters from the readers, I was in a trance. Everything around me seemed to fall still. I felt numb. My thoughts bounced in all directions. I was amazed at my achievement at this point of my life. Even though I had worked a year since my college graduation, I sometimes questioned how I got here. A year before, I had been hired on the spot after my first interview with the *Crazy English* chief editor. I had not planned to become an editor. Like thousands of students who graduated from a less prestigious university in Guangzhou, I had expected I would spend weeks, months, or maybe a couple of years hunting for a decent job. Unexpectedly blessed, I found a full-time job faster than many of my classmates in college.

My roaming mind kept returning to Father's urgent voice on the phone. The words, *Hospital* and *Mama*, flashed in my head at the speed of my nervous pulse. I shuddered. Daydreaming ceased. I flipped a couple of pages of the *Crazy English Teens* magazine, in an attempt to hone my concentration onto something to disguise my absentminded state.

The magazine name, Crazy English, originated from the concept of "To shout out loud, you learn" conceived by Li Yang, a millionaire entrepreneur and educator who used to suffer from low-grade English. He encouraged his students to go behind buildings or on rooftops to shout English insanely to overcome their shyness. His competitor, Earnest Corporation Ltd., registered the name in the mid-1990s for its bilingual audio magazines, including *Crazy English Teens*. The *Crazy English* magazines helped students from the fourth grade through university learn English by reading and listening. The monthly English magazines with Chinese translations included a wide range of subjects, from international travel to Hollywood entertainment. Each copy contained a CD disk with the magazine contents read in English by native speakers.

Working for *Crazy English* magazines then was a perfect fit for me. Since my childhood, I have had a penchant for foreign languages, particularly English, my first one. I don't know why. Perhaps I liked musical phonetics; perhaps I felt safe to keep my secrets in a language that my parents did not understand; or perhaps I loved the heart-pounding-cheeks-glowing-and-praise-singing ecstasy when I spoke English with the golden-haired-and-big-nosed foreigners on the street. My fever for English became extreme in high school. I translated some of the texts, particularly the technical terms, of the science textbooks from Chinese into English, in order to make the subjects more interesting. Knowing I was hopeless in dealing with figures and logical thinking, I chose English as my major in college. It seemed to be fate rather than a plan that my twenty-three years of living was closely associated with English.

English disturbed my normal feeling of being an only child. Whenever I introduced myself as an only child in English, in my early teens, my foreign listeners often expressed brow-raising disbelief, together with a sympathetic "Oh, really?" For a while I was puzzled. "Yes, really," I would reply firmly. After watching a number of American movies and TV dramas, I noticed it was not uncommon for an American family to have at least two children. One girl and one boy was the ideal. I had assumed everyone about my age in the office was an only child that was until my one-year-apart colleague, Tiffany, told me she had a younger sister. I used to envy my childhood playmate, Connie, who is one year older than I. She has a younger brother who looked after their parents while she studied in England.

Before I attended high school, my parents often sent me to the homes of other friends and families for my long vacations. I played with other only children—daughters of Father's friends, and my cousin Jerry who is ten months younger. I used to wonder why I visited my playmates but they never came to my home for a longer stay. After I grew up, I realized it was mainly because my small and run-down house was not capable of putting up any guests. My parents wanted me to have a memorable childhood with playmates instead of being alone.

My parents' friends probably thought the same. When all the kids played together, it was hard to tell whether they were siblings or only children. At a very young age, I became close friends with Ivy and Yip. They are daughters of Cheong's and Yu's.

"We hope you girls can stick together like sisters," said Cheong, one of Father's best friends, at a dinner. "Just like your fathers and I, we've been friends for forty some years. Our brotherly friendship is priceless." He raised his wine glass and toasted Father and Yu, who is Father's other lifelong best friend.

"The three of you don't have siblings, so it's crucial you support each other through difficult times in the future," Cheong said in a fatherly manner.

In our late teens then, my close friends and I were too busy pursuing our interests to meet as often as before, not until a few years later, I met them again by my mother's bedside in the hospital.

Cheong's speech resonated with me for a long time though, particularly, after I heard Father's tense voice on the phone; I realized how much I wanted to count on someone trustworthy, to tell that person how frightened I was and to draw strength and calmness from that person. A sibling would fit that role; a lover might as well. But I had neither of those. I did not even think of Ivy

15

or Yip, despite our sharing girls' secrets in our coming-of-age years. We no longer met as often as when we were kids. Instinctively, I prayed to my god, who had been in my imagination since I was a little girl. It was an intimate way for me to communicate with someone spiritually.

* * * * * *

The clock struck five. My desire to jump into a cab for the hospital grew. I packed my handbag too early, putting it on my lap as if I were a refugee vigilantly waiting to escape. I had already geared up as soon as the clock's minute hand touched six: to shut down the computer, grab my bag, run down the stairs, clock out on my time card and run straight to the pedestrian footbridge to flag a cab.

I ran like Forrest Gump toward the in-patient center after the cab dropped me at the hospital. This place was familiar. My parents had taken me to the First Municipal Hospital for treatment when I was ill in my childhood; most of the time we only visited the out-patient center, which was partly funded by the Hong Kong tycoon, Henry Fok Ying Tung. It was a ten-story building with comprehensive medical departments and offices. In daytime, the building was jammed mainly with the old and the young. Coughing, sneezing, groaning, bawling, shouting, chattering, a babble of voices filled the air of the lobby.

Unlike the out-patient center which was as noisy as a bazaar, the in-patient center was a peaceful sanatorium. I seldom visited the in-patient center, which was composed of several beige and gray buildings on the other side of the hospital. Concrete buildings of various heights lined both sides of a shady boulevard in the hospital grounds. Two gates on each end of the boulevard bracketed the road. Guards were on duty at the entrance as vehicles and bikes were restricted from entering. Although two busy main roads ran in front of the hospital, the city noise was reduced greatly in the hospital area, thanks to the old banyan trees. Their lush branches turned down the volume of the city noise. Patients in loose gowns strolled along the boulevard and rested in the vine-covered pergolas.

I found the Internal Medicine Building without any problem. Mother's room was on the fifth floor. I could have taken the elevator but I could not wait for it. Huffing and puffing, I skipped every other step up the staircase. The steps were wide, fenced by cold, stainless steel railings. I had not run so fiercely for a long time. I dislike running. I reject any sport that requires me to run. Since I had started working, I only ran to catch my bus to work. Living in big cities in China, you have got to be aggressive when taking a bus in rush hour. Buses never wait; since buses just frequently pull over before the stop, passengers have to dash for ten to fifteen meters to meet the arriving bus. If the bus is packed, but you do not have time to wait for the next one, you have to shove and squash and operate little tricks from martial arts to elbow in before the bus doors close. Otherwise, you may never get on the bus in time for work.

Seeing Mother immediately was like catching that bus in the morning. I could not think of anything except the one command blinking in my head: GO FORWARD. I gasped for oxygen. Mother used to say the hospital air was filled with germs. But the antiseptic odor in the staircase was pungent. My lungs must be aseptic after a deep breath. After spiraling up a few flights of stairs, I was already dizzy. Clenching the icy banister to support my fatigued body, I was afraid I would fall. I could not speak. My chest was blocked all the way to my throat. *I need water.* I thought. *I need to slow down.* I panted fast and deep. My breathing was so loud that my eardrums vibrated. Sweat trickled down to the corner of my eyes, under my nose and down onto my lips. *Mom, I'm here.*

* * * * * *

The fifth floor, a big circular sign read "5" at the entranceway. I stood, gulping the antiseptic air like a dog sticking out his tongue to cool off. I did not want my parents to see me red-faced and breathless. Mother would be worried, I thought. I wiped the sweat off my face with the back of my arm. For a moment, my legs were numb. If I had had a choice, I would not have wanted to have come here in such a mad rush. I did not know at the time that I would have to return to this place every day in the following three weeks. I did not know Mother's thorough examination would take longer than we expected. I did not know the results would be too obscure for the gastrointestinal specialist to determine a diagnosis. I did not know that the problem would compel Mother to finally turn to Western medical treatment, about which she was always doubtful.

Composed, I walked into her room. Lit by half a dozen white fluorescent lights, the room accommodated two rows of beds, four on each side. Several patients were lying in their beds. Some had visitors. The patients were women above fifty, presumably having various digestive problems. A color television hung up in the corner, blaring sound that nearly swallowed my exhausted voice when I greeted Mother from the door.

She was in a loose, white patient gown, sitting on her bed. Her short hair was disheveled over her tawny forehead. Her eyes were round and shining. Her full lips, dry and lusterless, relaxed between her sagging cheeks.

My lips bear a resemblance to Mother's. In fact, both of my parents have full lips. I inherited this from both. I used to hate this genetic trait about which my elementary school classmates teased me. They gave me an ugly nickname, Snout Witch, although they had mistaken a pig's nose for its mouth. The name followed me for six years until I separated from those mischievous rascals after graduation.

As soon as I saw Mother's face in the hospital, my pounding heartbeat gradually slowed to normal. Although she looked haggard, she flashed one of her comforting smiles. I recognized the dimple in her right cheek. Father sat by an empty bed next to Mother's. Mother averted her gaze to the flickering TV, as if she wanted to show me she was fine and watching TV as she did every day at home.

"Mom, how's it going?" I asked and hugged her.

"Fine," She answered wearily, releasing herself from my hug.

"*Baba*." I looked at Father's eyes and greeted him.

"So what's going on? Any results yet?" I asked.

"Well, Dr. Deng said he needed more medical proof for his diagnosis. He suggested she stay in the hospital for a thorough checkup. She has done a couple of tests today," Father briefed me.

"What are the tests?" I turned to Mother.

Neither of my parents is talkative by nature. They are chatty only when each is with friends. When they were in the same room, Father usually took charge of the conversation. If not, the room would quickly fall into silence. This had been my observation since I was a little girl, learning to recognize that these two reticent adults were my mother and father.

18

"I had a fingertip blood test, then an X-ray and a urine test. Tomorrow I'll have another blood work and a gastroscopy. So I have to fast."

"Have you eaten yet?" I asked.

"Yes. I had noodles and congee in late afternoon with your father."

"Do you need to take pills now?"

"Not yet, but very soon. Otherwise, how can a hospital make money?"

I chuckled at Mother's witty response and said, "You have a good rest tonight for tomorrow's tests." I looked around her night stand and opened the drawers. "Do you need anything from home? I can bring it to you tomorrow."

"Can you bring me two rolls of toilet paper and my comb on the cupboard next to the fridge?" She thought for a while and said, "Oh and my cell phone charger. I don't know how long I'm gonna stay here. I put the charger on the dresser in the bedroom."

"OK. I'll bring these things tomorrow. Just call me anytime if you remember suddenly what else you need overnight."

Mother reclined her head on the pillow. After a while, she turned from the TV and said to Father and me it was time to go home. I looked Father square in the eye and he agreed. So we said goodnight to Mother. I turned around as I stepped through the doorway. Mother looked petite underneath her baggy patient gown. Her gaze fell upon the TV in the room. Her sallow face was shrouded in an air of edginess. She looked in my direction.

"Mom, I'll be back tomorrow," I assured her.

She nodded.

* * * * * *

After Father and I left the hospital, I suggested we should grab a bite. I had not yet eaten. He took me to a diner, specializing in noodle and congee, a kind of rice porridge, across the street opposite the hospital. He and Mother went there in late afternoon. The small diner was called Zaam Gai, a colloquial way to name a Cantonese restaurant after the owner's name. In this case, the name means "Buddy Zaam." The diner served Cantonese fast food, including combo platters of rice and two or three different dishes. The patrons were mainly patients and their visitors as well as the hospital staff.

The hospital canteen also provided meals three times a day. The food choices there varied depending on the day of the week. The canteen staff delivered food in a stainless steel pushcart to every floor for the hospitalized patients. According to the dietary condition of each patient, food was basically divided into three categories: clear liquids, semi-liquids and solid foods. Mother had to order her meals a day before by filling out a menu sheet. In the drawer of her night stand was a wad of meal tickets, each of which was worth two or five *yuan*, the Chinese currency, also known as *renminbi*, people's money.

Although every day the canteen provided a dozen different food choices, ranging from fried noodles and plain congee for breakfast to stewed chicken soup and minced pork with preserved vegetables for supper, the repetition of the same choices on the same day of the week stimulated patients to dine out or order takeout for a change. So bakeries, fast food joints and restaurants mushroomed around the hospital.

Zaam Gai was a favorite diner in the neighborhood because of its prime location. It sat right at the corner of a T intersection, facing the guarded gate of the in-patient center across the street. The place was always crowded, and I waited a long time to get my food. During lunch and suppertime, the in-store phone rang non-stop for takeout orders. Boxes of takeout were piled on the cashier's desk, ready to be delivered. There was no air conditioning. Electric fans on the wall spun day in and day out. A big glass window separated the kitchen and the eating area. Patrons could see how the food was made while they were waiting.

The cooks in white were swamped: Cook A scooped soup into a bowl and passed it to Cook B who prepared the noodles in a deep, boiling pot. After he filled the bowl with strands of noodles, he passed the bowl to Cook C who completed the culinary procedure in the impeccable assembly line. She checked the order and added cooked beef or pork or other combinations, then sprinkled spring onions on top of the noodles. In less than five minutes, out came a bowl of steamy noodles in soup through the pick-up window.

The kitchen exhaust fans above the cooks blasted hot air. The steamer against the wall churned like a grouchy tuba player, accompanied with the clink and clang of the cooking utensils. On the other side of the kitchen, several other cooks were in the midst of conducting their own duet or trio of culinary masterpieces. White smoke enveloped the kitchen, veiling the sweaty faces of the cooks. Through the pick-up windows and the staff-only entrance, the cooking heat steamed out into the eating area. Since the diner was a storefront with no concrete divider, pedestrians could see the patrons dining inside Zaam Gai, and vice versa. The early-bird patrons usually sat by the street, where they could watch the hustle and bustle at the intersection and hear the clamor of the city while smelling the scent wafted by the steamy air from the kitchen.

"What did you have with Mom?" I asked, after Father and I were seated.

"Your mother had a bowl of plain noodles in soup and I had a bowl of congee with sliced fish and a dish of pork *Cheong Fun*," Father said.

"I see. I'll have *Cheong Fun*, too," I said.

Father and I were big fans of *Cheong Fun*, literally, the intestine rice noodle, because the stuffed rice noodle is like a long roll of intestine. Inside the stuffed noodles are sliced beef or pork or dried shrimp. Congee and *Cheong Fun* are typical snack foods in the Cantonese-speaking region of South China.

"Why didn't you tell me you were going to the hospital today?" I said while munching my beef *Cheong Fun*.

"We didn't want to disturb your work," Father said without a second thought.

"But this is a serious appointment. You ought to have asked me to join you."

"I was surprised myself this morning when your mother asked me to accompany her to the hospital."

"She did?"

"Yes. You know, she hasn't looked well for quite some time. Her face is sallow and she has been to bathroom frequently in recent months." Father took a sip of the brandy he had just bought and continued, "I've urged her to go to a comprehensive hospital for a formal checkup many times. But she never listens. She'd rather go to the out-patient clinic that her sister recommended. You know, she'd taken the traditional Chinese medicine."

The out-patient clinic Father mentioned was one of the branches of the Guangdong Hospital of Traditional Chinese Medicine, which was located near my aunt's apartment building. An old friend of *Yee-ma*, Mother's elder sister, introduced Mother to that humble clinic. It was small and dreary. Mother had been visiting there for solutions to her digestive problems and rectal bleeding. I had not been aware of the seriousness of the matter.

* * * * * *

Father's words reminded me that I had seen Mother making the distinctive ink-like herbal medicine from time to time at home. The smell was acrid. Mother had a fascination with traditional Chinese medicine. She stored a number of dried herbs in the cabinets and the fridge: Chinese yam, longan, red dates, malt, sweet and bitter almond kernels, ginseng, deer velvet slices and many other beans, twigs and cubes that I could not recognize. She used them for her Cantonese soup as part of Chinese nutrition therapy, which is common in sub-tropical Guangdong province.

When I was sick as a child, Mother usually took me to a Chinese medicine physician after I was cured by a Western medicine doctor. She believed Western medicines could cure symptoms, not the disease, but the Chinese medicines effected a permanent cure. In her opinion, a combination of Chinese and Western medical therapy could achieve the best results. However, Father thought she had blind superstitions without any scientific knowledge.

"Who cares what he thinks? He doesn't believe anything but his nitwit water," Mother blurted out one day after I told her Father disliked the medicinal smell. She was cooking the herbal soup while Father was not at home. The bitter odor pervaded the house. Mother often demonized Father's brandy as nitwit water. She thought the alcohol muddled Father's mind and inflamed his temper.

Mother would make Cantonese Cooling Tea at home if I had a sore throat, chapped lips, pimples or bad breath. These were signs of internal heat, according to Mother. Although her medicinal Cooling Tea sometimes tasted bitter, I admitted it was effective—my symptoms would be all gone after two or three days.

"The medicine is good for health and bitter for your mouth," Mother always said when she saw my eyebrow-furrowed face before I drank the dark liquid from a bowl. I believed that was also her motto—to strengthen her will to drink up the bitter medicine. She did not need any sweets to go with her Chinese black coffee—a term that was used after a Chinese doctor described what the traditional Chinese medicine tasted like. I could not do that. Having candy was my reward after drinking the medicinal soup when I was a kid. Otherwise, the bitter taste would remain in my mouth for an unbearably long time. In fact, Mother often told me she enjoyed the liquorice aftertaste.

* * * * * *

"So what'll you do tomorrow?" I asked, wiping my lips with my own tissue. It is wise to bring your own tissue because there are no free napkins in most restaurants in China.

"I'll go back to the hospital in the morning, in case your mother needs help during the tests," Father said.

"Should I come along? I can take a half-day off."

"No, it's not necessary. If I need help, I'll tell you."

"OK. But please keep me informed. We're family. I can help anytime. I'll be around." I stopped eating and eyed him firmly. I wanted to assure him I was standing by. Father said nothing. The tightness on his face loosened up.

Chapter 2

The Lost Generation

Father and I could not have known then that evening would be the beginning of a long, distressing journey for our family. We could not have known then that Mother would stay in the hospital much longer than she wanted, much longer than we could have imagined. I always thought Mother was so tough that she did not want others to care about her business; she refused to answer my questions more than once when I was curious about what she was doing.

"Don't ask so much. Go about your own business," she would say.

Returning to my math problems about functions, I felt like she had pushed me out of her world and slammed the door in my face.

Nevertheless, Mother was not unfriendly. She liked chit chatting with her lady friends—co-workers, old neighbors, relatives on her side, and wives of Father's long-time friends—but not me. I did not think she considered me her friend. There were probably a hundred reasons that she did not want to share her thoughts with me. But the main reason I figured was that our mother and daughter relationship might make Mother feel unable to confide in me. She might always think I was too young to understand her woes, or perhaps she was afraid to interrupt my life, seemingly occupied with my schoolwork or full-time job. Until my early twenties, I still foolishly believed she could take care of herself as well as she had taken care of me. I rarely paid attention to Mother's health unless she complained to me, mostly about her quarrels with my, in her words, "opinionated father."

A few days after Mother was admitted to the hospital, Father mentioned to me that she had abdominal pain constantly. He learned it from her conversation with Dr. Deng. Father looked defeated and agitated, as if he was too late to have Mother treated. Mother had told him that the traditional Chinese medicine was good for her diarrhoea and internal hemorrhoids. But Father had been suspicious of the effect. He disbelieved traditional Chinese medicine could improve Mother's health.

Once, Mother was preparing her medicinal soup when Father came into the kitchen. The strong herbal smell irritated him.

"Cooking medicine, *again*?" Father asked impatiently. He filled up his porcelain teacup with hot water from a stainless steel thermos.

I could tell his word "again" was full of sarcasm. I sensed the contentious sparks between my parents. Mother said nothing, preoccupied with making her medicinal soup. She opened a brown paper bag that contained a lump of dry twigs and leaves and grains. After she poured out the medicine into a big bowl, she filled up the bowl with water to rinse the herbs and then threw them in a clay cooking pot reserved for cooking traditional Chinese medicine.

"Make sure the medicine is not expired," Father said as he walked out of the kitchen, holding the three-quarters-filled teacup.

"*You are* expired," Mother muttered. She continued to fill the pot with three rice bowls of water and stirred the herbs with a pair of wooden chopsticks.

Father grumbled almost every time Mother cooked the herbal medicine. For that reason, she avoided making Chinese medicinal soup when he was around. Yet, that did not stop Father lobbying her to consult specialists in a big hospital. He was convinced Mother's health would continue to decline if she did not receive a formal physical examination.

* * * * * *

I visited Mother every day after my work at *Crazy English*, although both of my parents told me it was not necessary. The bus ride was about forty minutes. My parents were afraid the constant travel between my work and the hospital might tire me. I told Mother it was more convenient for me to come to the hospital from work than to go home. That lessened her concern.

Indeed, thanks to the fact that the bus terminal was only three blocks away, I usually could get a seat on the bus from my work place to the hospital. For weeks, my time card was punched exactly at five thirty for departure. How could I not be proud of myself for such punctuality? That was the moment I anticipated the most of the whole day. When I walked out of the office building, the sun would hang low in the western sky, radiating its last brilliant golden light. The street already teemed with people from all walks of life. Teenage students in school uniform, pre-school kids holding the hands of their faltering grandparents, men and women in casual wear, in business suits, or in working uniform, the bikers, the hawkers, the illegal rickshaw guys all joined the daily commotion of the urban rush hour. They swam through the sea of busy traffic toward their respective destinations.

Ambling to the bus terminal, I found pleasure at looking down at the pedestrians' feet. They walked fast as they went to work, as if their destinations had a magnetizing power. A fast pace has become a distinction of city dwellers. We think fast, talk fast, walk fast, eat fast, drink fast, read fast, and even love fast. *How often do we really slow down to feel the world around us? How much have we missed when we are so preoccupied with what we are doing?* I pondered whether I was living proof of the increasing tempo of modern life, whether I was among those twenty-and-thirty-something office workers who filled their vacant self with iPod music, e-book reading and to-and-fro text messaging.

Unconsciously, I became contemplative whenever I was on the journey to the hospital. Perhaps, seated comfortably on the bus, my mind went off leash for an instant without worrying about being pushed or shoved or stepped on. Perhaps my destination made a difference. Unlike most of the passengers, I was *not* on my way home, but traveling to visit Mother who stayed in a place of bleak future.

On most days when I commuted from my office to the hospital, the sun fell behind the skyscrapers. As the bus steered forward, a glaring golden spot bounced between the soaring glass walls. The sun cast a rugged shadow of the city skyline on the bus ceiling and the passengers' faces. Traffic became dense near downtown. On the worst days, the eight-lane East Wind Road—one of the main arteries in Guangzhou—was so congested that the traffic was like a paralyzed dragon without head and tail. The red, white, blue, gray, green, yellow and black car roofs glittered in the setting sun. Our bus was surrounded with unbreakable queues of sedan cars and taxis, as if we had been ambushed by the tiny people from Lilliput and Belfuscu in *Gulliver's Travels*.

The gridlock tried everyone's patience. Some drivers stuck out their heads to rubberneck; some stretched their left arms out of the windows with cigarettes locked between the index and middle fingers; some others grabbed the creased newspaper by the driver's seat and read the headlines to kill time. The passengers on the bus were getting agitated. Some changed their standing position while the others whined about the problematic city traffic.

"*Aigh*, what chaos!" sighed one female passenger sitting behind the bus driver.

"That's the price we have to pay for having so many cars on the street," another passenger interjected.

The female passenger sighed again, "The municipal government keeps encouraging residents to buy cars but the road infrastructure never catches up."

I was not surprised by such casual conversation. In fact, what the two passengers were describing had become a headache in a number of big Chinese cities. More and more urban people had been able to afford private cars in the last decade since the millennium. Purchasing an automobile was one of the first investments for the majority of white collar workers. With car factories such as Japan's Honda Motors, Nissan Motors and Toyota Motors, Guangzhou ranked at the top as the city with the largest auto output in China, surpassing Shanghai in 2008. Car ownership in the city had increased from about three hundred and fifty thousand to one million in the last ten years.

In the 1980s, we had an old saying, "If you know math, physics and chemistry, you will not be afraid to travel around the world." Twenty years later, I heard a new interpretation, "If you know computers, English and driving, you will be invincible in all competitions." That partly explained why driving schools in Guangzhou were prosperous all year round. In 2009, more than a quarter of the ten million Guangzhou residents had a driver's license.

Our bus inched forward with intermittent sudden brakes.

"The next stop is the First Municipal Hospital. Please get ready and alight from the back door," the recorded announcer spoke in both Mandarin and Cantonese.

The announcement jammed with static broke my chain of thought. I elbowed my way out, raising my voice, "*Ng goi! Yau lok!*" and repeated in Mandarin, "Excuse me! Getting off here" as more people understand Mandarin in public.

It was getting dark by the time I took the familiar route to the hospital. *Go straight, cross the road, turn left, cross the pedestrian footbridge, go on ahead, and turn right*...I had learned the directions by heart as if a biological GPS guided me in my subconscious mind. I began thinking of my parents as I walked. *How's Mother hanging in there today? Has Father visited her yet? When will he drop his guard and talk to me?* I wondered if it was my family tradition to always say no at first to a source of help, then, after polite compromise, to give in. For instance, a few times when Father talked on the phone with his sister and brothers, he repeated "It's not necessary." I assumed my relatives wanted to visit Mother or give us financial help. Father kindly declined.

Mother often said "It's not necessary" to me when I offered to help in the kitchen; I helped anyway.

Father said "It's not necessary" to Mother when he wanted to finish his work before having dinner. We always waited for him.

I probably said "It's not necessary" too frequently to remember. Like when I was in college and had to move into another dormitory. With no elevator in the building, it would have taken me hours to carry all my boxes of books to the new sixth floor dorm room. Thank heaven! Lee's boyfriend did not take my "It's not necessary" seriously. He helped me lift the heaviest boxes of books, and I moved as quickly as a slam dunk.

* * * * * *

We had hoped Mother would be discharged from the hospital within a few days, just as the words on the chest pocket of her patient gown suggested: "Have a Quick Recovery." The six Chinese characters were sewed in bright red thread. They stood out on the faded patient gown, as if the patients wore a scarlet letter A on their chests.

In the first two weeks, whenever I asked Mother if she needed anything from home or from the store, she said no.

"You really think it's a good sign to be in the hospital for this long?" she said bluntly.

I no longer asked her what she needed from home. I did not mean to irritate her. I looked at her anxious, sparkling eyes. She must be bored in the hospital. She must be restless at night. The wrinkles under her eyes were like two brown pouches. Her round

28

face seemed to have shrunk. Her unkempt dark hair grew longer, covering her earlobes. The skin on her arms and hands was chapped like the surface of an arid land. Her patient gown was getting bigger day by day. She often had to pull her collar and refold her sleeves and pant legs. She looked disinterested while I gave my pep talk.

"Look at my wrist, tanned and bony," she said, lifting her arm.

"It's OK. You'll have a comeback soon," I comforted her.

"*Aigh*," she heaved a sigh of frustration and said, "I've had liquid food for several days. I've lost my appetite."

"You'll have a normal meal after the tests."

"They draw my blood every third day. I've already had an X-ray, a colonoscopy, an electrocardiogram and an ultrasonic exam…"

I was overwhelmed with the tests that Mother listed. I had heard of these names but never sure exactly the function of each. The most familiar test was the X-ray exam. I had one when I was a student during our annual physical exam. Each of us boarded the X-ray bus in which we stood between a pair of big black gloves sticking out from "the wall." Later I learned that was the X-ray screen. We had to lean our chests against "the wall." The examiners slid their hands into the black gloves to position our bodies. After the test was done, they would pat our waists to signal us to get off the bus. I heard some naughty boys once gave a karate chop on the gloved hands, wounding the radiologist's hands.

Mother's tests were more complicated. She said she had never had so many medical tests. I did not know how to show my sympathy other than telling her things were going to be all right. But deep inside I had no idea if things would turn out well. What I said was just an expression, like "I'm fine. Thanks." We were taught to say so when asked, "Hi, how are you?" in my English beginner class, even though I was not fine at all. My English teacher explained the phrase was only a greeting. After all, nobody wanted to listen to your whining.

Everything will be fine. Will it? I hoped Mother had faith in what I said. As I grew into my late teens, I had found myself looking at almost everything as if it were gray. The Chinese proverb, "Things do not turn out as one wishes; the more you wish, the more you lose," had greatly influenced my pessimistic vibes. When in high school, more than once, I had hoped my hard work in science would lead me to a good grade. But I still did terribly in the subject. I did not know why. Gradually, I lost faith. I would rather have lower expectations with hope for a surprisingly good result. I was inclined to think less positively, or even negatively. That had been my way to overcome big disappointment. However, I told myself I must stay upbeat for Mother's sake. She deserved some good news after being so cooperative, abiding by her doctor's dos and don'ts.

I fidgeted. I did not know if there had been a side effect from the tests. Mother told me she had lost her taste for food. The CT scan, in particular, made her uncomfortable, after drinking lots of liquid that contained iodine. She had to go to the bathroom so many times that she felt sick of it. The night before the scan, she had had to fast. She disliked going to sleep with a hollow stomach.

I brought Mother a Walkman and a couple of books about food therapy. By accident, I found these books in a bookstore. The more I read, the better I understood the current situation. I had been ignorant about the human body. What's more, I hoped the books could pick Mother up. I knew she missed cooking. The smell of the kitchen had been her stimulus for food and joy for life.

"I'm sorry for not being able to make soup for you these days," Mother said every now and then.

"Never mind," I said. "I've grown up. I can take care of myself."

"Look at you." Mother's gaze fell upon my face. "You don't have much soup lately. Your lips are so red and you talk with bad breath."

I was embarrassed. I sometimes disliked her being so candid. But if she had not said so, I would not have realized how much I needed her soup. Soup was an important dish in my family. Cantonese called it *Lo Foh Tong*, meaning Slow-Cooked Soup. We had soup nearly every week, sometimes twice a week. Mother believed different seasonal soup could heal and strengthen our health. In summer, we had winter melon soup with duck, which was said to expel the heat inside us. In winter, we had spare rib soup with watercress and apricot kernels to nourish the *yin* and moisten the lungs. Mother would add Chinese herbs into a clear broth together with meat and other ingredients. She enjoyed selecting the right kind of herbs to match her recipe. She was like an experienced traditional Chinese medicine pharmacist, measuring the amount, breaking it into short pieces and grinding them into powder. It took two to four hours over low heat before the soup was done. However, the long preparation hours of *Lo Foh Tong* annoyed Father. He thought they wasted fuel and time.

I missed Mother's *Lo Foh Tong*. I began learning to make soup on my own in the hope that Mother could eat my soup after she recovered. Memories of the times when I was ill and tended by Mother rose up in my mind. I remembered once at the age of five when I had a high fever of forty degrees Celsius. She was by my side all night long. I rested on the couch bed in the living room, half-conscious. She changed the ice bag on my forehead every other hour, wiped my sweaty body and changed my drenched clothes. Every time I opened my fuzzy eyes during the night, I saw her frowning face.

"Are you thirsty?" Mother asked softly.

I nodded with difficulty as my neck muscle was quite sore. Mother slightly raised my head up with one arm, slowly tilting a glass of water to my mouth.

"Enough?" She asked after she heard my faint swallow.

"Ya," I answered feebly.

Mother sponged my lips with a hand towel and leveled my head down onto the pillow. "Close your eyes and go back to sleep," she whispered.

She must have fanned me for a long time as I fell asleep in a soothing cool breeze. I doubted Mother closed her eyes that night.

The next few times I visited Mother in the hospital I caught her reading in bed. The medical books must have enlightened her. She said reading helped her to sleep. She placed the books under her pillow and refused to let me put them away.

* * * * * *

I was used to thinking—I lived two months in advance of the calendar. The magazine production was a two-month-ahead schedule. I often forgot the present month while working on the future issue. But the November of 2006 was different. Every day, Mother counted how long she had been hospitalized. Her daily medication bill was dated. On average her bill came to forty *yuan* a day. It cost five times more if her test involved advanced medical devices, such as the CT scan and ultrasonography. Every once in a while, Father collected the sheets and calculated at home how much we had already spent on Mother's medical fees. Her retirement

31

medical insurance could cover forty percent of the expenses. My roughly three thousand *yuan* monthly salary could also share Father's burden.

The outside temperature gradually dropped. The northern wind defeated the "Autumn Tiger," a figure of speech that the Cantonese use to describe ferocious heat in October. The air became cool and crisp. Although trees remained green and lush in Guangzhou, their leaves fluttered briskly without the weight of the hot and humid air. The night chill made people stay in their beds longer.

I continued to pray to my imaginary god for Mother. It was also my way to talk to my inner world. Since I was a little girl, I had believed my god lived in the sky and the airplane was my god's messenger. If I heard a plane rumbling in the sky after I prayed, my message would have been received. I still believed so after I grew up, especially when I was in trouble, I prayed, I sobbed, I meditated. I hoped a plane would pass above my head afterwards. Nearly every night after visiting Mother, I prayed in my heart and looked forward to hearing a plane passing over. It was like making a wish on a shooting star streaking across the sky. Sometimes a plane did roar above me like thunder after I prayed. I was gratified. *Thank you, my prayer has been heard.*

* * * * * *

Going to the hospital after work was like my part-time job. On one of those days, I saw Father sitting on the bench outside the Internal Medicine Building with his two best friends, Cheong and Yu. They had been good friends since high school. Both Cheong and Yu were in their late fifties, about the same age as Father. Our immediate families were as close as kin. I called them Uncle Cheong and Uncle Yu.

Slender and myopic, Uncle Cheong started his own shipping business after he got laid off in the reform of the Chinese state-owned enterprises in the 1990s. The reform affected millions of workers, mainly those in their forties and fifties. After losing their jobs, many received insufficient compensation because of the poor or corrupt management and limited company resources. My parents were also among *The Army of Unemployed*, as the sacked workers ironically called themselves.

I was in high school when my parents lost their jobs. Ignorant as I was then, I did not understand completely the obstacles my family faced. Years later, I read in a news website about the state-owned enterprise reform:

> The central government decided to retain the ownership of between five hundred to one thousand large-scale state-owned enterprises and to allow small firms to be leased or sold. As a result, by the end of 2001, eighty-six percent of all state-owned enterprises had been restructured and about seventy percent had been partially or fully privatized. The reform improved economic performance, but it also created serious social problems. From 1998 to 2004, six in ten state-owned enterprises workers were dismissed.

Both Father's state-owned textile factory and the city's timber factory where Mother had worked for some twenty years were forced to close in the ownership reform. Working in the timber factory was Mother's first and only job. She had worked in the timber factory since her father, my *Gonggong*, passed away in her teenage years. Considering the financial difficulty in her family, the leaders of the factory allowed Mother to take over *Gonggong*'s position a year earlier than the legal employment age of sixteen. Even though Mother's job required a large amount of physical labor, such as lifting heavy plywood boards and piling large brown paper, she worked very hard to keep her "iron rice bowl"—a well-known Chinese term for a secure job with steady income and benefits. However, the good days did not outlast privatization. Mother's iron rice bowl was shattered.

Since I had become a working woman, I could *now* understand how Mother might have felt about her unemployment—the frustration, the anger and the loss. Perhaps that was why she was indifferent when I asked about her business in those years. I guessed most people who lost their jobs at that time had similar reactions. Perhaps these reactions had also propelled Uncle Cheong to work even harder to provide a good life for his family. Father said, Uncle Cheong was the most successful and industrious one among the three of them. He owned a private car and a roomy apartment of two bedrooms, one study and a balcony, three times as big as my home.

Uncle Yu was unaffected by the ownership reform because he did not work in a state-owned firm. He was fortunate to work as a senior driver in a municipal psychiatric hospital until he retired at the age of sixty, the legal age for men to retire in China. Because Uncle Yu had worked in the healthcare industry, he was knowledgeable about medical services. He often gave Father such insights as which hospital had better facilities for certain treatment, what the procedures were if a patient needed further examination, and how to get the best benefit as a retired worker from the government medical insurance. Uncle Yu cared about his health more than Father. He swam and went to the gym. He kept his body solid and healthy, and looked younger than his contemporaries.

* * * * * *

It was unusual for me to see Mother having other visitors in the hospital besides Father. My relatives would visit Mother during the day when I was at work. The warmth of appreciation overwhelmed my heart when I met with Father and his best friends outside the Internal Medicine Building. *Baba and I are not alone.* I thought. *Mom is also on the minds of our friends and family.* Speaking of who should come to visit Mother, Father and I disagreed with one another. He believed it was not necessary to inform everyone who knew Mother about her admission to the hospital.

"Telling so many people that your mother is in the hospital means we expect them to visit her," Father argued at home one evening. "You must consider that nowadays everybody is busy working for a living. I don't want to bring them *mafan*."

How come he thinks keeping others informed is bringing them troubles? I protested inside, noticing the no-further-discussion expression on his grim face. *Won't we receive more support if more people know Mother is in the hospital?* I totally disagreed with him that a phone call would impose on our friends and family, let alone waste their precious time for making a living. In the end, Father only notified our immediate families and his close friends, such as Uncle Cheong and Uncle Yu.

I greeted Father's friends and they smiled back at me. I asked Father about Mother. Surprisingly, he did not respond.

"I know today the result is out. How is it?" I asked in a relaxed voice. My heart thumped fast.

"She'll be alright," Uncle Cheong said, patting Father's shoulder. "You should think of the bright side."

I heard Father's whimper as he turned around, remaining speechless. *Something must have gone wrong.* I eyed his friends. At dusk, I could not distinguish the expression on their faces. The night was falling; pedestrians and traffic abated. The streetlights along the boulevard lit one by one. The November wind blew against my face hard and fast, leaving echoes between my ears. Father finally spoke.

"Dr. Deng said the tests show numerous polyps in your mother's colon. They're likely to be…" he choked at the last word, "…cancer."

What? The word, cancer, sounded familiar yet shocking. It jolted my senses, as if a defibrillator had electrified my heart. I said nothing, trying to hide my utter astonishment and ignorance.

"It'll be alright," said Uncle Yu. "The diagnosis is not yet confirmed. You should not speculate too much."

Father seemed to know what I was about to ask. He sniffled and said, "Dr. Deng said it's a complicated case. The examination results suggest several possibilities. He said even though the polyps might become cancer, they might be benign or malignant. But he can't tell at this point."

Under the yellow streetlight, I saw shimmering tears rolling down Father's cheeks. He must have summoned a great amount of courage to give out the information. In my recollection, he rarely cried. He was always a tough man in control of everything. He was born in the Year of the Tiger, so Mother often joked about his peppery temperament, a characteristic of his zodiac. She compared Father to a roaring tiger in the jungle when he was enraged. In that instant, I could not believe that the man in front of me whom I fearfully respected and adored in my childhood, who had weathered numerous storms in his life, who could fix almost everything in the house, was my father.

What kid does not imagine his or her dad a superhero—the kind who can rescue the world and suffering mankind like in the comic strips? I did. I wished Father could tell me that Mother's health condition was under control and that we could overcome obstacles. But he said nothing more. He looked down and breathed deeply. His heaving shoulders were silhouetted against the golden pink evening sky in the west.

Uncle Cheong and Uncle Yu suggested I visit Mother before we all went for dinner. They had met her earlier. Father asked me not to tell her she had cancer until the doctor confirmed her illness. I said "yes" and turned around to enter the building. My pace slowed as if I were a locomotive running out of fuel. I was deep in thought. *What exactly is cancer? What do polyps look like? How do polyps grow in her intestines? Why was Baba so shaken up? What shall I do?*

Unconsciously, my feet transported my body to the stairwell. Two strands of thoughts intertwined in my mind. On one hand, I was concerned about Mother; on the other, I was still captured in the moment when Father shed tears. An urgent sense of mission transfused throughout my body, as if I had been injected with a stimulant. *I'm their only child. I must buck up and take control now.* I was worried the news would defeat his strong will to deal with what was to come. On that particular evening, I thought about Father a lot.

* * * * * *

My father had had a unique life. From the stories he told me as I grew up, I understood he had been through many hardships. When I started to learn numbers as a kid, I counted Father's many skills. He had taught himself to make wooden furniture, assemble crystal and semiconductor radios, repair TV sets and other electronic home appliances, farm in the rural area, sell bus tickets, work in front of fiery furnaces in a ferro-silicon alloy factory, work in the high-voltage power workshop of a textile factory and also restore antique porcelain. I gathered these from the stories he told me. But I felt that he knew even more than what he had told me about being able to survive during difficult times.

In my eyes, Father could fix anything and everything. He was my superhero, Mr. Fix-It. In fact, he was so skillful that Mother and I were proud to tell our friends who had broken fans, radios and TV sets to have him examine them before they threw them out. He repaired everything in our household, from the TV set, electric fan, washing machine, rice cooker, my tape recorder to the leaking sink, the dilapidated shingled roof and my broken-heeled shoes.

Father was like a surgeon of electrical appliances. On his desk, he had screwdrivers of all sizes, pliers, tweezers, a flashlight, a mirror, and a box of tiny parts like bolt rings, nails, springs and screws. He had larger hand tools like wrenches, hammers and brushes in the drawers. No matter whether they were strangers or friends, everyone came to him and asked, "Can you fix this for me?" Because of Father's magic hands, I even made good friends with my teacher in elementary school. She sewed a beautiful floral dress for me in her gratitude to Father who fixed the constant glitches of her color TV set.

Yet, the news about Mother's condition struck Father as unexpectedly as the notice he had received at eighteen that his schooling was suspended. During the Cultural Revolution, Father and his contemporaries, like Uncle Cheong and Uncle Yu, were ordered to go to rural areas to assume peasant lives. For that reason, he did not complete his education in high school. He became a *zhiqing*, a knowledgeable youth, a characteristic Chinese name for those young men and women sent to the countryside to be educated about living in rural poverty.

Father told me little about his seven years of *zhiqing* life. Although I asked about it, he seemed never to be in the mood to remember those years. I knew Uncle Cheong and Uncle Yu had been with him when they were all assigned to Panyu, a district in Guangzhou that used to be rural and poverty-stricken in the 1960s. Six months after Father moved to Panyu, his older brother, who taught math in a local high school in Zengcheng, a *zhiqing* hub city near Guangzhou, helped transfer him to work closer to his family.

Among all the fascinating personal stories Father told me, he was extremely proud that he could ride a bicycle for more than a hundred kilometers back and forth between Zengcheng and Guangzhou. To save traveling expenses, he borrowed a bicycle from the village people to go home for short visits during the slack farming season. He also felt proud of his physical capability in his youth when he could swim in fast flowing rivers in the evenings and walk through dangerous jungles where poisonous snakes lurked. That was when he attempted to escape to Hong Kong, a destination to which the *zhiqing* aspired.

Between 1973 and 1974, he failed in all three escape attempts. He was captured by ferocious army dogs and once was tortured in prison for half a year. Because he was reluctant to say more, I could not get any more details from him about his dreadful past. However, the stories about his life I already knew became my close contact with China's contemporary history. I was fortunate not to

37

experience tumultuous times in my country. During my coming-of-age years, I was so protected that Father breathed no word to me about the world-shaking democratic movement at Tiananmen Square in 1989. That year I was only six. I was truly living in a no-news-is-good-news type of innocent childhood. After I went to college and learned about the June Fourth Incident through overseas media, I asked Father why I knew nothing about it. "You were too young then," Father said affectionately.

As a young adult, I completely understood Father's selective memories about his life. Who would want to keep remembering his miserable experiences? They were the incurable wounds in Father's memories that would make his heart tingle if he recalled them. As the only-children generation, we had no recollections or personal experiences of the Cultural Revolution. We learned it through our history books, mass media and probably through our parents or older relatives. Although I could not feel as indignant and poignant as Father's contemporaries felt about the Cultural Revolution. I did cherish more what I had in my life by comparing what my parents did not have in their struggling lives.

* * * * * *

After Father returned to Guangzhou in 1975, he took a laborious and filthy job as a steel worker. Low-end jobs were the only opportunity for *zhiqing* to work in the city after they returned from rural life. With low pay and long hours, he worked in a ferro-silicon alloy factory in Guangzhou for nine years. As a furnace man, he had to stand in heat as high as seventy degrees Celsius every day. Although there was a huge electric fan behind him, with his fiberglass helmet, thick denim overalls and long leather heat-resistant boots, the fan did nothing for his drenched body. The tangy smell of sweat pervaded the workshop.

Those days were terrible. But they were not as distressing as when in his fifties he lost his job at the textile factory because of the ownership reform. By then, Mother had already been unemployed for two years. She could not find a new job and became a full-time homemaker. Father alone took on the responsibility to raise a family of three. It was almost impossible for my parents, then in their forties and fifties, to find jobs again. Most corporations tended to hire the educated, the young, and the good-looking. As one of Mother's unemployed co-workers put it, "We are none of those."

After learning the term, "The Lost Generation" in my history class, I felt the term was also appropriate to my parents' generation. They had lost their youth in the impoverished countryside, lost their opportunity to obtain education and lost their jobs in their mid-forties and fifties. They had missed out on their happiness and dreams. They had devoted a good part of their life to the country's revolutionary changes. In my eyes, my parents were the typical Lost Generation in China.

* * * * * *

The first few years after both of my parents were unemployed in 2000 was one of the toughest times in my childhood memory. My parents' unemployment benefits could hardly support my schooling. I would have had to drop out of high school. Thanks to Father who turned his lifelong hobby of repairing antique porcelain into his full-time work, I could continue my education and my family could make ends meet.

He repaired the broken antique porcelain for individuals. Secretly picking up the skill from his middle-school classmate who had done very well in the business, he had worked day and night at his desk at home with different shapes of vases, plates and statues. He examined closely every fragment, as if it could talk to him in ancient Chinese. On his desk were not only hardware tools but also glass reagent bottles and an airbrush pen. He used chemicals to remake the missing pieces and recover the painting on the porcelain. He was like a plastic surgeon to the flawed antique china. In this respect, my father was genuinely Mr. Fix-It.

Thinking back, in addition to money, my poor science score was also Father's big concern. "How come your math is so bad?" he often said. It saddened him that I had not inherited a touch of his math-specialty gene or that skill from his side of the family. His older brother and sister and their children all had excelled at math. When I looked at my nearly failed exam paper in math, I felt disgraced. I tried to make Father happy again by working hard in high school, but my brain disappointingly did not react to science. I understood Father wanted me to attend university, although he had said many times to me he would respect whatever decision I made for my life. Considering his compulsory resignation from further education so early in life, how would he not hope his daughter someday could receive better and higher education than he had?

I often stayed up late for homework in my senior year. On those nights after Mother was asleep, I could see Father sitting in the living room alone with his cigarette in one hand and a glass of brandy in the other. I was sure Father had resorted to these habits for solace. Perhaps he felt alcohol would take him away from reality. Although he revealed little about his feelings to Mother and me, his distress was fully shown on his sulky face.

* * * * * *

That night in the hospital, I paused at a window in the stairwell. Outside, the long winter was swiftly devouring the fading daylight. The short distance to Mother's room had unusually grown farther than it had been yesterday. I wanted to see Mother, but I did not want to get to her room too quickly. I wanted to tell her what Father told me, but I promised I would not until the diagnosis was confirmed. I wanted to take a break from this day-and-night, back-and-forth interaction with people, but I must carry on because my parents needed me. In that full minute, I would like to take my time to climb those familiar stairs. Step by step, flight by flight, let my pace synchronize with my train of thought.

Through the window, I saw the highway not far from the hospital illuminated, as if it were a golden belt slithering through a cluster of buildings. Vehicles with headlights ran like fireflies on the highway. People must have returned home. The residential buildings looked festive with the bright lights inside.

Suddenly, I feared Mother might be able to read my perplexed face. I was afraid I would burst into tears in front of her. I took a deep breath at the fourth floor and said to myself quietly. *No matter what, you must be strong. No. Don't cry, not at this moment. Save your tears and reserve your strength because you're the shield of your parents now.* My thought jumped to Father again. *How is he doing now? If only I had a brother keeping him company.* It probably would be easier for him to reveal his feelings to a male family member than to me. He needed an emotional outlet. But I felt relieved that Uncle Cheong and Uncle Yu were with him at that moment.

* * * * * *

I could hear the TV clamoring as I entered Mother's room. It was showing the eight o'clock prime time drama series about a family feud over a wealthy man's legacy. I forget the drama name now. Played five episodes a week, the Cantonese drama series on the Hong Kong TV channels—TVB Jade and ATV Home—were big hits in Guangzhou. If it were not for the fact that Mother was sick, I would have been drawn like Mother's roommates to the gangster-chasing or dysfunctional-family-fighting soap operas.

Mother was chatting with her neighbor. Her innocent smile told me she did not know the doctor's prognosis yet. I greeted the patients next to her bed and said "hi" to Mother.

"How do you feel today?"

"Still the same." She scratched her scalp and looked away from me.

"Do you know Uncle Cheong and Uncle Yu are here?"

"Yes. They visited me just now."

"Good. I'm going to have supper with them and *Baba*. They're downstairs."

"Your aunt also visited me today." Mother noticed I saw the Nestle tin can and the apples on her night stand. She added, "She bought me milk powder and fruit."

"I see. Would you like to have an apple?"

"No. I don't feel like eating. Take some apples home."

For the past week, Mother had eaten only semi-liquid food, such as noodles and congee. I knew she missed rice and fish. She never tired of fish. When she worked in the timber factory, she used to consume three bowls of rice at every meal. She always said a dinner was not complete without rice.

"Soon you'll have rice again," I said as if I were a seer.

"*Aigh*—"she signed. "My stomach fails me. I have the runs after eating."

"The good thing is now you're in the hospital for treatment. You'll get better." I did not know what else I could say. So I repeated it often. I could tell Mother was fed up with my pep talk. My voice dissolved in the boisterous TV noise.

"Can I help you with anything?" I asked and eyed the pill bottles on the table. I lifted the stainless steel thermos to see if it needed a refill. It weighed heavily.

41

"Your father has filled up the thermos. If you can handle it, help me to get a stool sample from the toilet."

I was surprised at her request. This had been such a disgusting task that in my elementary school days, I left it to Mother to do it for me before my annual physical examination. The tables now had turned—I had to do it for Mother.

She must have read my mind. She said, "Come on! I've seen your poop countless times when you were a baby. Nothing to be afraid of, after all, we're mother and daughter."

I agreed. Not until I saw Mother's stool did I realize how serious her illness had become. It was mostly black liquid. She was right. She had diarrhoea. It was hard for me to find a solid excrement sample. I held my breath and removed the best sample I could find into a tiny plastic cup. I spotted blood in her excrement, too, which frightened me. I did not know what these symptoms meant. I assumed Mother already knew she had blood coming out of her. But why had she never told me? Did she really think she was only affected by an easy-fix digestive problem?

The image of Father's teary face reappeared in my mind. Tears trickled down along his nose. His lips had been sealed so tight that I imagined he could not taste his tears. *Blood, Cancer, Blood, Cancer, Blood, Cancer.* How painful was it to understand the relationship between the two? I did not know what cancer was but I saw it had made Mother bleed. My chest tightened, as if a big rock obstructed the blood flowing to my heart. How I wished I were with Father when he had learned the news from Dr. Deng. How I wished I had enough knowledge so that I knew what to do next. I felt like I was alone on an island. I did not know how long it would take before I found the solution to Mother's health problem. But I would keep trying. There must be a way, I thought, for me to ease Mother's discomfort, to cease her rectal bleeding, to save her from this affliction.

I regretted that I had not paid closer attention to Mother in the past few years. A wave of guilt overwhelmed me. My heart quickened. I felt my eyes were soaked. The raven mixture of semi-solid and liquid substance in the toilet bowl reeked of sewage, perhaps had an even stronger odor. The tiny dark red dots of blood looked like evil eyes staring at me hatefully. *How can I make it up to Mom? Am I too late?*

After collecting the sample, I washed my hands at the sink. As I looked at myself in the mirror, I felt a sense of obligation. *I'm Mom's only child. I'm not a little girl any more. I can make money to support the family. I can take care of my parents. It's time I should do something for them to show my gratitude for their love and care since my birth. If god helps those who help themselves, I should not be alone to seek a solution.* I prayed harder, hoping a soaring airplane would respond.

Chapter 3
Wai-kurh

A few days later, Mother was transferred to the Department of Surgery. Dr. Deng had said that the surgeons could give us a final diagnosis of Mother's condition. By then, Mother had undergone a battery of tests that resulted in her near exhaustion. To a patient, the diagnostic tests seemed to be the prerequisite for an individual visit with a doctor. My parents and I were not knowledgeable about these tests. We only did as the doctors instructed.

I often wondered if all the medical tests were useful or if they were only for the sake of increasing the hospital's revenue. After all, a majority of patients and their families knew little about the complicated medical tests, unless they had members working in medicine or nursing. There was no way that the doctors would tell the patients up front about the cost of these tests either.

In Mandarin, we call internal medicine *Neike* (pronounced Nay-kurh), and surgery *Waike* (pronounced Wai-kurh). Before Mother was transferred to the Department of Surgery from the Gastrointestinal Department, I did not know the difference between both departments. Literally, *Neike* means "in-department" and *Waike* "out-department." Why did Mother need to move from "in-department" to "out-department"? I thought the *Waike* took care of the visible problems on a patient like burned skin and wounded limbs? If so, Mother's *invisible* digestive problem inside her was supposed to be the *Neike*'s business.

Father said it was the surgeons' decision about whether Mother needed surgery to remove the polyps. A polyp is a small growth protruding from a mucous membrane. The CT scan showed hundreds of polyps in Mother's colon. If they were not removed in time, the polyps would eventually take up the space of the colon and block food from getting through.

I was shocked to learn of the urgency of the condition. At the same time, I found it difficult to comprehend the technical description of Mother's sickness. *Where is the transverse colon? What is the ileocaecal valve? Why do the little flesh bumps have such a massive impact? How can they grow wildly like weeds? Are they parasites absorbing Mom's nutrients?* The questions were like shooting stars falling in my murky brain. If only somebody could give me a 101 lesson about Mother's health problem.

The Internet had become as informative as the medical books I got; I googled things that I was eager to learn. From Chinese websites to English ones, from the origin of the disease to the treatments, I browsed countless webpages and took notes. Within a week, my computer's favorite list contained a long list of websites about polyp's removal, indigestion, patient diet, rectal bleeding and colon cancer. I compared the solutions at home and abroad, from traditional Chinese medicine and from Western medicine. Disappointingly, the explanation on the Chinese websites was not extensive. Some websites repeated the same contents. While on the English websites, frequently, the more I wanted to know, the harder the access became. I had to either sign up for a readership or obtain the information in person. Besides, the medical technology in the West was more advanced than in China. However, precautionary examination was quite common in Western countries but less practiced in China.

* * * * * *

Dr. Zeng was the surgeon who dealt with Mother's case. He seemed to be in his mid-thirties, stout and with spiky hair. He was one of the few surgeons in the office who could speak Cantonese. That made our communication easier, particularly between the doctor and my father.

My parents had lived most of their lives in Guangzhou, where Cantonese is the local dialect. It was a challenge for them to speak Putonghua, literally "Common Speech," also known as Mandarin, the official language. Father often told me he found it hard to pronounce *zh, ch, sh,* and *r* which in Putonghua required the tongue to roll. However, Putonghua was mandatory in school. I had to speak it in class.

As a Chinese saying goes, "There is nothing to be afraid of except a Cantonese speaking Putonghua." There is some truth in it. But as more Northerners migrated to South China for jobs and living, I heard more people speaking Mandarin rather than Cantonese in Guangzhou. Some old Cantonese even worried that the colorful dialect would die out in the land where it originated.

Dr. Zeng's office was on the same floor as the patients' rooms. He shared the office with eight other surgeons in two rows of cubicles. His was at the corner by the entrance. Three sliding windows lined the wall, opposite to the door. The office reminded me of the editorial office I worked in where computers were on each desk. Piles of files were next to the computers. The Post-it notes were either attached to computer screens or studded on the cubicles together with other loose paper. Some computers flashed with diagrams and Excel tables. But the seats were vacant. Alone in the office, Dr. Zeng was working at his desk. I decided to find a doctor to ask why Mother had been snubbed. After some time, we still had no diagnosis. As I pushed the door and walked in, the loud shuffle of feet in the hallway became muffled.

"*Nihao*, Doctor," I interrupted. "I'm Golden Orchid's daughter. I wonder if you have time to look into her case and give my family a diagnosis."

Dr. Zeng slowly looked up from the document. He saw me and Father who stood in the doorway. "Which room was she in?"

I told him where Mother's bed was and briefed him about her condition. I wrapped up my speech anxiously, "She's been in the *Waike* ward for two days but we haven't had a doctor talk to us."

"OK. I'll follow the case," Dr. Zeng said with an air of sophistication. "We're a bit hectic this month. So please be patient. We'll talk to you soon after the weekly *Waike* meeting."

The conversation was over. I thanked the doctor on my way out. Father waved as a gesture of thanks. I had no idea what the *Waike* meeting was but I truly hoped it would be finished as quickly as my first conversation with Dr. Zeng.

I noticed more silver hairs in Father's eyebrows while waiting for our next meeting with the doctor.

* * * * * *

The surgery rooms were on the tenth to twelfth floors. I remembered Father had been in one of the surgery rooms when he had his appendix removed. I wondered if it was fate that I returned to this *Waike* building. I did not want to experience those anxious waiting moments again. Father's surgery had lasted an hour and a half but I had felt like I was behind bars, facing empty walls for ages. I fidgeted even though it was a small operation. My mind had been split in half, and two voices were talking to each other in my head. *Will Baba be alright? How long do I have to wait? Is he in pain? No, he undergoes topical anesthesia. Can he eat and drink afterwards? Hopefully he can.* I sat for a minute, then stood and walked. I sat again, stood and walked. I sat, stood and walked. My back-and-forth pace finally got on Mother's nerves.

"Sit still, will you? You're making me dizzy," she said unpleasantly.

Since that time, I had learned that waiting outside the surgery room was as heart-wrenching as undergoing surgery. The patient temporarily felt no pain under anesthesia, but for the patient's family who waited outside the operating room, the anticipation stung like needles. Since Father's surgery, I had developed a deeper fear of surgery. The bright red light at the entrance of a surgery room reminded me of the pulsing red numbers on the timer of a bomb.

Mother's new room in the *Waike* was big enough for three patients. Three single beds with white sheets and pillowcases lay side by side. Next to each bed was a waist-high night stand with a drawer and a single-door cabinet. A private bathroom was attached, next to a balcony shared with the room next door. A TV set hung on the wall.

Occasionally, additional beds were lined against the wall in the hallway. The demand for bed space was much greater than the supply. It was so much easier for the patients who had good *guanxi*, or connections, with the doctors and administrative staff to be hospitalized. In the ordinary people's eyes, they also received better care. As true as is the phrase—*No Money, No Talk*—to describe the reality in contemporary China, *No Guanxi, No Way* is also common in all walks of life.

Mother was fortunate to be accommodated in the *Waike* right away without waiting for a bed. She stayed in a room opposite the station in which nurses were on duty 24/7. The day shift nurses outnumbered the night shift ones. In front of each bed was a call bell connected to the nursing station. Patients needing help could press the button to signal. But the nurses were usually too busy to show up immediately. It took them as long as five minutes to appear. So Mother usually would press the button five minutes before her intravenous injection was finished.

The surgeons were mainly men whereas the nurses were predominantly women in their twenties and thirties. The head nurse, in her forties, was probably the oldest and most experienced. Her pink uniform stood out among the white-clad nurses, whom Mother praised as white angels. I did not see the head nurse too often. She would show up on Monday mornings on bedside rounds, when all the surgeons and nurses of the *Waike* must attend.

At eight o'clock on Monday mornings, the director of the *Waike* would lead his team of surgeons to visit all the patients in the department. They walked into every room, inquired how every patient felt, and checked each one's report card. Sometimes interns would follow. The surgeon who was in charge of the patient would give an overview of the case to the interns. After the inspection, the surgeons would discuss the cases in a weekly meeting, including drawing out surgery plans for the following week. That was the weekly *Waike* meeting Dr. Zeng told us about in our first meeting. Similarly, the head nurse led the nurses to visit every patient after the surgeons' inspection.

Mother paid special attention to the Monday morning bedside rounds. She felt cared for. One Monday, I took a morning leave to be with her. It was 7:30 when I arrived. She was already sitting in bed.

"*Jousahn*," Good morning, I said to Mother. "You're up early."

"*Jousahn*," she greeted in a freshly sweet voice. She seemed in a good mood.

"Have you had breakfast yet?"

"Yes, an hour ago."

"Oh." I was surprised, and asked, "So what time did you get up?"

"Six. I'm ageing. I can't sleep long." She glanced at the watch by her pillow and said, "Soon the doctors will come to check rooms. Could you help me to tidy the table?"

"OK. Do doctors come every day?"

48

"Yes, but not like Mondays. The doctors with big titles will show up, too."

I quickly cleaned the night stand and put Mother's small items into the drawer. The carnations on the table caught my eye.

"Who bought you the flowers?"

"Mr. Liang. He stopped by last night after you left."

"How pretty they are."

Mother smiled.

After I finished organizing Mother's night stand, we waited patiently for the surgeons' inspection. When Mother heard footsteps echoing from the corridor, she would look out at the doorway.

* * * * * *

Mr. Liang was a warm-hearted, long-time family friend. My parents and I trusted him deeply, as if he was a family member. Lanky and slightly taller than me, he wore a pair of dark-framed glasses. His thin silver hair retreated to the back of his head. In his seventies, he was the youngest of eleven siblings. His only surviving sister was in America, as were his wife and five daughters and their families. But he did not feel lonely. He enjoyed hanging around with his friends and helping the needy. He had talked about his immigration application.

"It's my sister's biggest hope to see me in America," Mr. Liang once said. "She has done so much for me. It's time for me to reciprocate."

However, he was not as eager as most applicants would be. He said he had more freedom in Guangzhou with free transportation and free admission to museums and parks in the city. That was one of the benefits for senior citizens in Guangzhou.

When he was with my father, who had a potbelly, Mr. Liang often made fun of his slim body; he would tease, "When I stand next to Zhang Old Master, I look particularly malnourished."

Interestingly, although Father and Mr. Liang were so close that they found pleasure in mocking one another, they seldom addressed each other by their names. Instead, each gave the other a nickname—Father's was Zhang Old Master for his patriarchal demeanor, Mr. Liang's was Liang *Full-zi*, meaning Scholar Liang, for his erudition of Chinese literature. His bespectacled, studious appearance reflected his trustworthy personality.

From the first day I met Mr. Liang, I was told to call him Mr. Liang instead of Uncle Liang. It is common for Chinese people to call a non-related person "Uncle" or "Aunt" to show respect. We have specific family titles for the relatives depending on generation and gender. Father said that to address Mr. Liang as Uncle Liang would make him feel old. I guessed that was partly why Mr. Liang enjoyed the company of young people. One of the pleasurable moments I had with Mr. Liang was when he told me stories of the Chinese proverbs or when he recited excerpts of Chinese classic poems or essays.

"Have you read the Tang poet, Meng Jiao's *You Zi Yin*?" *The Song of a Traveling Son*. Mr. Liang asked once when he saw I was writing a Chinese composition about Mother.

"Yes," I nodded immediately. That was one of the most famous Chinese classical poems about a loving mother sewing the clothes for her son who was about to set out on a long journey.

"*How can a blade of young grass/ ever repay the warmth of the spring sun?*" Mr. Liang recited the last line emotionally. "This poem always touches my heart."

"Me, too," I interjected.

"The clothes that the son wears are made of stitches of thread in his mother's hand," Mr. Liang expressed. "How moving it is!"

I usually stopped what I was doing and listened to Mr. Liang, although he did not realize he had repeated himself. His understanding of Chinese literature and traditional culture was mesmerizing. Nobody had told me about the same subjects the way Mr. Liang did, not even my parents. I could not learn them at school either. Father always said, "The more you read, the more you will understand." So instead of asking Father about the origin of a Chinese idiom, I turned to Mr. Liang for more stories. I did not feel the barrier of a generation gap with Mr. Liang as much as I did with Father.

Mr. Liang was always there when my family needed help. He was one of Father's confidants. They could talk all night long. Mother also liked to chat with Mr. Liang. She found him understanding and amiable. She would complain to him after Father chided her. I was not around when she did that but I heard Father mention this.

"Mr. Liang's phone number has become your mother's complaint number," he whined half-jokingly. "She probably can remember his number backwards now."

Mr. Liang's rich experience in Cantonese cooking and in traditional Chinese medicine enlightened Mother. They also shared common interests—singing Karaoke of Cantonese opera and worshipping Buddhist beliefs.

* * * * * *

I had been waiting for the surgery notice after our first brief meeting with Dr. Zeng. The weekend passed, then a Monday, a Tuesday and on Wednesday, Dr. Zeng told me that he and the other surgeons had not decided whether Mother needed an operation. I was getting anxious and annoyed. *Come on! How difficult is it to schedule surgery for a critical patient? Mom should be the surgeons' first consideration.* Anger clouded my senses. I blamed those who had personal *guanxi* with the hospital staff. They could schedule surgery as early as possible. I felt my family was neglected. We knew nobody in the hospital and we were not knowledgeable about medicine and surgery. If only I had married a medical doctor.

I felt I had begun to lose control. Only surgeons could save Mother's life, I thought. They were like the reincarnation of Hua Tuo, a renowned Chinese physician in the Eastern Han Dynasty, who was considered a divine doctor for generations due to his mastery of medical skills. Dr. Zeng had undertaken challenging surgeries that lasted half a day or longer. A couple of times I saw his forehead was sweaty after surgery. Mr. Liang said that a surgeon needed to take risks and tolerate pressure, and that not everyone was cut out to be a surgeon because of the intensity of the job.

Every day I wondered if Mother's polyps would increase exponentially. At that thought, I had greater hope that an operation on Mother could terminate the growth of the polyps. I prayed day and night that Mother's case would not be pending for too long.

Mother seemed to do fine with her new roommates. She said her old roommates from the gastrointestinal ward came to visit her. They were about fifteen years her senior. One of them had just recovered from surgery on her stomach. Sometimes I wondered if their presence reminded Mother of her mother.

Father's visits alternated with mine. He usually came to the hospital at noon or early afternoon while I visited Mother after work in late afternoon. Some days Mother seemed to be more willing to chat with me alone. A few times during my visits, she revealed her thoughts of her own mother, whom I had never met.

"I feel sorry to see some daughters being mean to their mothers. They don't know how fortunate they are to have a mother," she often said.

"Do you miss *Popo* now?" I asked.

"Sometimes; I dream of her a lot lately."

"I wish I had met her."

Mother sighed. "She died on the surgery bed."

I was stunned. Mother had never told me about her mournful past. Did she sense something ominous? Father and I tried not to frighten her about her debilitating health. We told her she had polyps in her colon and the gastrointestinal doctor suggested she stay in the *Waike* for a possible surgery to remove the polyps. That was it. I did not know how Mother interpreted what we told her. She might be as anxious as I was about the upcoming surgery.

"She was like what I am now, sent to the hospital," Mother continued. "The doctor gave her an anesthetic shot and she never woke up."

"What was her problem?"

"Abdominal pain, she was about to have an operation."

"Did you have a chance to talk to her?" I asked hesitantly for fear she would suddenly withdraw her feelings.

"I wish. By the time I reached the hospital from the timber factory, she was already unconscious."

I did not continue my questioning. I was afraid the more she remembered her past, the more she would fear the same fate might happen to her. She was twenty-four when her mother died in the same hospital where Mom was staying now. How could she not think of *Popo*? During the hours when no visitors were allowed, Mother spent her time alone. That must have given her too much time to think and speculate. She was not like some patients who spent most of the time watching TV. The best time for her would be taking a walk with her roommates on the shady boulevard in the hospital. She liked chatting with older women. Perhaps they consoled her as a mother might. Although she did not tell me, I could feel her fear about having surgery. For a few days, she did not eat much. She was afraid she did not have enough time to fast before the surgery. While I was annoyed by the slow reaction of the surgeons, she asked me not to rush the doctors.

"They have their own schedule. Be patient," she said.

* * * * * *

The day arrived. That morning when Father, Mr. Liang and I went to visit Mother, she told us that Dr. Zeng wanted to see us in his office. Her face was as white as a Japanese *geisha*'s powdered countenance. She pointed to her night stand and said, "Dr. Zeng took away my CT scan result early this morning."

"Could you help me to take out a roll of toilet paper there?" she asked.

"Sure. How do you feel this morning?" I asked.

"So-so. I have a belly ache. So I only had half a bun for breakfast."

"If the breakfast in the hospital is no good, I can bring you food that you like in the morning," Father interjected.

"It's not necessary. Restaurants are nearby. It's convenient for me to eat out."

Father seldom talked to Mother in my presence. If he talked, it would be one of the shortest dialogues between husband and wife. Mother sometimes gave no response. I was already used to the awkwardness between them. They were like two gears with mismatched teeth, creating a grating sound. Sometimes I wanted to leave Father alone with Mother. He would rather go out to the balcony or the staircase where smoking was allowed.

The morning breeze reminded me that the temperature had dropped. I helped Mother put on a gray jacket before I went with Father and Mr. Liang to meet Dr. Zeng. He was in his cubical at the corner of the surgeons' office. He told us to wait for him in the meeting room next door. There I saw colorful posters on the wall showing human internal organs. Red, purple, black, yellow and blue represented different viscera and systems of a human body. The figures were more detailed than the ones in my high school biology class. I saw the English captions of lungs, heart, liver, stomach, spleen, pancreas and colon. I was usually pleased to read English, but not at that moment. A feeling of apprehension permeated the surgeons' meeting room. I felt like we were cannibals, discussing

53

how to anatomize Mother's body. I was anxious to find out more about Mother's illness, but at the same time I was afraid of knowing more. The innards in the figures were gloomy.

"Sit down, please." Dr. Zeng entered the room with Mother's CT scan result in his hand. "Sorry to have kept you waiting. You're Golden Orchid's family, right?"

"Yes. I'm her husband and she's her daughter. And this is Mr. Liang, our close friend."

"Good. And how may I address you?"

"My surname is Zhang."

Dr. Zeng pulled a chair to the table and stuck Mother's CT scan result on a white lit screen. The images of Mother's colon and liver were shown clearly. On that big negative were about a dozen small images at different angles among the organs.

"Mr. Zhang, I looked into your wife's test results carefully and we actually discussed your wife's case on Monday with other experts. The case is tricky. The growth tendency of the polyps makes it difficult for us to judge if they're cancerous or not. They grow densely around here and here," Dr. Zeng said, and pointed to the screen.

"You see, the size and shape of the polyps in the ascending colon varies greatly. Some are much bigger than the others." He pointed to the left side of the colon with a pen-like pointer. "We'll need to take a biopsy of tissue through surgery before we confirm if the patient has cancer."

"We've also discovered there is a tumor about three to four centimeters in diameter in her liver. See here." The pointer sat on the shadowed image of Mother's liver.

"This resembles the metastasis of a carcinoma. We assume the tumor has developed over two years at least. If the tumor is small enough, we'll be able to remove it. But the area here is getting bigger and over here," Dr. Zeng said, and pointed to the other side of the liver. "A smaller tumor is forming. It's too risky to do so."

I gulped. This sounded more deadly than I thought. *It is not true, is it? I am in the wrong room.* I eyed Father. He looked ghastly. The cheekbones stood out in his tan, sagged face. His thick eyebrows and the sideburns were salted with gray. His dark eyes were watery.

"So the tumor in the liver will continue to grow?" Mr. Liang asked.

"If cancer is confirmed, the tumor tends to spread faster in later stages. It's like a battle between normal blood cells and cancerous cells. The cancerous cells gradually get stronger for they've been absorbing the patient's nutrients. Eventually they'll take over the organ."

"Do you think a liver transplant will help?" A question popped out of my mouth. *Isn't that easy if Mom has a new liver?*

"No. Although we don't have a pathogenesis of the polyps to see if they contain malignant tumor cells, we assume the colon is the primary tumor. The tumor cells metastasize, forming a second tumor in the liver. There could be more areas infected. We don't know until we take a biopsy of tissues."

"What about surgery to remove the polyps?" I asked. This had been my primary question for a couple of weeks. How I wished Mother's problem was as simple as an operation could solve.

"Even when we operate, we cannot remove the large quantity of the polyps. They've grown everywhere in the colon. The areas I just pointed out to you have little space for solid food to pass through. That's why the patient has diarrhoea; the success rate of this operation is only 50/50."

"How bad will it be if she doesn't undergo surgery?" Father asked. His brows were knitted tightly, forming a Chinese character, 川, meaning stream. His face was darkened as if rain clouds hovered above his head. His voice was deep and hoarse. He had had rough nights for weeks. His shoulders sloped.

"Well, the polyps have grown fast. Eventually, they'll occupy the digestive tract in the colon. Food cannot pass through the colon and rectum, and be expelled from the body. That'll cause danger to the patient's life." Dr. Zeng paused and added, "When the patient reaches the later stages of cancer, we, as doctors, are now more in favor of maintaining the patient's quality of life than prolonging her life. In this case, it'd be better to have the patient eat whatever she wants. But now she can't because of the condition of the colon."

Hearing the words, Father immediately turned around, took out a tissue from his pocket, wiped his face and blew his nose. Dr. Zeng stopped. But Father did not want to interrupt the conversation. He soon returned to the table and gestured Dr. Zeng to go on.

"So, we'd recommend the patient to wear a colostomy bag. The patient's upper part of the colon is still in good condition," Dr. Zeng said. He drew the colon on a piece of paper. It was shaped like a big question mark without a dot at the end. He pointed to the upper part and highlighted a line outside the colon as a new outlet.

"We can separate the good part and connect a tube with the colon. On the other end of the tube is a bag receiving the food residue. After that, the patient can have a normal diet without worrying about the blockage of the colon caused by large food residue."

I was dumbfounded. What on earth was the matter here? It sounded like assembling a machine—you separate the original configuration, replace a portion, and put the machine back together. *I don't want Mom to have this surgery. No, no, not this one.* With or without surgery, Mother was doomed to living in misery. I could not picture her carrying a colostomy bag for the rest of her life. She would look like an extraterrestrial creature, with the waste coming out from an opening in her abdomen. How could she carry a bag to do morning exercises with her friends? How could she cook and sleep?

My ears refused to listen. I wished Dr. Zeng was talking about another patient, not Mother. I wished I was just having a nightmare. I wished I could stop this conversation that was filled with bloody anatomical lingo.

Mr. Liang was as calm as a Buddhist master. He asked a few questions and made some comments. By then, my mind was already somewhere else. Thank heaven that someone like Mr. Liang was still listening to Dr. Zeng. As the patient's family member, I should have been proactive and cooperative. I should have taken charge and posed questions. I should have stood up for my parents to look for a solution. But I was speechless, as quiet as Father.

Dr. Zeng's words were incredible. I had never thought the matter was so grave. I had no idea how to absorb every bit. *It cannot be true.* I kept telling myself. I wanted to escape. I wanted to rewrite this scene like a novelist who could determine the fate of her characters. I wanted Dr. Zeng to tell me word for word what exactly was happening. His speech became too fast for me to follow. I felt he was speaking a foreign language. His lips were moving but I had no clue what he was talking about. I could not help looking at the time constantly. Whenever I looked up I saw the naked, stomach-turning images of human internal organs on the walls, and I shuddered. Dr. Zeng's voice drew my attention again.

"I understand it's very difficult for the family. You may want to discuss the options with other family members and get back to me after a few days. The examinations show the patient is anemic. So I've prescribed some medicine and intravenous injections for her. It'd be better that her blood properties recover before she is discharged from the hospital," Dr. Zeng said.

We thanked Dr. Zeng and shook hands with him. As we were on our way out, Dr. Zeng remembered something.

"By the way, I wonder if you know whether the patient's parents had a similar problem. The overgrown polyps suggest they may be hereditary."

"I'm not sure but I know both of her parents had gastrointestinal problems," Father said.

"I suggest your daughter have a colonoscopy within a few years for the sake of her health," Dr. Zeng said and eyed me like a yellow traffic light.

What? I may also have cancerous polyps? I thought to myself in disbelief. *Great! Not only is Mom's health in danger, mine may be too.* I never knew cancer was inherited. Nobody told me what cancer really was. Mother had never told me how her parents passed away. Did she know she may have the genetic colon cancer? I was in a big black hole.

We left the meeting room. I returned Mother's CT scan result into her night stand. She was sitting on her bed, eyeing me curiously with her big dark eyes. She must have thought our meeting with Dr. Zeng was over. I told her we were still at the meeting but would be out shortly. Then I left her. I knew I lied but it was for Mother's good. Both Father and Mr. Liang wanted to discuss Mother's situation outside her hearing range. We were all afraid the bad news would make her even more worried.

* * * * * *

Father and Mr. Liang stood at the elevator entrance. Father had already found a corner next to an open window for a cigarette. His eyebrows were still knitted tightly. His eyes recessed into their sockets. The bags were noticeable under his fatigued eyes. He looked out of the window and breathed out smoke rings. He was in deep thought and did not notice my presence.

I saw a pair of concerned eyes behind Mr. Liang's dark-framed spectacles. He folded his arms on his chest and leaned against the wall. Except for an occasional nurse who went by, the place where we stood was so quiet that I could hear a pin drop.

"So do you understand what Dr. Zeng said?" I started the conversation.

"No. I only understand half and half," Father said honestly.

"Really, I saw you listening to him attentively," I said.

"I do that to show my respect to the doctor," Father said. "You know your father; it's hard to understand everything in that kind of environment."

"Yes, that moment was very hard for the family," Mr. Liang interjected. "In fact, tending the patient in the coming days is going to be more difficult. You have to be prepared for unexpected factors."

I nodded my head and said, "So what shall we do? I've never heard of colostomy. It sounds scary."

Mr. Liang explained patiently what colostomy was and agreed it would inconvenience both the patient and the family. The only merit was Mother could eat whatever she liked.

"Neither *Baba* and I are good at home nursing. I'm afraid the cleaning-up work of the colostomy bag will be a hassle," I said hesitantly. A spasm of shame chilled down my spine instantly. I dared not to imagine the bizarre looking person Mother would become. Who would want their mother to attract public attention resulting from her physical abnormality? I was awfully unprepared for this unpleasant and messy tending experience. *Cut it off!* The other half of my mind shouted. *She's your mother, your one and only mother. How can you let her suffer alone? How can you cop out when she needs you most?* But the more I envisioned the difficulty ahead, the less motivated I felt about the colostomy surgery. I added, "*Mama* might end up worrying about the filling of the bag during the night."

"That's true. Your father and I are both concerned about your mother's physical ability. She's too weak to undergo any surgery at the moment," Mr. Liang said. "Dr. Zeng is a surgeon. His point of view reflects his position. Surgeons are like butchers. They like talking you into having surgery. Selfishly speaking, a successful operation helps to generate income for the department and gain reputation. But not everyone is suitable for surgery."

I recalled *Popo* passed away during surgery. Yes, Mr. Liang was right. Not everyone is suitable for surgery. *What if Mother dies on a surgery bed, too?* I eyed Father. The cigarette in between his fingers was about to burn to the butt. He coughed a couple of times. I could smell the foul nicotine.

"Actually without taking a biopsy of tissue, we all know Golden Orchid has cancer. The surgery is just routine before the doctor files an official report," Father said gravely.

"Some people can never recover from surgery," Mr. Liang continued. "We often say once your belly is open, your *qi* will be greatly undermined."

I had heard of this traditional belief. The ancient Chinese believed *qi*, the flow of energy, was through the body. The incision on a body was like a punctured tire, eventually exhausting the air. I eyed Mr. Liang, gesturing him to go on.

"Blood is particularly essential to women. You see, more women are anemic than men. Since your mother is anemic, she'll pay a high price for surgery. I'd suggest a conservative approach: that is the illness is diagnosed by Western medicine and treated by traditional Chinese medicine.

"Surgery cannot solve all problems. In the case of cancer, it may in fact activate the cancerous cells and expedite their growth," Mr. Liang said. He mentioned a couple of real-life examples that happened to his friends to prove his point.

Surprisingly, Father listened to Mr. Liang patiently. He was not a big fan of traditional Chinese medicine. But Mr. Liang's charisma won our heart. He was so eloquent that his opinions weighed heavily in my family.

Mr. Liang studied medicine for a stint when he was young because his parents wanted him to be a doctor. He did not make it. But what he learned was of great help in his life. He told me he used to tend his sick daughters. Now his medical knowledge made us trust him as if he was our family doctor.

"I have decided not to tell her about her cancer," Father said. His words sounded like they had been discreetly chosen from an intense inner reasoning.

"She lacks rational judgment. The news will rather hit her hard than do her any good," Father continued. He had already tossed the butt in the tray.

"Um—" Mr. Liang thought for a second and said, "this is not a bad idea. She can get a good rest without the psychological burden. As an old saying goes, 'Thirty percent of cancer patients die of the disease while seventy percent of them die of fright.'"

At hearing Father's decision, I had a little debate inside. I had always believed every patient should have the right to know what disease she has, especially when dealing with a terminal illness. This is also what doctors should do—reveal the truth to the patient. Besides, having cancer is not a taboo in our society. I saw an increasing concern among Chinese on breast cancer, skin cancer, lung cancer and even prostate cancer in recent years. But if Father's presumption of Mother's reaction to cancer was correct, I would also not take that risk of ruining her hope of living. For that matter, I changed my opinion about what I had believed. We must make an exception in Mother's case.

"So, what shall I say to her if she asks?" I asked with concern.

"Well, we can just tell her she has polyps. She needs to take medicine to strengthen her body before she has surgery. She is anemic and it's not a good idea to have surgery now," Father summed up our discussion.

That was what we told Mother afterwards. She could go home after her body was recovered to the level that met the doctor's requirement. Hearing our explanation, Mother was as calm as a placid lake. She did not have any unusual reaction, nor did she ask questions. I wondered if she felt relieved about not having surgery, or if she was still haunted by *Popo*'s unexpected death. I wondered how she would feel about the patients around her being pushed in and out of the surgery room. Wouldn't she feel lucky that she was not like those sedated patients?

Chapter 4
Disillusion

A government survey in 2007 shows cancer had topped the list of the ten most lethal diseases for urban residents the year before in China. The cancer mortality rate in China has increased by eighty percent over the past thirty years. After the media had exposed the "cancer villages" in South China, where mining and industrial manufacturing polluted heavily the local air and water system, causing a skyrocketing increase of cancer deaths, the public's awareness of the worsening environment grew stronger.

I realized my awareness of Mother's health came too late. That night after meeting Dr. Zeng, I lay in bed but could not fall asleep. Father was in the living room alone with his brandy and cigarettes. The scuffling of his plastic slippers and the collision of his shot glass and the glass tabletop sounded loud in the small hours. Dr. Zeng's words resonated in my mind. Mother's days were numbered! The more I thought, the more panicked I felt. My nose twitched as if it sensed the pain of the imminent death. I felt a lump in my throat; for a moment I was breathless. My weeping interrupted Father's nocturnal contemplation. He walked into my bedroom and turned on the light.

"You're still not asleep?" he asked.

"I'm trying." I held my breath for fear Father would find out I was crying. But my trembling soft voice gave me away.

Father sat next to me on the bedside. "Don't think too much. Go to sleep."

A strange force pushed me to sit up and I wailed on his shoulder.

"Is it true that Mom will die? I don't want her to leave us," I cried.

Father patted my back and said nothing.

61

That was the only time after I grew up that I burst into tears on Father's shoulder. I cried uncontrollably as if my tears flowed out of a loosened fire hydrant. I had never felt so frightened. I grasped Father's arms tightly. My heart thumped fast. I could feel his deep breath at my ear. He did not stop me from crying.

"OK. Now go to sleep. You need to work tomorrow," he said feebly after my weeping ceased.

I slept through the rest of the night. The next morning, I saw two dozen cigarette butts in the ashtray, next to it was a palm-sized shot glass. Father must have stayed up all night long.

* * * * * *

Before Dr. Zeng revealed Mother's condition to us, I was fed up with the bureaucracy of the hospital. The long waiting for a conversation with a physician compelled me to send out emails for help. I wrote, "My mother is dying. Please introduce me to your doctor friends if you have any. I need professional opinions. I'll be very grateful."

I felt bad about my pushy language. But at that time, there was no other way for me to put it courteously without showing my anxiety. Thank goodness! My friends had read my message instead of deleting it like a phony spam. But I was heartbroken to find out my circle of friends had no one working in the medical sciences. The closest connection I could find was my high school classmate who was a veterinarian. After days of waiting for responses, I saw no hope.

Until the day after we met Dr. Zeng and were still in the midst of making the decision on what Mother should do next, I received an email from an American professor about his doctor friend in Guangzhou. A former Associated Press foreign correspondent, Prof. Zeitlin was in his fourth year of journalism teaching in China. His fast-expanding social network always astounded me. He told me in a message that his Chinese colleague's old classmate's husband was a radiologist at a local traditional Chinese medicine hospital. He was willing to put me in touch.

I was elated. I had not felt such pulsating excitement for a long time. As soon as I got home I shared my joy with Father.

"*Baba*, I'm introduced to a radiologist, Dr. Yang," I said. "I want to bring Mom's CT scan result to him for a second opinion."

"*Ho-ah*," Father agreed in a disguised thrill. He thought for a second and then changed his tone, "But it won't matter. The result is an unchangeable fact."

"I know. But since I worked hard to get to know a doctor, it won't hurt to hear more professional advice." I was afraid that Father would discourage me at the drop of a hat.

"Fine, give it a shot then."

* * * * * *

The evening before I met Dr. Yang, Father handed me a red packet.

"Tell your doctor friend," Father said, "this is your father's little token."

Astonished, I received the rectangular red envelope and said yes. Receiving lucky money in red packets from our parents and relatives was a dream for every kid during Chinese New Year. But the meaning of the red packet went sour today. People often say, we do not count it as a problem if it can be resolved by money. Giving someone a red packet might help us cut corners, build *guanxi*, conceal secrets and acquire all sorts of convenience immorally. Personally, I despised this means of appreciation. But he was my father and it was inevitable that we were influenced by the value of *No Money, No Talk*, I would do what I was told. I felt my appointment with Dr. Yang suddenly became an under-the-table bribe. I went back to my bedroom and peeped into the red packet. A red note of one hundred *yuan* was folded inside. I pondered, was that the worth of Dr. Yang's piece of advice?

The next day I went to meet Dr. Yang in the hospital. His office was in the Radiology Department, in the back of the observation room where a big glass window allowed me to see the testing patient in the room next door. Small and simple, Dr. Yang's office had a long desk and three chairs. There were no human organ charts on the wall. Thank goodness.

In his mid-thirties, Dr. Yang looked attractive with his thin, black-rimmed spectacles. He had a square face, straight nose, thin lips, and clear skin. He did not have Dr. Zeng's walk-the-walk-type zest but more a hint of scrupulousness and chivalry. He was about a head taller than I, slender but firm. His white gown gave an air of authority. After I explained Mother's problem, I handed him the CT scan result. He raised the big negative composed of small snapshots over the white fluorescent light on the wall. His eyes strained for a few minutes. I sat opposite from him across the long desk, waiting quietly for his one-hundred-*yuan*-worth statement. I could hear my breathing, heart thumping through my ears.

"Your mother's cancer is serious," Dr. Yang said in Mandarin. "How long have you noticed her symptoms?"

"About two months ago," I said after a quick calculation in my head.

"That's a late discovery," Dr. Yang said, looking at each snapshot closely. "According to the CT scan result, it takes at least two to three years for such tumor development.

"The sad news is", Dr. Yang put down the CT scan result, eyeing me with compassion, "it will grow faster in her remaining days."

"How long can she live?" I asked in a fragile voice, holding back my tears.

"Estimated conservatively, it'd be from six months to a year."

Dr. Yang's analysis was as final as a judge's decision. Mother and I used to watch the TV drama series about lawyers, in which the judge struck his gavel in the courtroom and announced the verdict. From that instant, I felt what I heard was no different from a death sentence. My heart sank into an abyss of dismay. I lowered my gaze at the CT scan result on the desk, wordless. I was in a trance for some time until Dr. Yang's voice echoed in my eardrums again.

"It must be a blow to your father and you," he said calmly. "Try to provide your mother with a good quality of life. That's the best you can do."

I thanked him for his advice. As I was about to leave, I handed him the red packet, saying exactly what Father told me. Dr. Yang immediately declined. I offered several times, in vain.

"No, no," he said firmly. "Keep this for yourself. Your family needs money now. You're our friend. So feel free to ask me for help."

A fit of indescribable emotion surged inside me—warm and soothing but also heart-wrenching and throat-burning. I had to depart quickly before tears dropped from my blurry eyes. Bidding goodbye, I willed my lead-filled legs to carry me to the exit.

That evening, I gave back the red packet to Father and retold everything I had heard from Dr. Yang.

"It's all expected" was the only thing Father said before he contemplated in silence all night long. The chilling darkness hovered over his sloping shoulders. One side of his cheek bones was glistening damp. He probably sobbed quietly. I could not tell, peeping through the gap of my bedroom door. I could not help thinking how many more nights would be like this.

* * * * * *

After my consistent persuasion, I successfully talked Father into joining me in a dinner with Dr. Yang and his wife at Prof. Zeitlin's invitation. Ever since Mother was admitted to the hospital, Father had turned down his social activities. Instead, he either visited Mother in the hospital or lost himself in work. I bought several books on colon cancer and therapy. Father's first reaction was "It's not necessary to buy these books; a waste of money." But a few days later, he started to read them as well. He then said, "Don't show these books to your mother. Our reading is one thing; hers is another."

The dinner with Dr. Yang was in a newly-opened Chinese restaurant near the campus where Prof. Zeitlin taught. Every corner was brightly lit; even the blind could sense the glaring gilded divider at the entrance. We were seated in a reserved room in which stood a round table big enough for eight people. The splendid décor of the restaurant matched the high food prices. The first page of the menu listed the rarest and the dearest cuisines: abalone, sea cucumber, shark's fins and fish maw. At exorbitant prices, they are considered the food for the rich in Guangzhou. Obviously, the restaurant targeted the upper-middle class customer. I have forgotten the exact dishes except that each of us had a mushroom as big as the brim of a mug with abalone gravy. We had to eat with knife and fork for that particular dish, an unusual experience for Father and me. Compliments about the food broke the ice and started the conversation. Dr. Yang reiterated his viewpoint about Mother's health in response to his wife and Prof. Zeitlin's questions.

"Surgical methods and chemical therapy won't cure her now," Dr. Yang said. "Let her rest more and enjoy life the way she wants."

"We're thinking of taking her to see traditional Chinese medicine doctors," Father spoke slowly in his imperfect Mandarin.

"That's fine," Dr. Yang replied. "You may take her to our hospital. It's not far from your home, is it?"

"Not far," Father said, pouring tea into everyone's cup. "Thank you very much, Dr. Yang, for your concern and time."

As constrained as I was, Father thanked Dr. Yang too many times to remember. To show his gratitude, he even vied with Dr. Yang for paying the bill. After a full minute of arms flailing and elbows nudging, Dr. Yang picked up the tab at last. Had Prof. Zeitlin not understood it was a Chinese way of showing hospitality, he would have been dumbfounded by the seemingly fistfight melodrama between my father and Dr. Yang. The body contact warmed the atmosphere. Everyone's face wore a smile and teacups were filled several times. Topics jumped from Mother's health to Prof. Zeitlin's experience in China. I translated for Father, Mrs. Yang for her husband. At last, Dr. Yang and his wife sent their best to Mother even though they had never met her.

"*Nin Tai Ke Qi Le*," Father thanked Dr. Yang again.

That was the first and only dinner we had with a physician.

* * * * * *

A few days later, Mr. Liang and I exchanged our ideas with Dr. Zeng while Father waited outside. He said he believed in Mr. Liang and me, that we could handle the matter. Our decision was Mother would not have any surgery. She would stay in the hospital until her health improved. Father and I would also look into the traditional Chinese medicine therapy. It may have disappointed Dr. Zeng that we decided against surgery for Mother. After all, it was my original hope. But he supported our decision. He handed me a document and asked me to sign. I read the contents—a surgery waiver. Basically, it said the hospital took no responsibility should the patient's illness worsen because the patient or the patient's representatives decided against an immediate operation.

The experience reminded me of the night before Father had his appendix removed. I had to sign an agreement on behalf of my family. It was more or less a disclaimer that the hospital had no liability for any surgical accidents. I had to consent to whatever anesthesia was given to Father before the operation could proceed. I studied the pages carefully for fear I might miss some terms that would disadvantage my family. Mother stood next to me and

66

scratched her arm anxiously. Father was in excruciating pain in the waiting room. Finally, I just glanced at the page and checked YES for all the "Do you agree" questions. *Come on! I just want Baba to receive speedy treatment.* I was tired of bureaucracy.

Of course, the wording in the document was in favor of the hospital. I signed the paper in front of Mr. Liang and Dr. Zeng. I felt I had just made a deal with a loan shark. What if Mother's health condition plummeted like a stock market index from this minute on? I would be the most reprehensible person. Fear lingered over me. My hands were as cold as ice. I had not felt so clear-headed for I knew I had to take the consequences if anything wrong happened to Mother. After we told Dr. Zeng that Mother was mentally vulnerable to the news, he agreed not to reveal the information about the tumor to her.

* * * * * *

For the very first time, I saw Father make *Lo Foh Tong* for Mother. Mr. Liang gave him tips on how to make the fish soup as it was good for Mother's rehabilitation. Father asked me to deliver the soup to the hospital. He said Mother would be happier if I served her soup. But I knew he wanted to avoid confrontation with Mother.

"How do you like the soup?" I asked after pouring the silky white broth into Mother's stainless steel lunch box. The soup remained steaming hot.

"It's a bit salty," Mother said as she sipped several mouthfuls. "Your father's cooking is always heavy on salt."

How I wish for once she would appreciate her husband's good will.

"*Baba* spent several hours making the soup," I said, wrapping the thermal lunch box Father gave me. "The soup is good for your recovery, please eat more."

Knowing I had not had *Lo Foh Tong* for days, Mother wanted me to finish the soup for her. I refused. She groaned about its salty taste and made an excuse that she had just had a full meal. I finally accepted. Without it being said, Mother truly wanted to share the best she had with me.

* * * * * *

Dr. Zeng said Mother had been malnourished for some time; she had glucose and other injections every day. She was infused daily with about four to six bottles of liquid medicine in various sizes of 250-500 ml. I admired her bravery in how she bore the pain of the needles. After two months in the hospital, both of her wrists and hands were tattooed with needle holes. I felt as if the needles pierced my heart. The back of her hands were bruised from long-time intravenous injections. Every time I visited her, I saw two colors—the fresh bruise was purple, the old one black. She did not want me to touch her hands for fear her hands would ache more. The only time I could observe her hands was when I applied slices of potatoes to the back of her hands. Some of her older roommates told her that fresh potatoes could absorb the bruise.

I made sure Mother had fresh potatoes every day. A potato usually lasted two days. I washed the potato and cut it in thin slices, the thinner the better. Mother was particular about it. If the slice was not transparent, she would say "this slice is not thin enough." I applied a fresh slice to the back of her hands. The potato juice cooled her hands.

"Are you feeling better?" I asked.

"Yeah, so comfortable," she said. She reclined in bed, closed her eyes and stretched her left arm to me.

When the slice was dry, I replaced another piece on the back of her hand. It lasted another half an hour. I did the same treatment every day. Gradually, the old bruises were gone, but new ones were always there. Mother's hands looked older than her peers'—coarse dark skin, short lean fingers and small palms. They were like dull leather furniture needing to be polished. The blue veins were visible in the back of her hands, as if they were water pipes dug out above ground. I measured my palm with Mother's. Mine was one third of a finger bigger than hers.

"*Mama* is getting old now," Mother sighed. "Look at my hands, no flesh at all, just bones."

She showed both of her hands to me and ringed her wrist with the fingers of her other hand. On her left wrist was a jade bracelet that Father gave her as a souvenir from Yunan province. The jade was rare, typically produced in Dali, an ethnic minority city. Mother had worn the bracelet ever since Father helped her put it on. When she first tried to put it on, it barely fitted. Father had to take her to a jeweler. With the help of soap and the jeweler's expertise, Mother finally put on the bracelet. Now she could take the bracelet on and off as easy as pie.

The fact that Mother could take off her bracelet effortlessly worried her. She knew she had lost ten kilograms from fifty-five kilograms in several weeks. She blamed her non-stop diarrhoea. After we told her she was malnourished, she immediately said, "No doubt. For months I had the runs every day right after I ate. The food was not yet fully digested, it was all expelled. *Aigh*, *Mama* is old. I'm useless."

No matter how tired Mother sometimes felt about her hospital life, she was an obedient patient who followed doctors' instructions. I thought because Mother was born in the Year of the Horse, maybe she possessed the docile nature of a horse. In Father's lexicon, she listened to the doctor as if the doctor's words were imperial decrees.

On the opposite, Father would listen to himself instead of doctors' advice. When he was still under medication after his appendix removal, he demanded the nurse take away an intravenous injection. He complained the medicine hurt his arm. He did not take pills on time and smoked while his wound was not healed. "That's how your father bosses around a nurse," Mother recalled. She said he was as vicious as a tiger in the jungle.

* * * * * *

One day on my way home after I had visited Mother, I overheard a conversation between a man and a woman in the elevator.

"How's your father doing? Can he eat now?" the woman asked.

"Yes, he's doing fine. The doctor suggests he take small portions and have several meals a day. You know, two thirds of his stomach is removed," the man said.

"Marvelous," the woman praised as they walked out of the elevator.

I followed behind, savoring what they said. I was amazed at how surgery could change a patient's way of living. How could a man survive with one third of a stomach? That was one of the weirdest things I had heard. How old would he be? Would he get hungry all the time because he did not eat much?

To some extent, I felt relieved that Mother did not undergo surgery. But she did not make this decision. We did. Did she like it?

How would she react if she knew we had hidden the fact that she had cancer from her? Would she live happily with an incomplete organ or a colostomy bag? That kind of life would be miserable for me. I felt as if Mother's pain was contagious. It pained me more every day.

Sometimes I wished Mother and I were not related, so I might see things through more objectively. I would be able to regard an operation on Mother or the organ donation after she passed away as strictly a medical research project, no affection attached. But the truth was I could not put aside my emotion to make an unbiased decision for her. I cared about how she felt if she had surgery, if she knew she was about to die, if she was attached to a colostomy bag like a freak. I did not want her to suffer more. I wanted to make up for every blood cell that was devoured by the cancerous cells in her body. I wanted to transfer all her tumor to me so that she could live well. I wanted to take her pain away. I prayed to my god day and night, more frequently than I used to. I had awful dreams. One of them kept coming back. I would dash ahead regardless of my safety to stop flying bullets shooting Mother. I realized how much Mother meant to me. When I thought of her, I felt warmth flowing through my body. I could not distinguish if it was love or courage or both. *Dear god, if my body could save my mother, please, please let me take those bullets instead of my mother.*

* * * * * *

The battery of tests in the hospital prohibited Mother from having a solid food diet for nearly a month. She often said the noodles and congee did not fill up her stomach. Pangs of hunger in the middle of night woke her up. We were told Mother had not gained enough nutrition via intravenous injections. Shortly after I signed the surgery waiver, she was permitted to have solid food again, but with high restrictions—no fatty or fried foods and no high-fiber or hard-to-digest foods, such as vegetable leaves, mushrooms, wheat products, chicken, pork, beef, bean sprouts and one of Mother's favorites, lotus roots. She could chew some food but not swallow.

The restrictions were hard on her. She chewed the food finely, swallowing only the juice. She had to eat less rice although she was a big rice consumer like Mr. Liang. I remembered in the past when

Mr. Liang came to our house to have supper, Mother cooked three times as much rice as she normally did. Father often joked that when Mr. Liang visited us, our rice container went empty quickly.

Mother understood she had to change her eating habits to prevent her colon from being completely obstructed. She ate like a tiny bird. She ate smaller meals four or five times a day as Dr. Zeng suggested. She sucked the juice of everything that could be in her mouth. When she opened her mouth to bite, I could see her throat muscle—no extra flesh under her chin and her wrinkled neck.

* * * * * *

One day, I went to her room after work as usual, and found her table bare and her bed empty, as if they were made for a newcomer. I was scared. *What happened to Mom? Is she in an emergency? Has she gone without bidding farewell?* The worst thoughts emerged in my mind. Her roommate, about Mother's age, was aware of my panicked face. She told me that Mother had moved in the morning to the room next door. Oh thank heaven! I found her.

Memory transported me to my kindergarten days. It was always difficult for the two-to-four-year-olds to separate from their parents. I was one of them. I attended the daycare in Mother's factory. Every day she sent me there on her way to work. One time, I took the chance when the teachers did not pay attention to me and I sneaked out of the fence. I wanted to run to where Mother worked and find her. I ran and ran and ran. I wanted so badly to see Mother. But Ms. Mai, one of the teachers, had spotted my escape. She followed behind, taking much bigger steps than mine. At last, like a swooping eagle, she grabbed me in her arms. I screamed hysterically "I want *Mama*." I struggled to loosen her tight grip on my belly, kicking my feet hard as if I were a chick caught by her enemy. She forced me to sit in the corner until I calmed down.

At the end of the day, when Mother came to pick me up, Ms. Mai told her what happened.

"Your daughter is very bold. She ran fast. If I had discovered her escape a bit later, I could have lost her," the teacher said. She was still shocked at my attempt. She talked excitedly and flailed her arms, as if I had challenged her physical ability.

"She's usually quiet and obedient in class. To my surprise, she ran away today. But anyway, she's a good girl. Don't beat her or ground her," the teacher finally said. She looked at me and smiled affectionately, "Don't run away again, OK?"

"Say yes and goodbye to Ms. Mai," Mother held my hand and said.

I did what I was told.

For years, I still could not forget that incident. During the weeks when Mother was in hospital, I missed her the most. I still had not completely accepted the fact that she had cancer. *I am going to lose Mom.* I said it to myself every day. I passed by beggars on the footbridge near the hospital. They were a mother and her teenage son. In the mother's arm was an infant. They looked dirty and desperate. They knelt and bowed to every pedestrian in the hope of receiving some merciful offerings. In front of them on the floor was a placard on which was written the hardship this family went through. Most people did not take such a scene seriously. They all knew ninety percent of the city beggars were professional crooks. I did not stop for the mother and children but a thought crossed my mind. The boy was even luckier than me. At least he had a mother. My mother was going to leave me.

I thanked Mother's roommate and ran to next door. There she was, lying in bed with her intravenous injection. She looked at peace. I did not want to disturb her. This room only had two beds. Mother's neighbor was a thirty-something woman. Around her were all sorts of machines and a number of catheters. One of the devices showed the heart beat and blood pressure of the patient. It beeped rhythmically. The patient seemed to be asleep, her back faced me.

I took out a potato from a plastic bag I had brought with me. I went to the bathroom to wash it and got ready for our potato therapy. I looked around. The room seemed to be bigger. The space between Mother's bed and her new roommate's was about three steps wide. Mother opened her eyes and said softly, "You're here."

"Yes. How do you feel today?"

"Good. Your father came this morning and helped me to move."

"I was wondering about that. Neither of you called me and told me about it."

"Well, it was a surprise. The head nurse told me this morning there was an empty bed available. She said I could have more space in this room. So your father and I moved here."

"Have you met Dr. Zeng today?"

"Yes. He was on duty last night and he came to greet me before he got off work." Mother was pleased.

"So he knew you changed rooms?"

"Yes. I think he suggested the idea before the head nurse told me the news."

"I see. Are you ready for the potato therapy after the injection?"

"Yep. Be quiet when we talk. She just had surgery and needs a rest," Mother pointed to the patient next to her.

"You know each other already?"

"Briefly, we greeted each other this morning when she was awake. I talked to her husband after she fell asleep. She's a middle school teacher. She had kidney surgery two days ago. Her family knew the president of the hospital so she was sent to this room. Originally, she could have had the room all to herself. But she wanted a roommate with whom she can chat."

"I see. So you're lucky to have a new roommate."

"This room is quite comfortable," Mother said. She thought for a while and continued, "The director of the *Waike* and several leaders of the hospital came to visit her this morning. Her surgery was successful. Hopefully she will be discharged from the hospital in a week."

"It sounds like her family has really good *guanxi* with the officials," I commented.

"You bet. Otherwise she couldn't have scheduled surgery so soon."

"And you can benefit from her *guanxi*, too." I added, "Perhaps the doctors and nurses will pay more attention to you."

Mother was more talkative than on other days. Perhaps she saw hope in the fact that she could room with someone who had a smooth surgical experience. Perhaps she felt warmth from the people who cared about her. Perhaps she was happy that she did not need to wait long for the bathroom. I loved seeing her big bright eyes when she talked. Her eyes rolled when ideas sprinkled in her mind. She asked me about how I was getting on and how was everything in the family.

"*Mama* is not at home. You have to take care of yourself and your father," she said. "Don't order too many takeaways. I know your father is too lazy to cook. Don't be like him."

"We often eat at home. Don't worry. I do the dishes after the supper and on weekends I clean up the house."

"You've grown up. You have to learn how to look after yourself. *Mama* cannot always be around with you."

Mother's words flooded me with an odd sense: Did she imply her last will? They almost made me shed tears in front of her. I told her I would be around for her all the time, no matter what. I told her I would earn lots of money to travel with her. I also told her after she was released from the hospital I would take her out to places that she wanted to visit the most. She beamed, revealing a dimple on her pinkish cheeks.

The November wind was chilly at night but warm in the day when the sun was shining. The trees were still as green as in the spring. Pedestrians began to wear long-sleeve clothes. The central air conditioning in the building was turned off. All the patients received a flyer reminding them to keep warm in the cool weather. Father and I tried to persuade Mother to wear socks but she preferred bare feet. She said socks made her uncomfortable. In the end, she wore the thin silky socks.

* * * * * *

It was mid-December of 2006 when Father, Mr. Liang and I met Dr. Zeng for the last time. The atmosphere in the meeting room was less stressed this time. Dr. Zeng gave us a report of Mother's health improvement. He said she was cooperative and optimistic about her prospects.

"That's very important. I think as her family you must have made a lot of effort to keep up her spirits. A good attitude is always of great help to a patient's recovery; sometimes it's even better than medicine can do," Dr. Zeng said.

"Thank you for not telling her about the tumor," Mr. Liang said.

"I respect the patient's family's decision. Everyone's response to cancer varies. As the family, you understand the patient's personality better than me. I'm just a surgeon who is responsible for healing my patients." Dr. Zeng said, beaming. "Once my last intravenous prescription for her is used up, she can be discharged. Just ask the on-duty nurse for the tablets to take home."

Father and Mr. Liang thanked Dr. Zeng. They nodded when Dr. Zeng repeated a list of foods that Mother should not eat. After the business talk, Dr. Zeng looked at me and said, "I heard you are working for *Crazy English*."

"Yeah, I'm an editor for the magazine." I was surprised that the doctor took interest in my job.

"That's what the nurse told me. I'm wondering if you know any English training classes for adults. We need to take the annual career qualification test. Part of the test is an English level test," Dr. Zeng said.

I was surprised that a surgeon had to take an English test. The connection between surgical skills and English would have never crossed my mind. But that was the fact. Most of the well-paid positions in Guangzhou required the staff to take an English level test. Civil servants needed an English qualification test, as did medical doctors, accountants and lawyers. Even Guangzhou taxi drivers could not avoid learning English if they wanted to keep their jobs. Within the last ten years, the fever to learn English was like an epidemic in China. Young parents sent their toddlers to English nursery school. Learning English had become more important for the Chinese than studying the national language.

Who had suggested Dr. Zeng come to me for advice? I bet it must be Mother's chatting about me with one of the nurses. If it was not because of Dr. Zeng's recommendation, Mother would not have moved to a more comfortable room. To some extent, Dr. Zeng was like a *guanxi* I had newly built in the hospital. I was also grateful to Dr. Yu, an orthopedic surgeon who treated my American teacher, Frank, when he broke his leg. Dr. Yu visited Mother and asked Dr. Zeng to take good care of her after he heard of Mother's illness from me. This was *guanxi* diplomacy in hospital. Whether or not Mother would return to the *Waike*, I should maintain my *guanxi*. Perhaps someday in the near future when her colon was completely blocked, Dr. Zeng would be of speedy help to my family. In those dragging two months, I had learned to prepare for the worst.

I gave tips to Dr. Zeng on how to improve his English and introduced him to several adult English schools in town. I also gave him my business card. I told him to feel free to contact me if he needed any help during his preparation for his English test. He walked us to the door like a friendly host. Father helped me get Dr. Zeng's phone number before Mother departed from the hospital. I felt secure that my cell phone had a personal emergency number— that was Dr. Zeng's.

Chapter 5

No. 14

The iron door of my childhood home No. 14 on my last visit in January 2007

Not a single day went by that Mother did not think of her parents. Among many things that she did as routine, worshipping my grandparents was on the top of her to-do list every day. She kindled three chopstick-length joss sticks with a cigarette lighter. She held the tuft of incense in one hand and fanned them with the other to make sure every stick was burning. The glowing ember on the incense turned into a red dot, then smoldered quickly. A puff of smoke and fragrance pervaded the room. She clutched the joss sticks between her thumbs and the rest of her fingers at chin level before her and bowed three times to the images of her late parents on top of the cabinet. She then planted the joss sticks in a censer on the balcony. She often did her worshipping before meals like a Christian saying grace.

"It's impolite to eat before your ancestors," she said to me when I did not wait for her worshipping and ate.

Mother believed the incense was like food to her late parents. She said the deceased *ate* incense. When the incense burned up, it meant my grandparents had completed the *meal*. She did not forget to worship them when she ate at home. After she returned home from the hospital, she offered incense to her parents even before her bedtime, as if her prayer was her sleeping pill. At times, I saw her lips moving quietly while she looked at the images of her parents, joss sticks clipped in her hands.

Those black-and-white images were engraved on square white tiles. Father had them made when we moved into the apartment. I was in my first year of high school. He and his pal designed and made a redwood cabinet for the display of his collections of antique china. Behind the two glass sliding doors were various shapes of vases, dark-red enameled teapots and blue-and-white plates. My favorite piece was the teeny snuffbox with a red cap from the Qing Dynasty. Reflected under the orange spotlights from the top, these gems glowed in the cabinet, making the corner of our living room most exquisite.

Father also changed the cabinet top into an elevated altar. On the altar were some of his precious treasures—a late Ming Dynasty fruit plate, a pair of small, green lion antique statues and an early twentieth century porcelain vase. I could not tell which part of these pieces had been repaired even though Father told me he had done so. He often bragged about his generosity of offering his collections, including a dark brown antique censer he put on the balcony, for Mother's worshipping. She also offered incense to *his* deceased parents.

Father had five engraved tiles made. They were images of Mother's parents and Father's parents and my paternal grandfather's first wife. I had met none of them except my Granny, my father's mother, who passed away in 1997, an eventful year that I remembered. Hong Kong's sovereignty was transferred from the United Kingdom to China. Princess Diana and Deng Xiaoping died in the same year. I had thought my Granny was blessed to meet these prestigious people in heaven.

For a long time, Father had been against Mother making the living room smoky when she lit the incense. He removed the censer to outdoors.

"The smoke contaminates the house like in a Buddhist temple," Father sputtered.

Mother did not retort but I knew she utterly disagreed with Father's opinion.

"What about his cigarette smoke? It's even poisonous gas," Mother sometimes snapped when we chatted.

Father bought her an electronic incense burner in which stood three plastic incense sticks. I later learned from Mr. Liang that offering three incense sticks represented our utmost sincerity and respect to our ancestors. So during holidays Mother would light a bunch of joss sticks. The number of the joss sticks was always a multiple of three. There were three small light bulbs on the tip of the plastic incense sticks. Once the power was on, the incense sticks would be lit red. The electronic incense burner looked real to me. I always thought offering incense was a Buddhist's thing. I was not sure if it was right for me to touch the joss sticks since I was not a believer. I usually stayed away from Mother's worshipping.

However, Father did not think of Mother as a Buddhist but as a blind follower. Older people with whom she hung around influenced, in his words, her "groundless, stupid superstition." Everything she did to pay reverence to her parents he condemned as superstitious activity. I remembered when I was in school, every Chinese New Year and Ching Ming Festival, a traditional Chinese festival to commemorate departed loved ones, she would burn ghost money and other joss paper offerings, such as paper credit cards, watches, clothes and houses.

"*Popo* and *Gonggong* will be happy to receive these and they'll have an affluent life in heaven," Mother often explained to me when she gathered the offerings in piles.

I was not sure I believed it but that was the saying I had grown up with. It was like Western kids who were supposed to believe there is a Santa. I found it amusing that the modern ghost money notes were all issued by the Hell Bank, the name printed on the bills. The Jade Emperor was pictured on the face of the note. As powerful as Zeus in Greek mythology, the Jade Emperor was the King of gods and mortals, ruling Heaven and Hell, according to Chinese mythology. The par value of the notes was as enormous as one billion *yuan* or one hundred billion *yuan*. Obviously, my grandparents could lead a more sumptuous life than when they were alive unless the ghost money was devalued in heaven.

The night before the ceremony, Mother folded the traditional ghost money in dozens of boat-like *yuanbao*, an ancient Chinese gold medium for exchanging expensive goods. She once taught me how to fold them. To make the *yuanbao*, we started with a piece of square, coarse paper, the center of which is a gilded square. I gingerly folded the paper in half and sealed the edge by rolling it twice. I then tucked two sides into the roll, and slightly pressed the pointed edges to make the roll curve like a smile with the gilded square facing up. It was done. I could not say I speeded up Mother's work but I helped a bit. She was so deft that the *yuanbao* from her hands were like incessant raindrops filling the big plastic bag between her legs. After a night's non-stop finger work, we gathered two or three bags of paper *yuanbao*.

The next day early in the morning she would prepare several dishes: stir-fried barbecued pork with bean sprouts and celery, white-cut poached chicken or oily red roasted duck and spring onions. In Cantonese folk culture, the sound of the word "celery" is similar to the word "industrious" and "spring onion" is similar to "clever." So worshippers pray for their family members to work hard and have smart performance at school, by offering dishes with celery and spring onions.

Mother would lay the table with three sets of mini red plastic cups and chopsticks. She filled the cups with Chinese white wine. In the meantime, she lit the altar and the doorway with red candles and a bunch of incense. Traditionally, if we worship our ancestors, we also need to worship the Earth God. So Mother sprinkled the wine on the ground and stuck joss sticks in the incense holder at the doorway. She bowed to her parents' pictures and sometimes I could hear her prayer: "Wishing everyone in the family good health and my daughter to be book-smart and obedient." After her prayer, it was my turn. And she would pile up all the joss paper offerings from large to small and burn them in a rusty basin at the doorway. From time to time, she stirred the burning paper with a long iron stick to increase the flame, followed by thick smoke.

I closed my hands to my chest. My eyes were closed as if I was about to make my birthday wish. I bowed three times while saying my prayer to *Popo* and *Gonggong*. *Please bless me to do well in school and to make my dreams come true.* The thick smoke from the rusty basin wafted to my face. As the wind blew, the smoke swirled up to the sky, as if it carried Mother's and my prayers to heaven. I did not know how Mother could bear the suffocating smoke. I found the song title "Smoke Gets in Your Eyes" couldn't be more appropriate to describe the scene—the smoke had blanketed my sight. Mother stood piously by the basin to control the flame until the joss paper was fully burnt. Afterwards, we could eat the food we offered to our ancestors.

* * * * * *

The religious ritual was harmless but to Father, he saw it as an evil practice of some superstitious cult. He would chide Mother unreservedly. In Mother's words, his fury was like someone "had stepped on his tiger's tail."

I remembered years ago once at supper, Father approached his seat at the dining table with heavy footsteps. I almost could feel my stool was shaking. He chinked his shot glass on the table. Something must have gone wrong. His face was overcast as if thunder and lightning was imminent. Mother sat next to me, helping herself to the dishes she had made.

"The house is about to collapse," Father snorted.

I eyed him and was startled by his opening remark. Mother continued to eat.

"The joss paper you've hidden in the loft, in the closet and in the kitchen will eventually give rise to a fire and overload the ceiling," Father said. "How many times have I told you not to hoard inflammable materials in the house? You never listen, but instead you're following those busybodies' instructions." Father disregarded Mother's elder friends, some of whom were close to *Popo*'s age. He thought their rooted superstition misled Mother, turning her into an unruly woman. Having filled up his shot glass with brandy, he lifted the glass and slurped a big gulp.

Mother said nothing. She lowered her head, seemingly enjoying her meal. The sound of her chopsticks raking the bottom of the rice bowl was in sync with Father's anger-loaded breath. The air around the dining table was frozen like a block of ice.

I was used to such an intense atmosphere in my family. Both Mother and I knew the best way to silence Father's enraged voice was to remain silent. We went about our own business after supper. From then on, Mother kept her ritual secret. She performed the ceremony in Father's absence. I had not seen her confront him about this matter. That made me wonder why she was so afraid of him even though she came to me to express her unhappiness. She would defend herself when she talked to me. Hardly did she complain in front of Father's face. What a shame, I often thought.

After the electronic incense burner came to our house, to make peace, Mother gave up her daily ritual of offering real incense to her parents for a while. But she privately lit the joss sticks during holidays. After she was released from the hospital, she resumed her old habit. Now both the electronic incense burner and the joss sticks in the censer on the balcony were used before meals. I was surprised it did not stir up Father's anger.

"Well, your mother is ill. I don't want to confront her. Let her enjoy her remaining life," he later told me.

What a change of attitude. I was taken aback to hear his subdued remarks. What would happen if Mother were not sick? Would he still think the same? He became much quieter at home, burying himself with his porcelain repair work day and night. I guessed that was his way of avoiding conflict with Mother.

* * * * * *

For five years after we moved into a new apartment, Father still worked in our old brick house where I had lived for the first fifteen years of my life. He turned the old brick house into his antique repair workshop. His clients would visit him at the workshop rather than coming to our new apartment.

Compared with many of my classmates and friends who moved often in their childhood, my family had moved only once. We moved just five bus stops away, but the decision cost my parents a large sum of their lifelong savings. With the financial help of Father's younger brothers who were accomplished businessmen, my parents bought a small, two-bedroom apartment in a suburban neighborhood. There lived mostly migrant workers and native Cantonese who could not afford the skyrocketing housing prices in the city. In the new apartment, I finally had my own *bedroom* instead of sleeping in a dank loft.

I had slept in two lofts as a child. One was in the old brick house and the other was in the opposite rectangular building. They were both part of my childhood home. In between the two properties was a narrow alley named *Wu Yue Da Jie*, literally, the Fifth Big Street. The alley was only big enough to allow a Chinese manpowered tricycle to pass. As a common means of delivering goods, the tricycle had a wagon-like open platform behind the rider's seat. I remembered those days before propane gas entered Cantonese households. It was a headache for the vendor who delivered honeycomb briquettes, to pedal his loaded tricycle in the alley. Once the tricycle was in the alley, it would block the pedestrians' way. What's worse, there was no room for the tricycle to turn around. The vendor had to pedal from one end of the alley and exit from the other. The ground was uneven. It was paved with all sizes of granite stone tiles, freckled with cracks. The tires of either bicycles or the Chinese tricycles could easily fall into the ruts.

Each family lived in two separate one-story buildings: the kitchen and bathroom were on one side of the alley, the living room and bedrooms were on the other. Both buildings faced each other. It was a bit like two lines of inconsistent houses in a row divided by a narrow alley. When residents went from one side of the house to the other, they sometimes crisscrossed with passers-by.

"Don't rubberneck. It's impolite to look into other people's homes while passing," Mother used to teach me.

So I looked ahead when walking in the beaten alley unless seeing a neighbor standing on the doorstep. I would look in her direction and greet *nihao*.

However, when strolling in the alley, I hardly saw the activity inside other houses. It was common for Cantonese households to have two different doors. One was a metal safety door, which protected the family from intruders; the other was a wooden door. In humid spring and summer, the alley residents would leave the wooden door open and the safety door shut, so a breeze could get through a grid of metal rods in the steel-framed door. That was also a good way to protect their privacy. The kitchen side of the building was simpler, having only one wooden door.

Nearly every spring and early summer after a torrential rain storm, the alley quickly turned into a thigh-high dark stream, reeking of sewage water. Styrofoam boxes, plastic bags, worn-out slippers and other littering junk floated along the current. Rats and cockroaches scuttled in the flood water; some drowned and drifted on the water's surface.

The households on the ground floor were the victims of the rain. Our single-story brick house with a slanted asbestos tile roof was one of the most flood-plagued houses because it sat in the middle of the alley, which was shaped like a bowl. On both ends of the alley, houses were built on a higher ground base. I called it "above flood level." So in the rain season, all runoff flowed downstream towards our house.

Flooding was a perennial nuisance to my family in that old house. Father elevated the ground base with sand under the floor tiles. He also built a knee-high threshold to prevent the water from flooding in. But if the flood in the alley reached as high as the house ground base, rain water could still seep through from the brick tiles on the ground. Everything in our brick house was elevated. The fridge, in particular, stood on a calf-high cement stand. When I was little, I could barely reach the handle of the fridge. Come to think of it, that was a good way to prevent me from getting into the habit of snacking.

The safest place to get away from flood water was the loft. Father had done several alternations of the old brick house after he moved in with Mother. He built a loft in the old brick house for storage, and then across the alley in the rectangular building, he redesigned a kitchen and a bathroom on the ground floor and built a loft as his and Mother's bedroom. I slept with my parents in the loft above the kitchen until I started school. Father then refurbished the loft in the old brick house. He divided the loft in half. The front part was my bedroom; the back space was reserved for storage. My bedroom was as cramped as a spacecraft capsule. A square plywood table, a one-door wardrobe, and a queen-size bed, which was handmade by Father a few days before his wedding with Mother, were all I had. They were in arm-reaching distance. During the rainy season, I would sleep in a symphony of rainwater dropping into the plastic pails and iron buckets. The sound from the mice scuttling in between the ceiling and the roof frequently accompanied the tune.

One rainy day, I sat at the edge of the loft, dangling my feet. I saw Father stooping down to shovel the floodwater out of the house.

"Shall I come down to help?" I shouted from the loft.

"It's not necessary," Father mumbled.

"I can help."

"You think it's fun? I've already got a handful."

"I just want to help." Father's rejection of my goodwill chagrined me.

"Stay up there. That'd be a big help." Father continued to shovel.

The kitchen and the bathroom could not escape from the flood after a rainstorm, either. I used to hear rasping scrubbing from the kitchen after the flood had subsided. Mother swept away the water with a bamboo broom. In my adolescence, I was studying in my parent's bedroom.

"Do you need help?" I shouted from the loft.

"No. Stay put. Do your homework," Mother said. Her hands did not stop scrubbing the kitchen floor.

I studied at an ebony wooden desk in the loft. This piece of furniture was *Yeh-yeh*'s legacy. Father said it was the only thing he had from his own father. The desk by the window faced the sewing machine. Like the kitchen that barely fitted two bicycles, my parent's bedroom in the loft was also small. Between the sewing machine and the desk, I would have to lean forward against the desk to give way to Mother passing behind me. A black wooden wardrobe handmade by Father shortly after he married Mother stood against the wall next to my parents' bed. They slept on an ankle-high slat bed. A pallet covered over the hard wood planks like the Japanese *tatami* flooring. A silky mosquito net hung above their cushioned bed. After I grew up, I realized my parents had given their best—their wedding bed—to me while they slept on a makeshift bed for years.

I liked looking out of the window when I studied. The window provided me with a superior vista of the low-rise houses in the neighborhood. I saw the brown shingles on the top of our old brick house. They were in rows like the scales on a grass carp. From time to time, Father had to climb up on sunny days to repair the leaking roof. But it was an ineffective job simply because the house was too old to repair. On the exterior side of the gray brick wall were countless streaks that looked like the wrinkles on an octogenarian's face.

It had become part of our everyday life that we walked across the narrow alley from our old brick house to the kitchen back and forth. As my legs grew longer, I made three strides instead of four or five to dance across the two points. One, two, three, I dipped, I straddled and I leaped; one, two, three, I dipped, straddled and leaped; one, two, three, dipped, straddled, leaped. I could not remember when I had no longer watched for the steps but crossed the alley by instinct.

Father said it was illegal to build the rectangular building on the other side of the alley because we did not own the property. We did not own the old brick house, either. We rented it. In fact, we rented it without paying rent for years. The history went back to the days when *Popo* and *Gonggong*, my maternal grandparents, were still alive. Mother used to tell me her parents could have owned a house but *Gonggong* gave up the opportunity. She never explained why he did that. Before long, her parents unofficially rented a single-story brick house on a narrow street with the house number: 14. We often referred to our home in *Wu Yue Da Jie* as No. 14. The landlady and *Popo* were good friends, so the rent was waived.

"Why was the landlady so nice to *Popo*?" I once asked Mother.

"They were close like sisters," Mother said. "So the landlady did not require *Popo* to sign lease papers. They only made a verbal agreement."

Then trouble happened. *Popo* and *Gonggong* lived at No. 14 until they passed away and Mother continued to occupy the house alone. I was surprised that Mother did not mention *Yee-ma*, her only sister, in this chapter of her life.

"Where was *Yee-ma*?" I asked.

"She moved out after she finished high school," Mother said dryly.

That made sense. I sometimes heard the old neighbors asking Mother about *Yee-ma*'s well-being. "How's Golden Phoenix lately? Has she come back for a visit?" They must have not met *Yee-ma* since she left No. 14. *Yee-ma*'s name was one Chinese character different from Mother's, Golden Orchid. Despite their names and the close resemblance of their faces, a subtle absence of feeling remained in their sisterhood. Mother talked little about *Yee-ma* living in No. 14. I understood the ten-year age difference between Mother and *Yee-ma* made them share few childhood memories. I wondered how distant their relationship was after *Yee-ma* moved out.

After the old landlady died, the daughter of the landlady took charge of the family property. She was not as friendly as her mother, nagging Mother to relocate. Mother pleaded with her as she had no place to live. She got permission to continue to live at No. 14.

Four years later, Father moved in after he married Mother. Landlady Jr. resumed the relocation issue. Even after I was born, she urged us to move out of her property. Father tried to negotiate and even offered rent. She just did not budge. Neither did she accept the rent nor did she take any legal action since she did not have any provable documents to evict us. The deadlock lasted for many years. Father continued to occupy No. 14 as his workshop until he found a new place next to our apartment.

"How can we live there for so many years without paying rent?" I asked Father after he finally returned No. 14 to Landlady Jr. in early 2007.

"*Aigh*," Father sighed. "This is a historical problem."

* * * * * *

We had a spiteful neighbor during the years we lived at No. 14. She was a sixty-something dark-haired woman with the smallest eyes I had ever seen. When she snickered, her pupils were like two black beans rolling in their sockets. Her high cheekbones and thin lips wedged into an inverted triangle on her face. When she murmured, her lips were shaped like a hen's beak mashing feed. The wrinkles under her chin quivered like the wattles hanging below the beak. Her narrow shoulders and her protruding breasts formed a steep slide down her front to her skinny ankles.

She lived next to our brick house with her youngest son and daughter-in-law. Although we were neighbors for a good many years, I never knew her real name. Mother might have told me but the name hardly registered. I was much more used to her nickname, The Bitchy Stuff, which was given to her by Mother. She used the name behind the back of the neighbor.

Mother said The Bitchy Stuff had been very mean to her and her parents ever since she became our neighbor. That was a long time before I was born. I never understood why The Bitchy Stuff had such a sharp tongue. Yet, she seemed to be nice to other neighbors. If the ones she liked passed by her house, she would greet them, "Hey! Just got off work?" or "*Sik Zo Faan Mei Aa?*" Have you eaten yet?—a casual greeting in gourmet Guangzhou, the phrase was as familiar as a nursery rhyme to me. I also heard neighbors asking the question "*Sik Zo Faan Mei Aa?*" to my parents when they passed by No. 14.

"Yes. Just did," Mother sometimes replied. "And you?"

"About to, forgot to get corn powder," a female voice echoed.

The neighbors had to raise their voices to respond as they walked away from No. 14. If Mother did her chores outside the kitchen, she greeted many neighbors, too. But she had never said "*Sik Zo Faan Mei Aa?*" to The Bitchy Stuff. Neither did Father and I.

According to Mother, The Bitchy Stuff married the owner of the house next to No. 14. They had three sons. However, The Bitchy Stuff did not love her husband. The couple often quarreled about money. She was so greedy and evil-minded that her husband eventually hanged himself. She did not grieve. After her husband's death, she became the legal inheritor of the property. She was increasingly imperious and often took advantage of Mother. Mother then was only a teenager, living alone with her ailing parents. When she was by herself after her parents passed away, The Bitchy Stuff filched cabbages or mushrooms that Mother dried in the sun in front of No. 14. Knowing she could not get her belongings back without a fierce argument, Mother just let it be.

After Mother was married, Father moved into No. 14. The Bitchy Stuff was less aggressive. But still, whenever she found an opportunity, she would make a mountain out of a molehill. Father said the neighbor had challenged him too many times to remember. "I was on the verge of playing a prank on her," Father told me years later after we moved.

In my memory, The Bitchy Stuff reproached Mother in public a few times. Once, years ago when I was in elementary school, on a scorching hot summer day, Mother splashed a few basins of cold water on the ground in front of No. 14, in part to cool off the pavement, in part to recycle the used water. The water was accidentally splashed onto the side of the alley in front of The Bitchy Stuff's house. She came out as fast as a whirring arrow and snarled at Mother, "You son of a bitch! You make my path so wet like peeing in your pants. Do you want a fight? You malevolent bastard, go to hell!"

Her voice was so thunderous that even neighbors living at the end of the alley could hear her bitter cursing. I could not imagine how much more hostile The Bitchy Stuff was to Mother before I was born and before Father moved in. But Mother seldom responded to her verbal abuse. She went inside the house while The Bitchy Stuff repeatedly spat out her mass vocabulary of vulgar words until some neighbors or her family asked her to forget about it.

For years, we two families never spoke a civil word to each other. Father said our neighbor had mental health problems. I could not agree more. I was taught to avoid her ever since I was a little girl. I avoided walking on the same path with her. If I saw her in the distance, I would run across the street and go the other way. I was afraid of looking into her black bean eyes. They were like Medusa's, turning my dreams into stony nightmares. The name, The Bitchy Stuff, was frequently mentioned in my childhood when Mother talked to me.

"Don't play in front of The Bitchy Stuff's house," Mother warned. I nodded.

"Close the door. The Bitchy Stuff is coming in this direction," Mother raised her voice when she saw me leaving No. 14's door open.

It was known that The Bitchy Stuff was extremely nosy. Her pastime was spreading rumors. During the day, she roamed in the neighborhood and chitchatted with other gossipers. Whenever she passed by No. 14, she squinted in our direction like a wily fox. She liked sitting by the window in her house to observe my family's activity. Sometimes when I was in the loft above the kitchen, I looked down through the window and saw that she had hidden in the dark behind the meshed iron door, staring into our kitchen. The red light on the altar in the back of her house gleamed in the dark, reflecting on her contours like a chunky ghost.

Mother often asked me to discuss matters with her indoors for fear The Bitchy Stuff could eavesdrop and gossip about it. Unfortunately, The Bitchy Stuff became friends with Landlady Jr. She took pleasure in speaking ill of my family to increase the tension between Landlady Jr. and us. I had always believed that if The Bitchy Stuff had not fanned the flames of trouble, Landlady Jr. would not have been so unkind to us for the sake of the sister-like friendship between her mother and *Popo*. As a little girl, I grew to develop a deep hatred towards The Bitchy Stuff because she bullied Mother. Occasionally, the insults reduced Mother to tears. After I grew bigger, old enough to ride a bicycle to school, several times I wanted to defend Mother but she stopped me.

"It's better to save trouble," she said calmly. "Arguing with her only makes her happier. Don't go crazy with her."

I comforted Mother and went to the loft to do homework. Mother's tolerance was admirable. How could she bear the ridicule from The Bitchy Stuff? Didn't she want to fight back and teach the neighbor a lesson? What was she afraid of? Was she afraid that she would lose her dignity? Or that we would be kicked out of No. 14? I found it hard to put up with the belligerence of The Bitchy Stuff. But Mother's resigned attitude dispelled my teeth-gritting-and-punching-her-face ideas. I swore to study hard and make lots of money to buy a new house for Mother.

* * * * * *

We had a green washing machine at No. 14. Its bottom was corroded with reddish-brown rust spots because of the annual flood. Father bought the washing machine to reduce Mother's load of housework. However, Mother had gotten into the habit of washing clothes by hand since she was a child. She handwashed not only her clothes but Father's and mine when I was a pupil. Every day she sat on a low plastic stool by a big red pail, knees bent like a pair of boomerangs. Her two small hands soaked in the soapy water for an hour or two. She kept scrubbing the clothes until her palms turned red. The water running into the pail dimmed the friction sound she made to get rid of the stains on the clothes. Her body shook in rhythm as her hands rubbed against one another. After the clothes were rinsed twice, she wrung them out and hung them outside.

In the early 1990s, dryers had not come into the Chinese market. Every household hung their wet clothes on the wires in front of their houses. On sunny days the alley was festooned with colorful clothes and sheets, as if multinational flags were strung above the alley. *Popo* and *Gonggong* left several clothes bars for Mother. They were long, yellow bamboo sticks tied under the eaves of No. 14. Mother cared for them very much. She only used them when she cleaned the bed linen and sheets.

One day, when I was about twelve, she frowned and chafed, "The Bitchy Stuff has stolen our clothes bars!"

Her announcement stopped me from my work. I went out and looked up at the eaves. She was right. The bamboo sticks were fewer than I remembered. I looked at the other side. A couple of yellow bamboo sticks were tied together with the brown ones under The Bitchy Stuff's eaves. I knew The Bitchy Stuff would not admit she had stolen ours. She probably would insist that our names were not tagged on, so there was no evidence to show the yellow ones were ours. Such a no-brainer response—even kids who took away my toys in kindergarten would say the same thing. In most cases of the neighbor's stealing, Mother was like a mute chewing goldthread root: No matter how bitter the plant she had to swallow, she would not say anything. But the loss of the clothes bars really drove her mad.

"Such an evil-hearted asshole! Only she would spray coal dust on our clean clothes hanging outside," Mother continued.

I stood next to her and asked, "When did she do that?"

"You were at school. That day, I saw the weather was nice and windy, so I washed a load of clothes and hung them outside. When I collected them after I came back from grocery shopping, I saw black spots on the clothes. If she didn't do it, who would?" The more Mother spoke, the angrier she became. A vein in her neck bulged. She even swore.

"Why did she do that? She's insane," I chimed in, trying to make her feel better.

"Insane as she is, she had been attempting to seek revenge after I poured the water on her side of the pavement," Mother revealed.

We never got the clothes bars back but I was astounded to learn of the neighbor's sinister attack. This woman was unbelievably horrible. I could not wait for the day that we could move away from No.14, away from The Bitchy Stuff's stare, away from her bitter reproaches, away from her range of eavesdropping, her gossip, her bullying, her habitual stealing, and her target for harm. We needed to live in a better place anyway, a place better than No. 14 so that we would not suffer annually from flood and leaks; we would not then cohabit with palm-size spiders, dark red flying cockroaches, creepy centipedes, mice, moths, silverfish, ants, beetles and scads of microscopic creatures; we would not huddle in a narrow loft which shook like an earthquake when a train rumbled through three blocks away.

Father used to spook me after he caught the spiders in his bedroom. He closed his hands over the dead spider. Just as he was about to throw it away, he jammed his locked palms at me and said, "Boo!" In the blink of an eye, I screamed. The first few times I was really frightened. Gradually, I did not fall for his trick. I would scream to pretend I was scared. I thought I would be as unfazed by the threat of the neighbor as I was by the spiders. But I was not that courageous. After we finally moved out of No. 14, I never again wanted to live the life that we had there.

Although we both lived through our childhoods at No. 14, Mother had bonded to the place as deeply as the indigenous moss that grew on its doorstep. The moss grew green and rich without our care, coating the steps every spring. Mother often had to remove the moss with a bamboo broom to prevent us from the possibility of a slippery fall. The first two years after we moved into the apartment, she still would rather do her grocery shopping in the market near No. 14 than at the one in walking distance from the apartment building. I understood it was partly because Mother missed her old life, and partly because we did not want Landlady Jr. to take back the house immediately after we moved. Father had not found a place for his workshop then. He left the old furniture in No. 14 and repaired antique porcelain there every day. It helped divert the suspicion of the neighbors and Landlady Jr. that the house was vacant. At night, Father would turn on the lamp in the loft before he returned to the apartment.

I always wondered if it was the environment at No. 14 that slowly changed Mother's temperament. There is a Confucius saying, "The company of good people is like entering a room of orchids. After a while, you become soaked in the fragrance and don't even notice it. The company of bad people is like going into a shop selling preserved fish. After a while, you don't notice the stink because you have been immersed in it."

As time went by, I became convinced Mother was accustomed to the harsh conditions, including The Bitchy Stuff's bitter tongue. Mother did not give a damn about the neighbor's overboard insults and pranks.

"So what, I've already lived here for so many years," she always said after I asked her why she did not react.

She had spent three quarters of her life at No. 14. Instead of changing the environment, she learned to tolerate the tribulations.

This was her way of living, strong and unfazed. This was her demonstration that silence is golden; truth needs not many words. Above all, she could not leave No. 14 without deep emotion, where every nook and cranny was laden with the memories of her childhood, her single adulthood and her seventeen years of married life; where she felt private with her parents; where she cradled her first and only child in her arms; where she experienced motherhood alone while Father was away as a breadwinner; and where she witnessed her husband falling in love with another woman.

* * * * * *

In my childhood memory, there was always a shadow of a willowy woman. Her long, wavy, dark hair tumbled down over her square shoulders. She was no more than one hundred sixty centimeters, a perfect size for Chinese women. When she looked up at Father, I saw a petite, pointed nose on her face silhouetted against the dim lamplight. Her shadow drew closer to Father's. At last, two shadows merged into one, as if a hairy beast was devouring a human. The mingling black shadows flickered on the wall, tearing Mother's heart to pieces.

I did not realize I had watched an extramarital affair live in front of my naked eyes until years later when I looked back upon my parents' marriage. No doubt, the little me had no idea what love was, what a-third-wheel meant, why Father held the hand of another woman alone in a park, why the woman pressed her moist lips onto Father's, why Father embraced the woman in his arms tighter than he hugged me, why Father's voice was soft and sweet to that woman but abrasive and abrupt to Mother, why Mother was sulky, hidden in the kitchen all the time.

For years after I tried hard to forget the woman's name, Lucky Lily. I considered her a thief who had stolen my childhood happiness. Yet, her name was indelible in my pea brain. I might forget the names of my middle school classmates, but never forget hers. I must have tucked her name along with my birthday and my identification number permanently in the back of my mind.

Mother sometimes called the woman The Fox Spirit, a common derogatory expression in Chinese that indicates a woman who seduces a married man by her beauty. A multitude of tales and legends in ancient China depict the character of the Fox Spirit, including Daji, portrayed in the Ming fantasy novel, *The Investiture of the Gods*, and infamously known to every Chinese household.

Daji was a beautiful daughter of a General in the Shang Dynasty (1600 BC-1046 BC). Just before she was about to marry the cruel tyrant Zhou Xin (pronounced Joe Sin), a calculating fox spirit entered into Daji's body and ruled her soul. Bewitched by Daji's gorgeous beauty, King Zhou complied with her atrocious scheme of torturing and killing legions of loyal ministers. In the legendary tale, Jiang Ziya once served King Zhou but hated the tyrant with all his heart. He was an expert in military affairs and hoped that someday someone would call on him to help overthrow King Zhou. The time had come. Employed as Prime Minister by King Wu of Zhou, Jiang Ziya fought against King Zhou's dynasty and exorcized the fox spirit from Daji's body. At last, King Wu of Zhou killed Daji, toppled the Shang Dynasty, and started a new dynasty of Zhou.

Mother and I used to watch the TV series called *The Investiture of the Gods*. That was a few years after Father's extramarital romance. When Mother saw Daji coaxing King Zhou on TV, her muscles were locked, veins bulged on her forehead.

"You sly Fox Spirit, even the devil will denounce you!" Mother exclaimed.

She clenched her fist and thumped it on her lap after the exorcism of Daji by Jiang Ziya appeared on the screen. "*Ho! Ho!* Serves you right!" She muttered "very good" several times.

It was not surprising that Mother had a strong reaction to the TV series. But I never understood why she did not accuse my father about his relationship with Lucky Lily. The adults' complicated relationships baffled me. I was like a little dot standing in the center of a square, whose four angles stood for my parents, Lucky Lily and her husband, Chee Ming. If I drew two diagonal lines inside the square to show the triangular relationship, how many triangles are there in this square?

* * * * * *

I remember one night when I was about four. Father must have sneaked to Lucky Lily's house, about five minutes' walk from No. 14. I was sleeping with Mother at the time. I woke to find myself alone in a big bed. *Where is Mama?* The house was quiet to death. She left the fluorescent light on in the living room. A shaft of white light thrust into my sleeping eyes. Stricken in panic, I scrambled off the bed and ran to the wooden doors. I pulled the doors with all the utmost strength I could muster, all in vain. The harder I pulled and pushed the doors, the louder the metal lock rattled on the wooden surface. The doors were locked from the outside. A pang of fear ran through me. *Mama is missing. I must be a bad girl so Mama doesn't want me.* My eyes bubbled with a fountain of tears. I tiptoed on a stool to look out of the open window. My cold, wet hands gripped the bars tightly like a criminal who felt unjust to be locked up. I bawled, "*Mama, Mama, Mama!*"

I could not remember how many times I cried out *Mama*. Exhausted, I felt a burning in my throat and heat in my swollen eyes. The sound of crickets and the sheer silence in the wee hours of the night filled the interludes between my sobs. I had never felt so pathetic. The more I thought so, the more I felt so. The idea of Mother deserting me planted itself in my brain. *That must be it. Or Mama won't leave me without saying goodbye.* The horrifying thought fueled me to cry louder.

"*Mama, Mama*, please don't abandon me. I'll be a good girl. *Mama, Mama*, woo—woo, woo," I cried and cried as if that was the only thing I could do to discharge the fear inside me. I must have thought the louder I cried the more likely Mother could hear faraway.

I did not know how long I stood by the window, probably a good hour. My hysterical wail flew as far as the ears of Nanny Fong, a kind-hearted neighbor who lived next door to The Bitchy Stuff. She walked out of her house in her pajamas to the window against which I leaned.

"Oh dear, what's the matter? Why are you crying so miserably?" She asked lovingly. Her tender voice, like a pacifier to a crying baby, soothed my tantrum.

"Ma-m-m-ma, Ma-m-ma doe-does nooo-t waaa-nnt me," I stuttered.

"No way! Don't be silly. You're a good girl. Why would your mother not want you? Are you alone?" she said.

I nodded and wiped my cheeks with the back of my hands. My nose was so stuffed that I could only breathe through my mouth.

"She's probably gone out for some urgent matter. She'll be back soon," Nanny Fong continued. "Don't be afraid. You just sit quietly at home. I'm sure she'll come back soon after she finishes her business."

I tried to breathe between my hiccoughs. I listened to Nanny Fong's words and sat on the couch, waiting. Not long after Nanny Fong left, Mother did return. I heard the metal lock rattling on the wooden doors again. Anxiously, I stared at the doorway as if I were a prisoner about to meet her most-wanted family. The doors opened in a loud rasping sound. As Mother entered the house, I darted to her like a frog hopping to catch a flying mosquito with its long tongue. I clasped her leg so tight that she stood still for a while.

"Why aren't you sleeping at this hour?" She sounded upset.

"*Mama*, *Mama*, please don't leave me," I started to sob. Mother's cotton pants rubbed against every inch of my facial skin. I missed Mother's make-me-feel-good aroma.

"Don't cry. You're waking up the neighbors," she said worriedly. But she did not know my powerful weeping soundtrack had already woken up Nanny Fong. "Come on, go to bed. It's very late." She hushed me and untied my arms from around her leg. She never told me where she had gone and I did not ask her either. But the question had lingered in my mind for many years. *Where on earth had she gone that night?*

* * * * * *

I never thought I had a happy childhood but I surely had an unforgettable one. I could not remember how long Father's love affair lasted, probably two or three years. His attitude towards Mother got worse during those months. The way Father talked to Mother was more like The Bitchy Stuff than a loving husband. One day, I was in the bedroom which at the time was at the back of the house, divided by a faded pink curtain. Unexpectedly, I heard Father's voice in rage.

"Who asks you to do that?" Father bellowed in the living room. I peeked through the crack of the curtain. Mother was sitting on a wicker chair, sewing. Father stood in front of her.

"Are you happy now? You've done your job to squeal on me," Father yelled. His loud voice scared me as if thunder thumped inside my chest. I could not recall if I had seen Father in such anger before. This part of my memory was stored in the very beginning of things that I could remember.

The house was uncomfortably quiet after Father's ranting. Suddenly, a sharp crunch scratched the appallingly grim air. I ran out to the living room. A loosely-attached photo frame lay on the floor. Its glass was shattered. Shocked as I was, I lowered my eyes at the picture of Mother, Father and me. Mother put down her sewing, grabbing me immediately into her arms.

"Don't get too close. The glass will hurt," she said nervously.

"Please, please, don't yell at *Mama*," I implored. Tears gushed out of my eyes. I eyed Father and reiterated my pleading.

Father stomped off. Mother swept up the broken glass on the floor after Father left. I stood aside, recovering from the panic. I watched the back of Father's figure dwindling until it went out of my sight.

From that day on, I realized my family was no longer what it should be. Father seldom came home for supper. If he did, he was quiet like a dead fish. I knew he hung around with his drinking buddies, including Chee Ming, Lucky Lily's husband. They drank, laughed and chatted for hours. On the rare chance I did see Father before my bedtime; his bloodshot eyes told me he had been on a binge. His face was red like a Cantonese opera performer. I hardly recognized those Cantonese opera singers on stage after they painted their faces with striking, thick colors. Each combo of colors represents the personality of the character. Red often stands for heroic protagonist. Yet, Father was hardly heroic to me. A sense of protecting Mother arose in my young mind. I hated Father shouting at Mother. I would quickly turn myself into a mediator. "Hey, stop it! Can you two talk to each other calmly?" I said matter-of-factly. I thought my responsibility to make peace in my family would prepare me to do well in the United Nations after I grew up. From time to time, I wondered if it would be easier to deal with the situation if I had a brother or sister. Perhaps my sibling could stand on Father's side while I would be on Mother's. That way Father would not be alone. I had decided to back up Mother in every fight they had. I was Mother's ally. We were as staunch as the relationship between the United States and the United Kingdom.

Almost every night Father would come to kiss me after he returned home. By then, it was after my bedtime. His foul alcoholic, heavy breath and his hard stubble often awoke me from my slumbering dreamland. So I tried to stay awake in bed until he kissed me goodnight.

That was why I witnessed such a violent scene.

One night, I was sleeping with Mother in the loft. Father's pull on the light string suddenly dispelled the darkness of the room. I heard impatient footsteps clumping up the wooden stairs. The next thing I saw as I opened my eyes was Father's muscle-tightened arm reaching for Mother's head. She was lying in bed, head facing the stairway.

"Get up! You think I don't know about this," Father bellowed.

"Ahhhh—" Mother screamed out of pain. Father's hand had already intertwined Mother's wavy short hair. The mosquito net was askew.

I rose and cried instantly, "Stop! Stop pulling *Mama*'s hair!" I slapped my small hand on Father's strong arm and pulled his hand off Mother's hair. "Stop it, stop it, stop it…" I kept saying.

"You think you can sleep tight after you screwed this up?" Father finally released his hand and stood by the staircase.

I looked up with my blurry eyes through the silky mosquito net. He was definitely drunk. His breath reeked of tobacco and alcohol. His face glowed in red as if a big tomato had grown above his neck. He kept demanding Mother get up to straighten out something. I had no clue what he was talking about. I did not know what Mother had done to provoke him. But I guessed it must be about Lucky Lily. Father had detested Mother's intrusion in his romance. I loathed Lucky Lily sabotaging my parents' marriage. To protest my indignation at the home wrecker, I refused to visit Lucky Lily's home and made no friends with her niece of my age. I knew my behavior embarrassed Father, especially when I rejected Lucky Lily when she gave me food or presents.

"Are you OK?" I asked, rubbing Mother's scalp. I noticed tears were welling up Mother's eyes. *She must be in pain but she bears it.* I comforted her, "Don't be afraid. Everything will be over soon." I looked at Father's bloodshot eyes and pleaded with him, "It's late. Could you please leave us alone?"

"No," Father rebuffed. "Everything should come clean tonight! Your mother has done so many things behind my back."

"Who's talking? How many things *you* have done behind *my* back?" Mother retorted. "Have you thought about how this has influenced your daughter?"

"All right! All right! No more quarrel between you both!" I snapped just before Father was about to counter. "I want to sleep!

97

Pleeease—*Baba*, let *Mama* and me get rest. You can talk about anything tomorrow," I said in a tone of firm finality.

Father became resigned. The room returned to darkness after he switched off the light and left. It took a while before the humid evening air absorbed the smell of tobacco and alcohol in the loft. I doubted Mother had a good night's sleep but at least she could have a moment of peace.

I was not sure if the incident had toughened Mother's tolerance or had weakened her faith in marriage. She seemed to turn a blind eye to Father's cheating. After that night, she did not say much, at least not to me, about how she felt. When I asked, she always said, "You're too young. You'll understand after you grow up." She worked even harder in the house. Cooking, mopping, sweeping, dusting, washing the dishes, the clothes and the bedding, she took care of all the housework like a never-sit-still maid. She did not want any chip of space in her mind laden with the images of Father and The Fox Spirit. She needed to be occupied with something, something that required her daily attention. Housework definitely could distract her from thinking of the unhappiness.

Mother devoted her time and energy to care for me. She was there when I had an inflammation of the tonsils, resulting in high fever and coughing. She was there when my clothes were too small for me. She was there when I was frightened by the thunder. She was there when I accidentally tucked a cold pill into my nostrils. She was there when I fell off my bike and skinned my knees. She was there when my baby teeth were loose and she pulled them out. At this early age of life, I thought I was living in a single parent family.

* * * * * *

During those years in the late 1980s when the Economic Reform and Open Policy was in full swing, the breeze of overseas Chinese pop culture swept over the Middle Kingdom. Father not only drowned his sorrows but also soothed his mind by listening to music. He had a good collection of compact disks on the shelf he had made. Mozart's violin concertos, Strauss' waltz, Schubert's sonatas, *The Butterfly Lovers* by Yu Li Na, *The Yellow River Piano Concerto*, the theme score of *The White-Haired Girl*, Han Bao-yi's *Winter Love*, Qi Yu's *The Olive Tree*, Tsai Chin's *Lover's Tears*,

Zhang Ming-min's *Country Road* and a myriad of pop songs, light music and classical. One of Father's beloved singers was Teresa Teng, a Taiwanese pop singer who captivated listeners of Father's age. Because of her attractive appearance and mellow voice, Teresa was the heart-throb of millions of Chinese fans. Her melodic ballads constantly pervaded every corner of No. 14. Father turned up the music as long as he was at home. I listened to the tunes so many times that I could also sing along. A couple of Teresa's song lyrics came from the well-known Chinese poems, such as *Climb up the Western Tower Alone*. The lyric goes like this:

> *Silent I ascend alone the Western Tower*
> *The moon is like a hook.*
> *The desolate Chinese parasol tree shaded inner courtyard*
> *locks in the lucid autumn.*
> *Snipped, it breaks not.*
> *Unraveled, it entwines again.*
> *It is the sorrow of separation,*
> *Not the usual sort of flavor to the heart.*

The poem was composed by Li Yu, one of the emperors in the late Tang Dynasty. I had to learn the poem by heart when I was in elementary school. Teresa's charming song helped me remember the lyric quickly. The rhythm echoed in my mind when I recited the poem in class. Although the poem reflected the poet's melancholy for leaving his crumbling kingdom at a tumultuous time, modern Chinese quoted the line, "Snipped, it breaks not. Unraveled, it entwines again," to denote the emotional entanglements between lovers.

When I was a pupil, I used to make sentences out of the phrases we newly learned in class as homework. I once wrote: *The adult relationship is indeed snipped, it breaks not; unraveled, it entwines again.* It was exactly what happened in my family then—Mother was chagrined; Father was upset; both of them lived together like strangers. Father visited Lucky Lily frequently. When Mother bumped into Lucky Lily on the street, both of them smiled embarrassedly to one another and continued on their own way.

Mother sometimes encountered Lucky Lily's husband, Chee Ming, in *Gaai See*, also known as the wet market, where puddles of water scattered on the floors and the streets. The vendors sprayed water on the vegetables to make them appear fresh. Butchers washed their bloody cutting boards before chopping the scarlet red raw meat. Live fish wiggled their watery tails as the fishmonger swiftly grabbed them out of the tank.

"Buying groceries?" Chee Ming would say. His voice was dissolved in the clamorous noise from *Gaai See* instantly.

"Yes. You too?" Mother said, beaming.

"Yeah. It's good to come early, not so crowded."

"Of course. Well, don't wanna stand in your way. Enjoy your shopping."

Chee Ming waved. Both of them walked in the opposite direction, disappearing in the crowd quickly. Mother seemed to be friendly with Chee Ming. They smiled when chatting with one another. No disguise at all. I noticed Mother said more words to him than to Lucky Lily. So every day I pondered the same question: *Does Chee Ming know about the affair between his wife and Baba?*

My concern eventually got an answer. The entangled triangular love affair came to an end after Lucky Lily's husband discovered it. That day, when I was on the doorstep of my house after school, a man's shouting resounded inside.

"Why are you doing this, huh?" the male voice sputtered.

I walked into the house, there on the couch sat Chee Ming. His face was red like Father's when he got drunk. His bulging eyes blinked fast, as if they were fanning the hot steam leaking from his eyes. His potbelly heaved with difficulty at a rapid pace. Father was on Chee Ming's left, kneeling. He looked nervous and guilty.

"I know, I know. I'm stupid. I'm a bad ass," Father said.

"Screw you! I've been treating you like a brother. How can you betray me like this?" Chee Ming breathed through his mouth. His legs were folded and spread apart, hands propped up on the knees. His pose reminded me of the Kung Fu fighter. "I've been suspecting," he sighed and went on, "you and my wife of cheating. Huh! I just can't believe my eyes. This is real!"

"It's my fault. I'm an asshole. Come on, you can slaughter me." As soon as Father finished, he dashed to the kitchen. Mother was watching on the side. Her face went pale after she heard what Father said. She tried to get in his way.

"Don't! Don't! Are you crazy?" Mother shouted, pushing Father back.

Father broke through her hold like a wild bull. In no time, he came back with a cleaver in his hand. The silver blade glittered in my eyes. I was petrified. I could hear my heart beating through my ears. *Baba is serious.* He delivered the cleaver to Chee Ming. Mother scooped me up in her arms. I felt her body was trembling, heart thumping on my spine.

"Take this cleaver and kill me. You can make a clean break today," Father said forcefully. His face was tense like an expressionless mummy. He sounded determined. Why was he so gritty? Was it because he had undergone torture after he was seized for escaping to Hong Kong? Was it because his impoverished life in the countryside had prepared him to confront any life-threatening moments? Or was he emboldened by the excessive drinking? When I inhaled, his alcoholic breath singed my nostrils.

"You think that can solve the problem? You have no idea how it feels that my wife has given me this green hat to wear," Chee Ming said sadly. He fetched the cleaver from Father's hand and put it down on the tea table in front of him.

My heartbeat raced, as if I had just watched an acrobat in a heart-gripping performance. I was puzzled—wearing a green hat—a phrase I had never heard of before. I thought of the kids wearing green hats in kindergarten on June 1st, Children's Day. But Chee Ming's words must be more serious than a party. Years later, I caught the phrase again in a Cantonese television series. The husband in the drama found out his wife had an affair with another man. He scolded her with that slang. Then I knew "wearing a green hat" meant to cuckold, a man whose wife is unfaithful.

"Even today if I spare you, you'll be condemned by your conscience," Chee Ming choked.

The news had spread fast to Father's mother, my Granny. Perhaps Mother had called her on a public telephone located in a small store at the end of our alley. Living with Uncle Sahm and his family, Granny must have been frightened for us. She sent Uncle Sahm, Father's younger brother, to visit us. Ranking the third among Father's brothers, Uncle Sahm was a tall, solid-built man with a pair of golden-framed glasses on the straight bridge of his nose. He rode his motorbike to No. 14. After he switched off the humming motor, he entered the house with a helmet in one hand.

"*Yee Gor*," Second Brother, Uncle Sahm said. "*Yee Soh*." Second Sister-in-law. He eyed Mother. He also nodded to Chee Ming coyly.

"Please sit," Mother said. She pulled up a chair for him and filled up a cup of tea and placed it in front of him.

"*Ng Goi*." Uncle Sahm thanked Mother. He took a sip and said, "*Ma* asked me to come here. Are you all right?"

Father snuffled and kept nodding his head. I had never seen his head bowed so low, like a giraffe laboriously bending down to drink in the pond. Seeing the cleaver on the table, Uncle Sahm must have been as shocked as I was. He pulled my kneeling father up to the chair.

"You have a good wife and a good daughter," Chee Ming said. "You don't cherish them. Shame on you!" As his last words reverberated around the living room, Chee Ming stood and stomped out of the house.

Mother and I walked him to the door. By then, a few neighbors had stood in the narrow alley, wondering what the noise from my house was all about. Curious eyes sized up Mother and me. Seemingly, we were the laughing stock of the day and the headline for the gossipers. I did not like their staring, particularly The Bitchy Stuff's black-bean eyes. Nanny Fong came to Mother and inquired, "Golden Orchid, what's the matter? Why is your house so noisy?"

"Nothing. It is only a small argument. It's over," Mother said, embarrassed. She quickly went into the kitchen, followed by Nanny Fong.

"I know it's hard on you," Nanny Fong said kindly at the entrance of the kitchen. She eyed me and continued, "and on your daughter, too."

"Take it easy. Give him a chance to change," she comforted. Nanny Fong seemed to know what was going on in my family. She retold what happened that night I woke up alone at home and cried hysterically for Mother. I looked at Nanny Fong from the doorstep in front of No. 14. Her black hair was salted with gray. The brownish-yellow felt sweater draped over her lanky shoulders. I could not see Mother. She was inside the kitchen. I looked around. The neighbors had dispersed. Yet, out of the corner of my eyes I could still see The Bitchy Stuff's figure. I turned around and eyed her hard.

102

"You little skunk, serves you right!" She muttered and retreated to her house.

I hissed and walked inside. Father lay on the couch like a puppet whose strings had been snipped. He looked miserable. The corners of his eyes were damp, glistening under the white light. His breathing was short and heavy. Uncle Sahm sat next to him, saying something to Father. I lowered my gaze to the cleaver. How quietly it was sleeping on the table. But what happened ten minutes before re-ran on my mind, scene by scene, like a shaky documentary film.

I cannot remember the other things that happened during the rest of that day. I thought the episode was the end of my parents' marriage. The word "divorce" was as vague as "make love" to me. I only knew if Father disliked Mother, he would walk away and I would not see him at home any more. I cringed at the idea that my parents would separate permanently. Surprisingly, they did not break up. Things returned to normal quite quickly two days later. Father sat around the dining table with Mother and me. I glanced over at my parents. They looked calm. *OK. Just another quiet supper.* I thought.

"I went shopping with your mother today," Father said to me, breaking the ice. "We bought you a gift."

"A gift? You went shopping?" I was astonished. *How can that be after the scenario the other day?* I raked the rice in my mouth, as if the rice could sandbag my pounding heart.

"Yes. We went shopping in the department store and bought a new blanket and a bed sheet," Mother said, smiling.

"You take a look at the gift after supper. It's on the desk by the window," Father chimed in.

My gaze fell upon the dishes on the table. The white-cut poached chicken was scrumptiously sliced in pieces. By its side was a small saucer filled with spring onion and ginger dipping. My family did not often have white-cut poached chicken. It was usually served when a guest came to our house for dinner or at Chinese traditional festivals. Cantonese believe a banquet is not complete without a chicken dish. So when we had white-cut poached chicken in an ordinary potluck dinner, I always thought there must be something special to celebrate.

Mother had made my favorite pan-fried eggs with sweet and sour vegetable. Just looking at the crisp, golden egg white laced around the orange yolk, my mouth was already watering. The shredded preserved vegetable—cucumber, red ginger, white ginger, onion and lettuce—was sprayed on the top of the fried eggs like confetti. Because of the five different vegetables, we named the dish "Five Willow Fried Eggs." The tangy smell of sweet and sour whetted my appetite further.

Munching the delicious food, I forgot all about the disagreement between my parents. They were miraculously on good terms. I had no idea why, and I did not have courage to ask either. I wondered if my parents' resumed relationship would end my role as a mediator. I wondered if the peaceful days would last. I wondered if Mother was happy after Father came home for supper every night. I wondered if Father had learned his lesson and would care about us for good.

In the meantime, I talked to myself a lot, as if my mind and heart were split in half. I was curious about the relationship between men and women.

Please give me one more chance. I really love you. My mind said.

No. You already have her. Why do you come back to me? My heart said.

Come on. I promise I will not leave you again. My mind said.

Go away! I do not want to see you ever again. My heart said.

I even wrote to myself, pretending I was the vulnerable one and requesting for a breakup with the other half of me. I felt as if I were talking to a transparent, heartbreaking ghost. What if I had a brother or sister? I wondered if I would be so crazy about talking to myself.

Father saw Lucky Lily no more. In fact, neither of my parents mentioned anyone from her family. It had been a while since Father had talked to Mother in a pleasant voice. When that happened again, their words warmed my heart. Father still drank during meals. He confessed he could not and did not plan to quit the bad habit. The shot glass was like his beloved side dish. He said without it, his taste buds were numb. I was used to setting the table before meals, including placing Father's shot glass at his place.

After the incident that nearly annulled my parents' marriage, I understood more whenever I looked at their black-and-white wedding photo. It lay underneath a glass desktop in the living room. The wedding photo was very plain. There was no wedding gown, no formal suit, no tie, no flower bouquet, no guests, no makeup. The half-length photo showed two young faces smiling into the camera. Mother's round face looked fresh like a blossom. On her right cheek appeared a dimple. Her full lips were closed. Her thick dark hair was always the envy of a hairdresser. Since she had had her hair permed, it looked dense. She wore a tidy floral shirt, possibly the best in her closet. Father was next to her. Both of their heads were tilted toward each other. Father was more slender in the picture than in reality. He looked like a young man just graduating from college, although he had never gone that far in his education. He wore a suit jacket over a white shirt. He tried to smile without showing much of his ridged front teeth. His mouth was slightly open with a smile. I had always loved looking at this picture when I did homework at this desk. I felt I was loved by my parents. Without them, without me. I was not in their wedding picture but I saw myself there, something about to happen.

The only wedding photo of my parents in 1980

Chapter 6
Mismatch

My mother in front of a fake Christmas tree at the Garden Hotel,
Guangzhou on Christmas Eve of 2006

At the end of the year, everywhere in Guangzhou was festooned with the Christmas colors of red, white and green. A two-story tall cartoon figure of the Fortune God balloon in red was tethered to the ground in front of the Trust-Mart store near my office. Trust-Mart is one of the largest supermarket chains in China. The retail giant Wal-Mart acquired a thirty-five percent stake in the corporation a year later.

December is one of the most, if not *the* most, decorative months in stores and restaurants in Guangzhou. To some extent, its festivities overwhelm the Chinese New Year, which usually falls in January or February. The salesgirls and servers wear plush Santa hats. Loudspeakers chant Christmas carols day and night in the malls and Western restaurants. Plastic Christmas trees with sparkling ornaments tower at the entrance of hotels, office buildings, and any public places that are allowed. Real poinsettias wave to the guests with their eye-burning red in the doorways.

Only in recent years had Christmas become significant in the Chinese festival calendar. But it was pretty much commercial, with little impact on our private behavior. Young people might take the opportunity to throw parties. It was the merchants' gimmick to promote businesses around some holiday titles, both Chinese and Western: the Valentines' Day romance dinner, the Buy-One-Get-One-Free Mother's Day special, the Mid-Autumn Festival mooncake package, the National Day's auto sales and Halloween carnivals. Nearly every month I was reminded of a holiday through the media. Well-informed as we were, young Chinese had surely "kept pace with the times," one of the slogans from the central government.

Father and I were happy about Mother's coming home from the hospital. In the past two months, the vacancy of Mother's seat at the redwood dining table was like the missing piece of a jigsaw puzzle. The emptiness of the house pricked my heart. I had longed for her voice echoing in the living room.

Unaware of her cancer, Mother looked forward to turning over a new leaf in her life. She perked up after she said goodbye to the antiseptic inpatient center. Although Father and I were uncertain about how long the remission would last, Mother's temporarily improved health eased our highly-strung minds. Her cheeks gleamed baby pink. A tinge of gloss rejuvenated her face. Her big round eyes illuminated hope.

"I should have a change of luck," she prayed with joss sticks in her hands. "May the bad things be expelled from my body. Good health from today on…"

Every day, she murmured for a while in front of my grandparents' pictures. She then bowed and offered the joss sticks in the censer. I barely caught what she said. She probably thought her health was on the right track even though she could not swallow much food.

"You can't swallow oranges, vegetables or pulled pork," Father emphasized several times in the first few weeks after Mother returned home.

"I know," Mother said.

"Anything chewy is no good for you."

"Alllllll right. Don't be so long-winded; even nursing homes won't accept you."

Days later, Father brought home an electric juicer. It was not a Christmas present but it was on sale in the store during Christmastime. Father spent a night fiddling with the new machine. Modern home appliances frustrated him. Although he used to be an electrician, his experience did not allow him to figure out the multi-buttons on the gizmo more quickly.

"*Wah!*" I exclaimed. "What have you got?" A dull whirr of a machine buzzed in my ears.

"I bought a juicer for your mother," Father said, examining the configuration of the white cylindrical machine. His reading glasses slipped down on his nose.

"Nice. How do we use it?"

"I'm still experimenting. There're too many functions on this machine. You should take your time to read the manual and teach your mother."

"It looks complicated."

"Well, the salesman showed me in the store," Father said after a puff of the cigarette, "that the juicer can make all sorts of drinks, orange juice, soy milk, carrot juice, apple juice and many others. So your mother will be able to absorb different nutrients without chewing the food."

"You're right," I said.

It took much longer for Mother to chew her food. She spat out the residue of the chewy food after she ground it between her teeth a hundred times. That was how she sucked the juice without swallowing certain food. It concerned us that her jaw muscles would be painfully overused. At the end of every meal, out came a heap of mangled dregs in front of Mother.

Father left the juicer on the tea table in the hope that Mother would use it frequently. He counted on me to teach her the basics. In his opinion, Mother was more receptive to whatever I said than to his remarks. So the ball was always in my court. Father usually said, "You have more patience than me." That quickly dispelled my attempt of asking "Why me again?"

The end of the year was a busy season in the editorial office. I totally forgot about reading the manual and teaching Mother to use the juicer. Mother was uninterested anyway. She thought Father often shopped on impulse, such as buying the CD player, the ironing board, the microwave and the stereo amplifier. But that was Father's way of making our life better by updating our home appliances. I was disappointed when Mother said "It's not necessary" to have the juicer. She was oblivious to it when passing by. The machine sat on the tea table for weeks, untouched. One day, Father asked why we did not use the juicer. Mother and I were both quiet as if we were too busy to talk to him. Off he went. Then, Mother scorned, "Another spur-of-the-moment purchase."

Weeks went by. We totally forgot about the juicer and having been used only once by Father, the machine at last spent the rest of its life in the cupboard together with the unused tableware.

* * * * * *

The business district around the Garden Hotel, one of the several five-star hotels in town, was adorned with a spectrum of colors during Christmas. Santa on a sleigh drawn by reindeer and electric fireworks glittered on the outer walls of the high-rise buildings at night. The area was bathed in brilliant neon lights, attracting many expatriates in the city. It never snows in Guangzhou. But some people liked to spray artificial snowflakes on the windows.

After Mother returned home from the hospital, I wanted to share the joyful atmosphere of Christmas with her in the hope of keeping her in good spirits. I suggested we eat out and see the lights. Invited by my American teacher Frank, Mother and I went to the Liwan Market Restaurant in the Garden Hotel. Father did not join us. He said he felt restrained in a fine restaurant—he could neither smoke, nor could he bring his own brandy to the restaurant. I thought it was only an excuse to let Mother enjoy herself without being under the stress of his presence.

A three-story high Christmas tree was centered in the hotel lobby every December. It was probably the first time Mother had been so near a giant tree with countless red, gold and silver balls. She was all bundled up. All I could see was a red scarf tucked in a cardigan sweater and a jacket. I bought her the clothes after I began working, a change from what we used to do when Mother usually paid the bills. Perhaps these garments were Mother's favorites, or perhaps they were the only suitable clothes she had for that winter. She wore them frequently.

Ever since my personal meeting with Dr. Yang, I had found it difficult *not* to think of the remaining time I could have with Mother. Mr. Liang had already told me in private to cherish the moments whenever I could. He said, "You should do all you can to make your mother happy. In the future, these things are your sweet memories, and you won't have regrets." His words resonated with me for a long time.

Watching Mother's face glowing with joy, I knew I was doing the right thing. I took out the digital camera that I brought along whenever I was out with her. I realized the best thing I could do was to keep the memories through the unchanged photographs.

"Mom, may I take a picture of you here?" I pointed to the twinkling Christmas tree in the hotel lobby.

"*Ho-ah*," Mother agreed with a pleasant smile.

She stood in front of the tree, at the bottom of which were colorful wrapped gift boxes. I fell back a couple of steps to capture the big golden star on the top of the tree. The richly carved wall behind the reception desk blazed in gold. Mother had just had her hair cut. She looked refreshed. Her hair remained dark and thick. She posed with a smile, showing her half closed lips and a dimple on her right cheek. The collars of her red sweater and jacket were tightly zipped up under her chin, as if they were the red petals of a blooming lotus. I had to give up a full-length shot because of the height of the tree. Mother's blue jeans were partly shown in my camera. The contrast was bizarre: The big Christmas tree made Mother look small, the way she looked in her roomy hospital gown. I got down on my knee like a professional to better angle a small person and a huge background.

"All right. Ready?" I shouted. "One, two, three, smile."

Ka-cha! My finger released the shutter.

"Great!" I was pleased. I stood up and approached Mother. "Would you like to take a picture with me?"

"*Ho-ah*," she said. Her voice faded in the muffled noises from the lobby.

I passed my camera to Frank and said, "Could you take a photo for us? Forget about the tree; a close-up will be fine."

"Sure," Frank said. He wobbled with his paunchy body to the front of the tree, facing Mother and me.

I held my right arm around Mother. She leaned against me. As I grabbed her shoulder, my heartbeat halted for an instant. A thick, soft surface sprang back against my fingertips. Mother was padded with layers of clothes. She was not as solid as she looked. My heart stung like iodine on my wounded knee as a child. I clasped Mother to me for fear I would lose her as quickly as the festival lights would soon blink. Facing the camera, I mustered a cheerful expression to disguise my deepened sorrow.

"OK?" Frank shouted, one of the few English words Mother could understand.

Mother and I both grinned at the sound of Ka-cha.

* * * * * *

Mother told me a few times that Father's smell of tobacco and alcohol jolted her awake at night. For some twenty years, Mother had put up with Father's sleeping habits, but no more. She spoke out about her discomfort. I wondered if because of her illness, she was more aware of surroundings that might be detrimental to her health. She would ask Father to smoke elsewhere or she would walk away if Father was smoking. It was not uncommon for the Chinese to smoke indoors if they felt it was convenient. Father observed the smoking rules in public, though. Where there was an ashbin, there was his standing figure. But at home, he was lax.

"Your father's cigarette ashes are everywhere in the house," Mother often complained.

One day, after she said so, I looked on the floor and around the redwood furniture. They shone in luster. The glass tabletop by the window reflected the partly cloudy sky.

"I spent a whole morning in mopping the floor and wiping all the furniture in the living room," Mother revealed, as if she had noticed I saw the difference.

"You shouldn't have done the work by yourself," I said. "Ask me to do it."

"You're busy at work but I have time at home," Mother said, averting her gaze to the corner where the desktop computer sat. "That corner is always filled with layers of dust and ashes. Every morning is like that."

Mother meant that in the evening, usually after she had gone to bed, Father hogged the computer until the small hours of the morning. He always placed a stool next to him, on which were his pack of Double Happiness cigarettes, a lighter, an ashtray, a teacup and a shot glass. He liked surfing the web at night. As autumn slipped into winter, the evening chill seemed to affect him little. The prolonged dark silence, however, lured him to stay up. He retired to bed so late, leaving behind a floor dusted with white and gray ashes.

While Father snored soundly at daybreak, Mother rose from the bed. The shuffle of her slippers, the flush from the bathroom and the gurgle of the water cooler had become my morning alarm. Mother would switch on the electronic incense burner to begin her day. After she offered incense to my ancestors, she turned on the water cooler to heat water. While waiting for the hot water, Mother sometimes fetched a broom from the kitchen and swept the floor, particularly the computer corner.

Speaking of the water cooler, Father bought it for Mother. The white cylinder machine had two nozzles—one for cold water, the other for hot water. Tap water in China is not for direct drinking. Although water coolers had been popular in Cantonese households for several years—mainly because urban people were more concerned about health, my family still used the traditional way of boiling water before drinking.

After Mother was released from the hospital, Father bought the water cooler to make her life easier, since she drank warm water to take pills every day. Mother accepted the convenience while Father continued to boil water. He said the hot water from the water cooler was not hot enough to make tea. He was a lifelong tea drinker. Tea and brandy were his only two drinks. For sixteen *yuan*, we could get a five-gallon barrel of drinking water, which lasted three to four weeks for Mother. But it would not last long if Father used it to make tea. He could drink at least two domestic vacuum flasks of water every day. I believed he made an excuse to assure Mother of having a good supply of the distilled water.

* * * * * *

I continued to learn about how to tend cancer patients through reading and internet research. One thing I learned was that the white blood cells coming from the human immune system can defend the body against both infectious disease and foreign substances. They are like the brave soldiers in our bodies. Once bacteria, viruses or fungi invade, the white blood cells, also known as leukocytes, will charge at the enemy and attack them. Often referred to as the immune system's army, the number of white blood cells will increase if a person gets sufficient sleep. Sleep assists the body to heal wounds and to develop a strong immune system, which can identify and kill pathogens and tumor cells. It explains why we are supposed to rest more when being sick; and why we are more prone to catching a cold or having a headache if our sleep is deficient.

I was galvanized about my findings. If the white blood cells multiplied, that meant Mother's immune system would have more soldiers to battle against the tumor cells. *I must do something to maintain Mother's sleeping quality.* I came up with an idea. I suggested Mother sleep in my bedroom which helped her escape from Father's smell of cigarettes and alcohol. Sleeping separately from Father, Mother felt her sleeping quality was improved. She not only slept eight guaranteed hours every night but also developed a habit of taking naps. She rarely napped before she was sick, although I had recommended it before.

"How to nap?" Mother used to say. "There's so much to do in the house. Only your father thinks that I'm idling at home."

She had lost her full-time job then. Even though she had received nursery school training as part of the municipal re-employment scheme, she could not find another full-time job. Her age and her primary school education disqualified her. She could only become a homemaker. Cooking and cleaning occupied her life, seven days a week with an occasional day off. Every day after I returned home from school or work, hot dinner would be served on time at 7 p.m. When winter came, Mother made each of our beds warm and cozy with a blanket and comforter. In late spring, she would change our beds with rattan mats and air the quilts before putting them away.

Father and I had taken for granted the convenience and comfort that Mother made. After we knew she had cancer, things changed. Father did not want Mother to do housework any more. He decided to hire a caretaker who could also cook and clean for us. On a sunny December morning, I accompanied Father to a community service center to look for a caretaker.

The market for housekeepers was in great demand in Guangzhou in recent years. Urban people were either too busy or too lazy to do housework. And the migrant workers were willing to take the dirty chores in the cities. I often thought it was a feudalistic thing to have servants and maids. Shouldn't we feel ashamed to be served at home while our hands and feet were healthily attached to our moveable bodies?

Thinking back, I thought I grew up in a family that served others rather than being served. There was a time when Mother helped Uncle Sahm's family cook and clean after Granny passed away. Granny used to take care of the housework when she was living with Uncle Sahm's family. Mother did not like to commute five days a week but Father insisted.

"It's fine that I cook and clean for his brother. When I do that for my sister, he just goes berserk," Mother once complained to me. "Where else can you find such a man who has double standards?"

* * * * * *

I did not know Mother had helped *Yee-ma* do housework regularly until Father mentioned it. Mother did that before she got sick. Every now and then, she would go to *Yee-ma*'s to wipe tables and chairs, dust the ceiling, sweep and mop the floor and even climb up to clean the aluminum sliding windows and the kitchen exhaust fan. I would not be surprised if she cleaned the toilet for *Yee-ma* as well. When it came to housekeeping, no one I knew could work harder than Mother.

Yee-ma and her husband, *Yee-jeong*, lived in a two-bedroom apartment. She had three children, two older daughters and a younger son. But they all moved out because of marriage or jobs. Like the wide age gap between Mother and *Yee-ma*, my cousins were about twenty years older than I. The oldest daughter, Soaring

114

Swallow, married the guy who ran a mom and pop business with her selling Cantonese Cooling Tea. Mother used to take me to her store to have free sugarcane juice with herbal medicines. It was a popular drink, suitable for all seasons.

Yee-ma's second daughter, Graceful Swallow, moved to Hong Kong after she married a local auto mechanic. Since then, visiting Hong Kong had become not only a touristy thing but also a family visit for *Yee-ma*. My parents and I would also make a stop at my cousin Graceful Swallow's house when we visited Hong Kong. I remembered they stayed at Graceful Swallow's on their first trip to Hong Kong in 2003, when the Individual Visit Scheme first kicked off, allowing travelers from mainland China to visit Hong Kong and Macao on an individual basis. Before the government introduced the Scheme, few mainland people traveled to Macao and Hong Kong because they were colonies of Portugal and the United Kingdom. Taking the geographical advantage, the residents of Guangdong province were the first beneficiaries of the Scheme. With a blue Special Administrative Regions (SARs) Passport, we could travel once or twice a year to both places. The Scheme has not only promoted the economy of the SARs but also opened the Chinese travelers' eyes to the dazzling capitalistic worlds of Las Vegas-style casinos in Macao and copious luxury goods in Hong Kong.

"The toilet is ritzy," Father lauded after his first and only visit to Hong Kong. His cheek muscles lifted as if they were a pair of brackets hung on his face.

"That day, I was on the street sightseeing," he continued. "Suddenly I had the urge to pee, so I went to a restroom in a tall office building in Central. *Wah*, the inside is palatial. It has automatically flushed commode and a suit-clad bathroom attendant offering me a hand towel."

One of Father's scores of idiosyncrasies was being aware of the gizmos that were new to him, including the toilet technology. Although he had never been abroad, he acquired up-to-date information through his daily habit of reading newspapers, watching TV and surfing the web. He always admired the Japanese who designed their commodes like intelligent robots. He once said bathroom users in Japan could appreciate having a deluxe hands-free experience simply by controlling a panel of buttons on the side of the commode. I could not imagine such a toilet until months later I found a picture in a Japanese magazine. It met Father's description.

Next to the sit-on toilet was a thin remote control box. With my rusty Japanese, I figured some buttons were for the flow of the water spray to the buttocks. There was a button for drying the soggy bottom. Father took pleasure in showing me his discovery.

"So did you give the attendant a tip?" I asked, intrigued by his discovery in Hong Kong.

"No," Father said, "I didn't know until I saw some gentlemen gave him money."

I could not help chuckling.

"Yeah, I was like Granny Liu entering the Grand View Garden," Father said, showing his self-deprecating humor.

In the novel, *Dream of the Red Chamber*, one of the four Chinese great classical novels, Granny Liu was a character who enters the Grand View Garden, a gigantic landscaped interior garden built to receive the visit of the Imperial Consort. Granny Liu had never been to any kind of grand building. Stunned and bewildered, she was a country bumpkin in a five-star hotel.

"Where's *Mama* then?" I was surprised that Father did not mention Mother while he was in Central, Hong Kong. I had known Mother sprained her ankle in Macao a few days before. Mother told me on a long-distance phone call from Hong Kong that she followed after Father and got off a bus in a hurry. That was how she missed a step and twisted her ankle. Father did not think it was a big deal. They continued their sightseeing.

"She's with your cousin to see Po Lin Monastery and the Big Buddha on Lantau Island," Father said.

I visited the twelve-story high bronze Big Buddha the year before on my first trip to Hong Kong. That was a magnificent site for the tourists and Buddhists.

"You weren't with her?"

"No," he explained. "I'm not interested in the Buddhist attractions. Plus, your mother would feel better with your cousin if I wasn't around."

Like Father said, Mother indeed had a close relationship with her nieces. Both of my female cousins, particularly Soaring Swallow, loved chatting with Mother. It was probably because her age was much closer to Mother's. I did not see her too often, maybe two or three times a year during Chinese New Year or on her parents' birthdays. But every time I met her, she praised Mother to me in private.

116

"Your mother is a great person," she said one time when Mother was out with her son. "I'm so thankful to her for caring for my mother."

"Your mother is so considerate," she said another time at a family dinner. "She always thinks of my son and buys stationery for him when she visits us."

I could not remember how many times Soaring Swallow had shared her gratitude with me. I was touched every time. Mother must have done many good deeds for everyone in *Yee-ma*'s family. However, she seldom mentioned them. Nor would I ask as long as she was content with her life. She could not get away from Father's questioning, though.

"Where have you been today?" Father would ask if he did not see Mother at home during the day.

Mother was usually busy doing something as if her chores at hand had taken all her attention. After a few seconds of silence, Father would draw his own conclusion. "Your sister has *three* children. They can take care of her. Only she dares to ask her own sister to clean her house." He stomped out of the living room and said, "Ridiculous."

Father's criticism came regularly as part of our everyday life. His voice would simply dry up towards the end of a thought and a long silence would follow.

"Why does he always question my whereabouts like interrogating a prisoner?" Mother often said in Father's absence. "I have to notify him about everything I do but he *never* tells me where he has been with his pals." She let her words sink in and went on, "Yeah. It's me who should stay at home every single day, doing the domestic chores while he and his friends eat and drink so happily that he doesn't even remember what his mother's surname is. That's perfectly fine for him.

"I don't even want to call his phone now," Mother said, getting angrier. "He always complains that my chicken-feather-garlic-skin trifles aren't worthy of making a phone call. So what about his chit-chat with his friends on the phone? He could have called to tell me he's not coming home for supper. But he always does that at the last minute when the dinner is already made.

"The next day he'd complain the food is not fresh," Mother lamented. She poured out her chagrin. She said, "Had I known he wouldn't come home for supper, I wouldn't have made so much food."

I was used to being a cushion for Mother's full venting of her feelings. I'd rather she let off steam this way. If only I could build a bridge for my parents to communicate heart to heart. But they were not that kind of couple who wore their hearts on their sleeves. They knew they disagreed on almost everything yet they seldom ironed out their disagreements together. The big wonder to me was how they had stayed married for so long. I observed tolerance on both sides rather than compromise, a cold war rather than a hot battle. Mother would reel off complaints if I sat still and listened to her attentively with occasional woodpecker-like nodding.

"Come on," I would say. "Don't be upset. Let's see what good program is on." Watching TV helped relax her. I flipped the TV stations to search for Cantonese Opera, one of the few programs that could intrigue Mother. I knew little about this form of art except to notice that the artists had peculiar voices, either as high-pitched as nails scratching across the blackboard or like a deep, gruff voice rasping at me. I was not sure if Mother understood Cantonese Opera to the level that she could critique the show. But she could follow the story with the help of the subtitles.

* * * * * *

During the years, Graceful Swallow brought a lot of gifts from Hong Kong on her visits to *Yee-ma* and *Yee-jeong*. Besides nutritious products and medicines, she also brought spiritual items like posters and beads. She was a devout Buddhist. She volunteered to bring volumes of Buddhist prayer books to monasteries and temples on her trips to mainland China. In her apartment in Hong Kong and *Yee-ma*'s in Guangzhou, bundles of Buddhist literature were often piled chin-level high against the walls, under the table and on the wooden couch.

Under Graceful Swallow's influence, everyone in *Yee-ma*'s family was more or less involved with these religious beliefs. *Yee-ma*, in particular, turned herself into a vegetarian. Beef was a taboo in her household. I did not know why until I was told oxen and cows were holy in Buddhism. I remembered several times when we ate out with *Yee-ma* and her family, Father had to order a separate beef dish for me.

118

It was a daily ritual for *Yee-ma* to offer incense and pray at home. She had a long table as her altar. A gold-edged, porcelain Kwun Yum statue, Goddess of Mercy, posed in the center. She is the most recognizable goddess in China. Wearing a white flowing robe, she holds a golden jar in one hand and a willow branch in the other. She sits in a meditation posture—one foot folded upon the opposite thigh—on a pink lotus. Her eyes are half-closed as if meditation has taken her to another world. She has long earlobes which signified longevity. She has a small red dot on her forehead and tiny red lips in contrast to her big round white cheeks. On both sides of the statue were big porcelain vases holding fresh gladioli and chrysanthemums. *Yee-ma* was a flower lover. She changed the flowers in those vases frequently. In summer, the fragrance of white ginger lily was pervasive in her home. Mother liked that flower the best. She also often arranged white ginger lily in our house in late spring and early summer.

On Buddhist holidays, *Yee-ma* usually worshipped piously at temples. Mother sometimes accompanied her. They would have Buddhist vegetarian food afterwards.

"Let me take you to have vegetarian food one of these days," Mother often said to me before she got ill. "*Yee-ma* and I ate in a new vegetarian restaurant the other day. That place was quite good."

I had tried the Buddhist vegetarian food a few times. Made from wheat gluten, tofu, agar and other plants, the vegetarian dishes closely mimicked various kinds of meat such as red barbequed pork or the eye-popping grass carp. I often thought they were good substitutes for the carnivorous people to deal with their weight problems. Or it might work the other way—since the Buddhist vegetarian dishes look almost the same as the mouth-watering meat dishes, they could increase the vegetarians' hunger for real meat.

Over the years, Mother would never tell Father that she went to temples with her sister. She was afraid it would deepen his misunderstanding that *Yee-ma* and *Yee-jeong* had implanted superstition about spirits into her.

One time, Father found a Buddhist prayer book underneath Mother's pillow in their bedroom. He said disappointedly, "I bought you women's magazines; you never read them. Instead, you read the *Diamond Sutra* every night. It'd be a miracle if you understand the ancient Chinese. I doubt that even your sister understands it. How can that book do any good to you? I try to influence you to be a modern woman but you'd rather become a sorceress. You're hopeless."

"Yeah, I'm hopeless," Mother said wryly. "You should marry another woman who can meet your expectations."

If it was not because something graver happened in our family, my parents would never come to a truce. In the first few months after Mother returned from the hospital, Father became much milder to her. It reminded me of the mysterious reconciliation between them years ago after Father's extramarital affair.

Mother kindled the joss sticks to worship her parents prior to every meal. Father had no objection. Mother made big portions of dishes which lasted several meals. Father had no objection. Mother stocked up herbal medicine in the fridge and cupboards. Father had no objection. Mother also started to listen to Buddhist prayer songs at home. Father had no objection.

* * * * * *

After a couple of interviews, Father and I finally hired a woman caretaker whose age was close to Mother's. Her family name was Kong, so we called her Kong Yee, meaning Auntie Kong. She came to our house six days a week to prepare lunch and supper. Father paid her eight hundred *yuan* a month, including lunch. Kong Yee came from Nanhai, a suburban district in southern Guangzhou.

"I'm good at cleaning. I can cook simple meals. But I'm not sure if my cooking suits your taste. Please feel free to correct me," she said in her accented Cantonese to Mother at their first meeting.

"Fine, fine," Mother said, scratching her nape impatiently.

Several times Mother confessed to me that it was not necessary to hire a caretaker. "Your father made a fuss about my illness. I have digestive problems but I'm not crippled. Why does he waste money this way?"

"He feels you could concentrate on your health without worrying about housework," I explained.

"It's more troublesome to ask someone to work for you than to do it yourself," Mother muttered. "She asks all the time. I have to teach her from scratch."

I understood Mother was not a lecturer-type of person. In the past when I asked her how to cook or how to knit, most of the times she just asked me to stay out of her way.

"Don't ask so much. You'll know in the future."

It sounded to me like the skills that were important for women to learn were supposed to come naturally without being taught. As the old saying goes, "The way to a man's heart is through his stomach." Didn't Mother want to teach her only daughter to make a delicious meal to entice her future lover? Didn't she want me to have nimble hands like hers to take care of my future family? Or would she rather let me be a tomboy, learning to assemble furniture and fix electric appliances from Father? After I started university, Mother said something new to avoid my asking.

"You're a college student. You can figure that out, can't you?"

She believed a university undergraduate would know anything and everything. After I kept throwing at her pellet-like questions of whys and hows, she finally got annoyed.

"Mama is like this. I'm cultureless. You go ask your father."

The word "cultureless" wrote off her mistakes if she ever did or said something wrong. It was also her disclaimer of not being able to answer. *Culture* in Chinese carries varied meanings, signifying literacy, knowledge, education, art, science and even common sense. When Mother said she was cultureless, it implied, "I'm illiterate. Excuse me. I can't help you, nor can I understand what you say. Accept who I am but don't judge me" or it could be as straightforward as "Back off!" depending on the circumstances.

So I figured it would take a long time for Mother to get along with Kong Yee and instruct the caretaker step by step on what to do. I did not have an impression of Kong Yee except for her broad shoulders and rough skin. She was a bit taller than Mother and much sturdier. I did not see the caretaker often as I had to work during the day. After I came home from work, she had gone and supper was ready on the dining table. Mother had usually already eaten. But she sometimes joined us at the table. She may have soup or chew fish bones. The 7 p.m. TV news was a must-watch program. It melted the frozen air in the house.

Father and I did not tell Kong Yee that Mother was a cancer patient for fear she would be too frightened to take the job. Anyone else might have asked for a larger salary in this circumstance or even quit immediately to avoid the responsibility. Father was more worried about the latter because it was not easy to find someone who was at about Mother's age and honest. So we only told Kong

Yee that Mother had polyps which required her to have a strict diet and sufficient time to rest during her rehabilitation.

"I don't want to tell Kong Yee about your mother's condition because I'm afraid she would tell your mother about it by accident while they chat," Father said to me in private later on. "I hired a caretaker not just to have her cook for us. The most important thing is she can keep your mother company during the day." He took a deep draw on a cigarette, white rings of smoke steaming out of his nostrils. He continued, "I can't talk to her, neither does your mother want to talk to me. So I hope a caretaker who is close to your mother's age will have common subjects to talk about."

I nodded. Father's eyebrows were furrowed deeply. Gray hairs sprung out in his brows, sideburns and the back of his head. He resumed his repair work. In his left hand was a glossy blue and white porcelain plate which I assumed was from the Qing Dynasty. Father used to tell me that that period was the prime production period of the blue and white china. He scrubbed part of the plate surface with a small piece of sandpaper in his right hand. He rubbed as hard as Mother washed the doormat. Smoothing the flawed antique was a paramount step in Father's work. He often called his porcelain repairing as "sandpaper scrubbing".

Together with my savings and his, Father bought the one-bedroom apartment next to our apartment in 2006, one year after I got a full-time salary. Father tore down the walls in the apartment and refurbished it into a big room with a modern bathroom containing a sit-on toilet. The apartment became his new workshop. It shared the same doorway with the apartment we lived in but had a separate entrance. The new apartment was more than Father's workshop. It was his private man's world where he could listen to his favorite music, receive his clients and friends, watch his own TV programs, feed his fish, read the newspaper after dinner and sit on a rocking chair smoking and drinking freely.

"Now we each have our own space," Father said to Mother after he moved his workshop into the new place. "You can do whatever you like in Room 303 while I spend my time in Room 302. The sit-on toilet is more comfortable. You can even shower in the new bathroom."

For years, we only used a squat toilet. It was such an ordinary part of our life that I did not even mention it to our first American guest, Frank, when he came to our house for dinner.

* * * * * *

That was not long after we moved into the apartment, and he was then visiting China in the summer of 2000. To receive the first American guest in our house, Mother made more dishes than we could consume, including fried Wonton, sweet tomato with eggs, steamed fish and white-cut poached chicken.

"Ah, you've made so many dishes," I was shocked to see a table of seven steamy dishes. Their stimulating aromas wafted into my nostrils.

"You're like your father," Mother said while filling the bowls with soup. "You haven't eaten yet, but you already comment about too many. Your American teacher has given you so much help with your English. How can a potluck like this reciprocate him enough? Please ask him to come to the table."

Neither of my parents spoke English. The best Father could say in English was "Happy New Yor" for "Happy New Year," "Happy Bir-day" for "Happy Birthday," and "Fan-que" instead of "Thank you." But my parents' charming smiles and attentive hosting, continuingly filling Frank's rice bowl with food and his cup with tea, conveyed their feeling of gratitude and hospitality. I was the interpreter between them to tie up the Sino-US friendship. I could not remember the exact details of the conversation but Father did mention Mr. Kissinger's epoch-making visits to China and the Ping Pong Diplomacy that paved the way to President Nixon's visit to Beijing. Father highly regarded President Nixon's achievement of formalizing the diplomatic relations between China and the United States.

At the end of the evening, Frank excused himself to leave early after he learned that our house did not have a toilet with "modern facilities." I realized our bathroom did not meet the "American Standard." From then on, whenever Frank came to our house for dinner, he consumed much less liquid. I surely understood why. My professor in college once told us that foreigners, particularly the ones who live in the developed countries, did not know how to squat. "If you don't believe me, go ahead and ask a Westerner to squat," he said matter-of-factly. "They're never taught how to squat. They only learn how to sit on the toilet."

My mind fixed on the image of the Kung Fu postures. *That must be hard for the foreigners who cannot squat to learn the bend-*

down kicking. My heart said. I chuckled at the clumsiness of the imitation. The new sit-on toilet was indeed a revolutionary facility in my family. Before too long my parents were accustomed to using the new bathroom. Father even said it was difficult for him to squat after he enjoyed the comfort of the sit-on toilet, especially for his sturdy potbelly. Mother also enjoyed the convenience after she was discharged from the hospital. She had to use bathroom frequently every day as a symptom of her ailing digestion.

* * * * * *

In Mother's eyes, it was excess spending that Father put a tank of fish in his workshop. At the beginning, Father bought new fish every other week when the old ones died. They were red palm-size fish with a protruding forehead like the one of the Longevity God's. Father said he hoped the fish could enliven the house especially when the Chinese New Year was around the corner.

"Most importantly," he said, "the lively aquarium may lift up your mother's spirit."

I doubted Mother understood Father's good intention. I sometimes looked at the fish swimming freely in the aquarium, trying to figure out how many of them there were. But I was never sure. They made their way underwater too fast. The water pump gurgled all day long. Chains of bubbles in the water distracted my counting. One day, a pang of fear loomed up in my mind. Mother's tumor cells probably grew faster than the oxygen bubbles. But they did not disappear like the bubbles. They stayed with her and accumulated their fatal power. The situation was as if toxic bubbles in the aquarium eventually poisoned the living creatures inside, all of them—the red fish and the algae suckers and the microorganisms that they lived on. How long would it take before the dark power took control within Mother? The indefinite waiting began to gnaw my morale. How many days are left when I can come home from work and find Mother all right?

The serenity before a storm worried me. Everything seemed to be in place—Mother was rehabilitating in the care of Kong Yee; Father was repairing antique porcelain every day, and I worked in the office five days a week. But a million thoughts ran through my mind: *How can I be working when Mom is sick? What else can I do in this phase? Are we together waiting for her death? How can I leave her alone in the care of an outsider? Where are our relatives? Where is Yee-ma?* I had not seen my aunt visiting Mother in our house.

Perhaps if I tended Mother instead of Kong Yee, Mother could live better. Perhaps if I kept her company more often, I would gain more trust from her. Perhaps if I was at home, the day for my parents would be easier. Nearly every day when I was by myself, I buried myself in deep thought about Mother. I talked to myself a million times, praying and praying in the hope that my imaginary god would be moved by my heartfelt wishes together with my incessant warm tears.

Chapter 7
Pilgrimage

My parents posing as a loving couple in front of a Buddhist convent in Shaoguan, Guangdong province in January 2007

In my college years, I read an English book named *Sophie's World*. A few lines had influenced me. It said, "We as individuals are microscopic insects burrowed deep in the rabbit's fur. A relative few crawl up the hairs. Most are content to remain in the depths of the fur, or else, having climbed to the top, crawl back down into its safety. The true philosopher climbs up the hair to look into the eyes of the magician."

Never do I want to be only content with a life in the cozy fur. My parents were gratified that I had found an editorial job which provided me with stability and security. But I had hoped I could work as a foreign correspondent, traveling to country after country, and maybe covering news at the battlefields. This idea of *me* being a reporter did not appeal to Father at all. He once said, "It's too dangerous for you, as a girl, to work in the front line of strife. You'll have to do too much legwork." He did not say exactly "I don't like it" but his tone insinuated strong disapproval.

Father had his point. I am his only daughter. Traditionally, tending to a family should come first above a career in a Chinese woman's life. As a city girl, I was lucky enough to finish tertiary education, a far-reaching dream for many country girls. They had to give up schooling and usually work from an early age to support their underprivileged families. Even though I was not inculcated with the Chinese women's ethics like the women in feudal China, I understood the social responsibility for a woman is to be a virtuous wife and a good mother. I watched Mother set a good example in my upbringing.

On a personal level, what Chinese parents at Father's age would want their only children to undergo the many tribulations they experienced in their lifetime? I was given a Chinese name, meaning to turn peril into safety, which mirrored Father's heartfelt blessing.

But my dream of seeing the outside world never ceased. For my parents, being stable was happiness; for me, being mobile would lead to opportunity. The yearning for a change of space and routines continuously burned inside me. But after we found out Mother had cancer, for once, I had to slow my pace of chasing my dream. I had to be by her side. I had to assist Father. I had to forgo my application to grad school, unwillingly letting my life be a yo-yo between home and office.

* * * * * *

Traveling had become a popular pastime on vacation in China. I would have three days off for the New Year. So I proposed our family, together with Mr. Liang, Frank and Prof. Zeitlin, have an outing to celebrate.

"Aren't there too many people traveling together?" Father said doubtfully.

"Well, the more the merrier," I said. "Mom loves joyful crowds, why not?" I was afraid Father would veto the idea. He loved tranquility. He would rather spend a quiet Chinese New Year at home than visiting family and friends.

"Look," I said matter-of-factly, "I don't know how many times are left for us to take Mom out. I think it's a good opportunity for us to cheer her up through travel."

"*Ho-lah*," Father said after a second thought. "Let's take your mother to some Buddhist temple. She'll find peace there. I'll call Mr. Liang and you invite your teachers."

Father's approval dissolved the stone of my worry. I started to arrange the family trip. Everyone agreed to join the trip to Shaoguan, a northern city in Guangdong province, known for the Nanhua Temple. Its history was traced back to the North-South Dynasties, more than fifteen hundred years ago. The Sixth Patriarch of the Chan School of Buddhism, the Great Master Hui Neng, lived and taught in the Buddhist monastery for thirty-seven years. It was said after Hui Neng achieved parinirvana, a Buddhist term for death, his real body became immortal and mummified. It was worshipped in the temple's Sixth Ancestor Hall.

The history of Buddhism did not appeal to Mother. She wanted to worship in a Buddhist temple the most. She was elated for several days after I told her we would travel together. She probably wanted to go out alone like she used to. But Father made sure the caretaker Kong Yee was with her in case of an emergency. She had been complaining to me about Kong Yee's cooking and her large consumption of water. Since the caretaker worked in our house, the bottle on the water cooler had quickly gone empty. It did not bother Father. But Mother was upset.

"I don't drink much water except taking pills," Mother said. She glanced at the water cooler and said, "Kong Yee is a water-guzzler. We've had to call for a new barrel in less than two weeks! She's also a *Dai Fan Tong*."

A big rice bucket, Mother meant, because Kong Yee ate so much rice, just the way Mother used to be—three big bowls every meal. That explained why our rice container, as big as a milk maid's bucket, needed a refill often. However, I thought Mother also used *Fan Tong* to refer to Kong Yee's slow learning because the phrase is a metaphorical insult, meaning an idiot or a simpleton.

Other than a small amount of rice, Mother could also eat steamed eggs, tofu and steamed fish. They were highly nutritious and easy to digest. But preparing steamed eggs often caused friction between Mother and Kong Yee.

"Remember, use cold boiled water to steam eggs," Mother would reminded Kong Yee, pointing at the water cooler. "Never use the tap water."

"She always forgets things I told her," Mother said impatiently when she and I were alone in the living room. "She's good at cleaning the house but when it comes to cooking, she's a bull in a china shop."

"Take it easy, Mom. We're going away in a few days. I hope you'll feel better."

"I can't wait. Your father will scold me for being unkind to the caretaker if he hears me speaking a tiny bit louder to her." Mother was short of breath. She lamented, "But my illness is like this. I'm easily agitated."

"Right. I understand very well. So please don't get upset, or it'll be detrimental to your health."

"Who's the patient here in this house? She's an employee. She should learn to tolerate criticism. I've cooked for this family for many years. Your father seldom grovels to me the way he does to Kong Yee. He's really a good actor."

"Please, Mom. Don't think so negatively. Relax. We all want you to be happy now. Let's hope we'll have a good time in Shaoguan."

Mother was quiet but I knew being misunderstood discomforted her. I tried a few words of consolation, but she still had to face Kong Yee in daytime. How could she simply escape from being at odds with the caretaker? Although both were similar in age, they did not click the way Father hoped. If only Father could realize the fact soon. I was concerned that Mother's life was not improving because of the unsatisfying meals prepared by Kong Yee. My thought of resigning from my job and tending Mother full time grew stronger. Yet, the other half of my mind told me to wait and see. *How about not making any ultimate decisions until after the trip to Shaoguan?* I listened to my conservative self.

* * * * * *

With Mr. Liang's help, we got the train tickets to Shaoguan. I had not taken a train for at least ten years. When I was little, Father used to take me by train to Zengcheng, where he spent several years of *zhiqing* life in his youth. Standing at the entrance to the train station, I felt this trip was monumental. A burst of sensation surged in my ribcage, as if my blood was boiling throughout my frigid body. I passed by the train station numerous times, but none of those times had moved me the way this time did.

Built in 1974, Guangzhou Train Station was a witness to the rapid change of the city. In the 1990s, in particular, millions of people from all parts of China flooded into Guangzhou and its neighboring regions for jobs. It was like the Gold Rush in the American West. Most of them came by train and transferred to bus. A new name to identify this group of people was born—they were *migrant workers*. They migrated from their rural hometowns to coastal cities for employment. At the end of every lunar year prior to the Chinese New Year, Guangzhou Train Station would turn into a Great Wall of people. Every migrant worker was anxious to return home in time for the reunion dinner on the Chinese New Year's Eve. So the throngs of workers put the Guangzhou Train Station in the limelight during the frantic "Spring Rush" in modern China.

Looking at the flocks of migrant workers at the train station, I recalled a wry remark I had heard long time ago by an American tourist about her trip to China. She said, "No kidding that China has too many people. It was so crowded on the Great Wall and there was always a long line in the ladies rooms." As a Chinese, I marveled at those who ruled the huge country for centuries. With such a large population, it was amazing that our emperors maintained order in the Middle Kingdom.

As was written in the Confucian classic work, *Da Xue*, Great Learning, "The ancients, who wished to manifest the enlightening character of spiritual power to the world, would first bring order to their government. Wishing to bring order to their government, they would first bring harmony to their families. Wishing to bring harmony to their families, they would first cultivate their personal lives…"

How profoundly did that great truth influence us for generations? Not everyone had such wisdom to make peace in a family, let alone in anything as large as a country. I had found it difficult to moderate peace between my parents, let alone trying to run a country of one billion three hundred million people.

The huge sign reading "Guang Zhou Zhan" (Zhan means station) in bold red Chinese characters stood proudly across the top of the station's concrete tower. Below the characters was a big clock reminding the scurrying passengers it was time to get on board. The station name and the clock are signature landmarks for China's railroad station postcards. I liked taking pictures of the train stations I had been to, such as Beijing, Shanghai, Chongqing, Jilin, Changchun and Nanchang. They all seemed to have an immensely crowded square in the front. Big as five soccer fields, the station square in Guangzhou transported me back to the times when New China was just founded; architectural style was simple and solemn.

We were waiting for Mr. Liang to double check the boarding gate. Father helped carry both his and Mother's duffel bags. He asked me to look after her on the road. In the meantime, I interpreted for Frank and Prof. Zeitlin. To some degree it was quite odd. Neither of the two American teachers spoke Chinese. But Mother seemed to understand them through body language. She would stick out her right forefinger to mean "attention," or point at Frank's pant legs to remind him to roll them up. She was always worried that the floor-dragging pants would trip Frank up or the half-stuck-out notebook would fall out of Prof. Zeitlin's back pocket. If she was pleased with the communication, she would show a thumbs-up to them.

In return, both of the Americans flashed a smile. Would people in the train station wonder why two foreigners—one was stout and short, the other was a head taller and robust—were gleefully kidnapped by a bag-loaded Chinese family? They were probably the only Caucasians within a fifty meter radius. Luckily, their silver hair could mingle with the Chinese black heads. Blondies in China often aroused attention in public, although more and more Chinese preferred dying their hair gold.

The sunlight started getting into my eyes. The station square was inundated with people. They stood, squatted, sat and slept on the floor, waiting for time to pass. Since it was a long way for the homesick passengers to get to the train station, they often arrived hours or a day earlier for their trains. Renting a hotel room was too costly for their meager salaries. Some of them just stayed overnight outdoors in the chill near the train station. Their bronze skin and black-rimmed finger nails implied they had taken hard outdoor jobs. Their weary faces suggested they had had a rough bus ride overnight. Their worn-out clothes and luggage denoted that they scrimped and saved to give the best to their loved ones at home.

The non-stop city traffic hummed in the background. On the eastern side were bus and taxi terminals. Subway Line Two connected to the train station underground. Small as I was in the wide-open station square, I felt the rhythmic pulse of the metropolis. Father often said, "Without the migrant workers' industrious effort in our city, Guangzhou will not progress so rapidly." I could not imagine how desolate the city would be if all the migrant workers had left the town for good.

* * * * * *

Our train finally started off. Father and Mr. Liang sat together. Mother and I sat across a table by the window on the other side. Frank and Prof. Zeitlin sat next to us on the aisle. We were all bundled up, so the seat seemed crowded, especially for the big-boned Americans. I once teased a group of foreign visitors that by Chinese body standards, the seat in the cable car could fit three people. But for the big fat foreigners, it could fit two or only one.

I had told Mother that the endearing nickname of the late, overweight Hong Kong comedian Fei-fei was translated as Fat in English. She quickly applied the name to Frank since both names began with the letter F. Pronouncing Fat was surely less challenging to her than saying Frank with a trilling *r*. Frank happily accepted his new diminutive.

"Shall we play cards?" I asked Mother. She brought a deck of poker cards with her. She liked playing cards with Frank, as if the game shared a mutual language between them.

"*Ho-ah*," she nodded, reaching her hand into her pocketbook. After a few seconds, she handed me the deck of cards. She swiveled around to look at Frank and then said, "Fat Fat." She showed her two chapped hands fumbling, as if she shuffled the invisible cards.

"OK," Frank said.

"Do you want to join us?" I asked Prof. Zeitlin while laying the cards on the small table.

"No. Thanks." Prof. Zeitlin said disinterestedly, turning his gaze upon the novel in his hands.

The train rattled along on the track. The scene outside the window flew by quickly, looking as if only gray and green parallel lines streaked by. I heard the train whistle in the distance, and sometimes the loudspeaker inside the train. Train attendants walked to and fro from one car to another, selling boiled corn, chicken thighs, beverages, maps, newspapers, magazines and cigarettes. Everything was overpriced on board. It cost five *yuan* for an ear of corn, which was equivalent to the price of nine or ten ears in a supermarket. Prof. Zeitlin bought one, quenching his mouth-watering yen for the steamy, juicy corn.

I was a constant card loser. Mother had some good hands of cards. She cheered when her hand beat Frank's or mine. I was in charge of shuffling the cards. After Mother glanced at all her cards, she said sympathetically, "Oh, you have stinky hands. My cards look so bad. You must've stolen my luck."

"Who has the lowest card?" I asked, ranking my cards in order.

"Not me. My cards are awful. Fat Fat?" Mother called.

Frank showed his cards and said in Mandarin, "*San*," meaning three. As a math professor, he could utter a few numbers in Chinese. But his Chinese was not improving in China. He blamed his diligent students who preferred to speak English rather than teaching him new Chinese words.

Mother often won because as she said, "To win takes strategy." She would reserve her ace in the hole at times to make her opponents happy by mistakenly thinking they were in control. Then just in the blink of an eye, she played her ace and terminated her opponents unexpectedly.

"Oh my!" Frank cried. Having realized Mother won again, he tossed hard the leftover cards on the table as if shouting he was dumb. The game was over. I pounded lightly on the table with my fist. But my disappointment at losing the game was not heartfelt. Quite the opposite, I felt as sweet as chewing candy. What could be more rewarding than making Mother happy? Especially at this period of her life, she needed to be surrounded with joy the most. Thank heaven for letting luck stand on her side.

* * * * * *

After several rounds of card games, the train arrived at our destination. The January wind brushed my skin like icicles grazing my neck. The temperature in Shaoguan was at least ten degrees Celsius lower than in Guangzhou. I had reserved hotel rooms in a hot spring resort near the Nanhua Temple. Our three-day schedule was to visit the Temple and have a hot spring bath. Father liked bathing in hot springs which was a relaxing pastime in winter. I had never been to one. I was more attracted by the scenery. We all needed to relax in our own ways while boosting Mother's spirit.

The Nanhua Temple was about twenty minutes by taxi from our hotel located in the town of Caoxi. Surrounded by a lush South China evergreen forest, the Temple covered acres of land, harmoniously including pagodas, ponds, footbridges, stupas, gardens, ancient Bodhi trees, gazebos, shrines, pavilions and livestock enclosures. I had traveled widely in China and Southeast Asia by then. But I had not paid much attention to the scenic spots in my own province. Why did I seek far places and neglect what lies close at hand? Were it not for Mother, I would have never come to a historic and holy place like the Nanhua Temple. The high saffron wall, the gold-gilded traditional Chinese characters imprinted on the name plate above the gate, the symmetrical red lanterns and the fanlike palm trees at the entrance beguiled me.

While I was appreciating the details of the architecture, Mother, in the company of Mr. Liang and Father, had walked ahead to the Grand Hall which stood in the center of the temple. Covered by glazed tiles, the Grand Hall housed the statues of Sakyamuni Buddha, Medicine Buddha, and Amitabha. The gilded figures were giants, about three-story high. Although I had seen colossal Buddha statues before, my eyes still popped, my mouth opened in a shape of the letter O. "Wow!" would be the appropriate expression for a kid admiring something fantastic. My wow factor echoed inside me quietly.

Sanctuaries of any religion have always intrigued me. Whether I am in a church, a Buddhist temple or a mosque, the sublimity and majesty quickly engulf little me. I feel a deep, spontaneous veneration, like a magical power that impels me to be silent.

The seal-your-lips magic inside that house of worship mesmerized me. No wonder anyone in trouble would come to such a sanctuary to pray and calm an inner disturbance. I needed to hide myself from reality in a corner of this Buddhist shrine. For too long, I had worn a mask of a strong person; I had to make everybody believe that I was in control and old enough to be the backbone of the family. But what if I doubted myself? What if I was spiritually weaker than my parents? My exhausted mind rested in that peaceful sanctuary. My faith was restored.

I remembered another trip when I sat in a Catholic Cathedral in Macao to seek peace of mind. I was on my way to buy imported honey for my ailing Mother. I listened to a Sunday mass in Portuguese. Although I did not understand the language, the musical tones of the priest's spiritual sermon soothed me like a mother stroking her restless child. I heard the word, "morte." *Doesn't it mean death?* My senses broke. Two streams of tears rolled down my cheeks. Did the priest read my mind? *Indeed, I am here for Mother. I want to gain strength. I want to give her hope to live on. I need blessing.*

The seal-your-lips magic in that Cathedral was like an invisible counselor. I easily revealed my feelings silently under the heavenly high ceiling. I felt psychologically lighter as I walked out of the church. Since then, I understood better about Mother's perseverance in going to the Buddhist temples after she was released from the hospital. She might also have found the seal-your-lips magic. Like me who knew little about the origin of Christianity, Mother only recognized several well-known Buddhist gods and goddesses. Both of us sought peace and consolation through some kind of belief. With or without the religious meaning, our beliefs helped us put our life together and regain hope for tomorrow.

Visitors crowded around a big round incense burner, which was studded with thin red stubs from the burnt incense sticks. I saw no room to plant new joss sticks there. Mother meticulously lit a bunch of joss sticks she had brought with her. She said offering the incense from home showed her sincerity. Like the way she did at home, she held the joss sticks with two hands and prayed. I could not hear what she said but I was sure one of the prayers was for good health. After her lips softly murmured, she bowed three times and planted the sticks in several chest-high burners.

The thick white smoke swirled along the wind, wafting to every nook and cranny in the yard. I stayed away as far as I could for the smoke had smothered my breath and watered my eyes. Some worshippers burned incense coils and big joss sticks. They were certainly more expensive and smokier than Mother's home incense. From a distance, the worshippers were like celestial beings. Instead of mounting to the clouds and riding the mist in the immortal world, the white smoke near the incense burner diffused over the worshippers' heads.

We roamed around the compound from room to room, hall to hall. About five hundred clay sculptures of Buddhist arhats, the spiritual practitioners who had attained enlightenment, were on display in the Grand Hall. The most precious cultural relic in the Temple was the mummified body of Hui Neng. The Sixth Ancestor Hall where the relic was exhibited received swarms of visitors on that day. I could barely get to the front to observe.

The relic in a glass box was somewhat shrunken, smaller than a normal modern man. A tour guide said the body was about eighty centimeters. That is half of my height—at most, to my waist! Wrapped in a saffron kasaya robe, the body was waxy dark. He sat in a lotus meditation posture with eyes closed, lips sealed and both hands folded in the front of the abdomen. It was said Hui Neng fasted and sat like that while he was dying. When all the nutrients and liquid were exhausted inside his body, he achieved parinirvana.

I did not stand too long as people kept pushing and squeezing in. I felt like I was on a sardine bus again. With some effort, I rescued myself from the crowd. Mother and Mr. Liang already stood outside under the bulky Bodhi tree. She attentively listened to Mr. Liang's lively commentary, and nodded with a smile. Mr. Liang kept talking with hand gestures.

"Do you know this is Bodhi tree?" he asked as soon as he saw me.

"Yes," I said and looked up. The tree must have grown for some years. The dense leaves were tiny like green stars above me. The roots joined together with the trunk. It was hard to tell which was root and which was the trunk.

"The Bodhi tree is a symbol of the Buddha's presence," Mr. Liang said. "You can find this type of tree in Buddhist temples. It's also an object for worship."

"I see," I marveled, processing the English translation in my mind for my American teachers. They sat waiting for us, overwhelmed by the crowd. I repeated to them what I learned from Mr. Liang. "Ah—" was their response. Good enough, we continued on our way.

Father had to smoke from time to time. He now always kept a good distance from Mother when he smoked. Knowing Mr. Liang and I were in Mother's company, Father walked behind us, making sure nobody in our group was left behind. He sometimes paused for a few minutes to appreciate the Buddhist relics. His sharp eyes could distinguish the era of the antique exhibits after a brief perusal.

"The Buddhist arhats figures were gems," he said to Mr. Liang after he stepped out of an exhibition room. "The wooden carvings were from the Northern Song Dynasty."

"Yes, the historical relics are well kept here," Mr. Liang remarked.

As we walked uphill, Mother sang, "Let's paddle together/ and the boat will push away the waves./ The beautiful White Tower is/ reflected on the sea,/ green trees and red walls are all around…"

"Haha," Mr. Liang was surprised and said, "it looks like you're in a good mood."

"Of course," Mother stopped her tune and said, "new year, new spirit. I shall have a fresh start."

"Right, right," Mr. Liang agreed.

"Last year was lousy. I want a good body and live healthily this year."

Mother Nature must have heard Mother's wishful New Year resolution. The wind grew stronger, startling the birds on the trees. The evergreen trees rustled in the breeze as if they gossiped about Mother's pure hope. The knee-high weeds bent towards one side, gazing upon this gutsy woman who was trampling on them. The winter sun lazily crawled from behind the thick clouds. For an instant, rays of light shed upon Mother's body as if she had turned into a radiant Buddha. She smiled. The dimple appeared in her cheek. I wish I had been quick enough to capture that moment with my camera. Her dark wavy hair quivered in the January chill. So did my body. But Mother seemed not to be affected. She praised it was a good day to go out.

I hated to think Mother was as gullible as Father claimed. That was why we decided not to tell her she had cancer. She was too quick to believe what she heard. She was naïve. She was innocent. She had no opinion. She lacked good knowledge. She was irrational. She was obedient. She was fragile. Was that why we throttled her chance of knowing the truth? Was this how we kept her away from getting hurt? Or was it only for Father and me to deal with the sticky truth unharmed? How hard will it be to keep a secret from the one I love?

Whenever Father briefed our relatives and friends out of Mother's earshot about her health issue, he never forgot to warn them, "Do NOT tell her about cancer." We were plotting a conspiracy of silence, excluding Mother. However, looking at the good side, I did not want to come clean. If what we aimed to do could maintain Mother's quality of life, I would go all out for it. *Dear god, I'm an honest small potato. Am I committing a huge crime of lying? I don't want to lie to Mom. But I have no choice, especially seeing her so optimistic about her future health. I don't want to ruin her faith. I want her to live on. Whatever I can do to keep her spirit going I will do so, by all means. Please punish me but not her. Bless her and rescue her. She deserves it.* As the days went by, my prayer unconsciously became a confession of my guilt. I felt bittersweet—happy for Mother that she picked up her spirit but deep down, I was in a penitential mood.

"How about I take a picture here for your whole family?" Mr. Liang suggested. His words disrupted my deep thinking.

"Great!" I said and swiftly pulled my parents to me. "Could you also use my camera?" I passed my Olympus digital camera to Mr. Liang as he was adjusting the lens of his old Konica.

When it came to photography, Mr. Liang was a serious amateur. He was like a director, telling my parents and me where to stand and how to pose. Not until he was satisfied did he press the shutter. That usually took a couple of minutes to get ready. But the quality of his photography was guaranteed. Standing still with his cheeks lifted, Father teased Mr. Liang, "Hurry up! My pose won't last long." His words eased Mother and me, widening our beaming cheeks. I rested my arms on my parents' shoulders, left on Father's and right on Mother's. Mother's head leaned a bit towards me. I could feel her hair tickling my neck but I liked it—a sense of her existence. As soon as Mr. Liang called, "Ready? One, two, three," we all mustered the happiest expression on our faces. Off went the sound of Ka-cha.

"Done! Very good," Mr. Liang praised.

* * * * * *

Following the map of the Temple, we continued sightseeing. Wherever Mother saw a shrine she would leave her footprint of prayers and offerings. We stopped by a Buddhist convent on the way out. Mother offered incense there as well. This part of the Temple was surprisingly quiet. The murmur of the trees grew louder. I could hear the echo in the yard. Fewer visitors traveled here. While Mother was busy with her ritual, I walked around as if I were paparazzi sniffing for a sensational scoop.

The Buddhist nuns were in gray cassocks, slim with shaved heads. The young ones looked in their teens while the old ones had weathered faces and wrinkled hands. The seal-your-lips magic prevailed throughout the convent. Their chanted sutras were like a repetitive soundtrack. The senior nuns knelt on hassocks, buttocks on heels, eyes closed, mouths babbling, a string of black beads rolling counterclockwise between their fingers. I always wondered about the state of such a religious meditation. Could the nun hear me passing by? Was she preoccupied in her contemplation? Were all her urges and sins resolved?

Noise outside the convent interrupted my thoughts. I quickened my pace and strode across the threshold at the entrance. My parents were in front of the chest-high incense burner. Mr. Liang stood sideways.

"Ha, can't you put down your Old Master's airs for just a second and please your wife?" Mr. Liang said half-jokingly.

"All right, all right," Father laughed. He received the joss sticks from Mother and kindled them with his cigarette lighter. He marched to the center of yard, facing the Buddha statue at the entrance. Humbly and earnestly, he bowed ninety degrees three times with both of his hands clutching the lit joss sticks. Holding his breath, his face tightened, as if it were his way of showing his utmost respect to religion. He then discreetly planted the smoldering joss sticks into the incense burner.

"There!" Father finally relaxed and said, "I'm also pious."

Both Mr. Liang and Mother laughed.

"Zhang Old Master is truly a man of action," Mr. Liang noted, patting Father's shoulder as old buddies did. "You deserve high esteem from humble me."

Mr. Liang was a joker in my family. I was used to his ancient style of speech when he teased Father. In return, Father would say something funnier in old Chinese to challenge Mr. Liang. Their back and forth arguments always entertained Mother and me. Although neither of us would ever utter such out-of-date syntax as "Your substance is too distant from propriety," or "I only abide by the words as written," we knew Father and Mr. Liang had a good time in debate.

I felt sorry that I could not translate the essence of Chinese humor to Frank and Prof. Zeitlin. Bewildered, they craned their necks to look at us, as if they were children wanting to know more. After I told them what happened, they smiled. If only they could understand that the Chinese sense of humor is usually subtle and spontaneous.

I remembered I had a classmate in middle school whose family name was Xu. Its Cantonese pronunciation was the same as the verb "to take off." Some mischievous classmates were inspired after Xu was elected as vice-captain of a soccer team. The word "vice" sounded like "pants" in Cantonese. So out came a new nickname: Captain Pants-off. I did not get the joke the first few times when hearing the name. Neither did Vice-Captain Xu. He thought he had earned a respectful title. But it certainly did not mean that.

Just before we departed from the Buddhist convent, I invited my parents to take a photo at the gate. Arched under a square top, a stone tablet at the center read "Wujin Convent" or "Eternal Convent" in traditional Chinese characters. The name read from right to left, like ancient Chinese literature. A turquoise shingle-embedded roof with tilted ends covered the top of the gate. The green roof extended to the worn red walls on the perimeter. A pair of knee-high elephant statues made of white stone guarded the gate. A green pine tree, emblem of immortality, towered next to one elephant statue. Father embraced Mother like a passionate lover. Mother rested her head on his right shoulder. She looked protected and loved. That sweet smile, that longing intimacy, that indescribable bliss on both of my parents' faces jogged my memory to the black-and-white wedding photo I saw years before. How could I prolong this heart-warming moment? Did it come too late? Was it an illusion? *No, take it, right there!* Whatever it was, I had recorded it with my camera.

During the rest of our trip, not only did I take pictures of Mother in different poses, I also took candid shots. She beamed. She chuckled. She laughed wholeheartedly by the stone lion statue, against the railing, in the shade of the banyan tree and in the hotel lobby with the rest of us.

"Coming here to worship really makes me comfortable and relieved," she said happily more than once.

* * * * * *

The family photo was developed! It looked unexpectedly satisfying. Father praised it. So did Mother. I enlarged the photograph, framed it and hung on the wall in the living room. In the backdrop of a rocky mountain range, at the bottom of which were green subtropical trees, I stood between my parents. Father was on my left, crossing his arms behind his back. His forehead appeared pronounced with his retreating hair line. Silver hair sprang out of his thick dark brows. The lines underneath his eyes were deeper than his eyelids. As he beamed, scads of lines—short and long, straight and curved, solid and dotted—emerged expressively as if a convoluted map of life was drawn on his face. He wore much less than Mother and I, only a corduroy long sleeve shirt and a gray jacket. The zipper was half closed on his potbelly.

I was wrapped in a purple windbreaker and a red felt scarf. A white canvas bag with two light blue straps hung on my right shoulder. It was a present from Mother in celebration of the 2008 Beijing Olympic Games. I remembered on the day when we stood in front of the glass counter in the mall; she said to me, "Get it or you'll regret it for a long time." Knowing it was overpriced, I was about to change my mind. Mother knew me too well. I would have had deep regret had I missed the purchase.

"Come on. Let's show our support for China's sports achievement," she added, fumbling in her pocket. Out she took a ball of ten and twenty *yuan* notes. She unfolded the creased notes. "Twenty, thirty, forty, sixty, seventy and ninety," she muttered. "Here, take it. Get yourself the bag," she said and tucked the money in my hands. I bought the bag and I only use it on special occasions.

In the picture, my right hand is on Mother's sloping shoulder. Her beaming face makes me forget how weary she is. She is in a black jacket with a red collar, zipped up to her neck. Two red stripes on her jacket go straight to the sleeve. Her hand is almost hidden inside her sleeve. Her newly-trimmed, short raven hair enhances her refreshed look. Her eyes narrow into slits, setting off her right dimple. I can vaguely see her double chin lines.

In less than a year, I would realize this was the last photograph of my parents and me. It recorded a contemporary Chinese nuclear family, a rare united moment, an extra-special occasion in my life, a sweetest memory in the most difficult time, and an indelible past that I could look back onto time and time again to regain faith as life moves on.

The last family photo of my parents and me taken in Shaoguan, Guangdong province in January 2007

Chapter 8

The Closure

The last time I visited my childhood home on Wu
Yue Da Jie, the Fifth Big Street, in January 2007

After returning from Shaoguan, Mother was in a good mood for
several weeks. She talked softly with the caretaker, greeted people
she knew on the street, and hummed songs while getting ready to
shower. Smiles were on her face more often than I remembered. She
submitted to Father's suggestion to do grocery shopping together
with Kong Yee. Walking to *Gaai See*, the Wet Market, was a
moderate exercise for her. She wished she could do morning
exercise with the female neighbors again.

In the past when Mother was healthy, she joined half a dozen
retirees to practice Tai Chi in the public garden of our apartment

building. They met around the fountain in the center of the garden in early mornings. One of them brought a cassette recorder and all had their silk fans and extendible swords. Along with the rhythmic music from the recorder, they practiced a full repertoire of Tai Chi, which lasted about thirty minutes.

I had watched Mother doing Tai Chi several times. She and the other women always did the movements in unison. They sometimes slid across the floor with two-step wide strides and bent their knees; sometimes moved their arms softly like pushing invisible waves, eyes fixed on their open palms; sometimes rotated their closed silk fans and suddenly "*chup*—" all fans in their right hand opened at the same time as though a flock of peacocks had unfolded their plumage simultaneously.

After Mother was released from the hospital, she was more cautious of her health.

"Good health is priceless," she always said. "I've been through a bad year. After seeing a ghost, who will not be afraid of darkness?"

She was afraid the January chill would invade her body. Instead of doing morning exercise, she walked at noon when the sun hung above. She often took a long afternoon nap and retired at night early even though her sleep was interrupted by her bowel movements. She ate exactly what her doctor allowed her to eat. She cherished her feeling-good body more so than before.

One day, Mother bumped into a Tai Chi partner. They chatted a little on the street.

"Haven't seen you for a while. Are you all right?" said the neighbor who was in her eighties. Hunchbacked and slim, she quickly held Mother's hand. I could not remember her name. But I always called her Popo, the same Chinese character as that for a maternal grandmother. It was polite to address unknown elderly women as Popo in Cantonese.

"Getting better," Mother said. "My aged body failed me. I was in hospital for two months."

"Was that serious?" Popo looked surprised.

"Small problems; there's something wrong with my digestive system. I'm afraid I can't play with you all for a while."

"Don't worry. Take good care of yourself. You're always welcome in our group."

Mother did not tell me about her feelings. But I knew Popo comforted Mother as a mother would inquire about her daughter. In return, Mother was extremely kind to the silver-haired neighbor. They used to do grocery shopping together or have morning tea after doing Tai Chi. One time when I invited Mother for a Western buffet, to my surprise, she brought along Popo. She said her friend had never tried buffet. We should share the experience together. I remembered another time Mother knew I was going to visit Hong Kong, so she asked me to buy an over-the-counter medicine for Popo. The medicine was not available in mainland China. Mother felt good if she could help the elderly.

* * * * * *

Traveling helped lift Mother's spirits. Father and I both wanted to take her on an excursion when she felt better. Before Chinese New Year, Father signed up a package tour to Beijing for Mother, Mr. Liang and himself. Visiting Beijing had been Father's dream. He hoped Mr. Liang's presence would ease the tension between him and Mother on the journey. That was not a bad idea. Mr. Liang always brought peace and laughter to my family. Besides, he could communicate with both of my parents better than I did. So we counted Mr. Liang in many family activities in the following months.

Mother had been to Beijing on business in the 1980s. Yet, she looked forward to an outing regardless of the destination. After their one-week Beijing tour, she said appreciatively, "There has been a dramatic change in Beijing. With so many tall buildings built there, I can't recognize the city anymore." Mother's words verified what I read in the news that only one third of the traditional *hutongs*—a neighborhood of narrow streets and alleys—remained in Beijing because of the rapid urban construction. On my last visit to Beijing a year before, I saw the business district in the capital was no different from that in Shanghai, Guangzhou, Chongqing or any other big cities in China. Blocks of glassy, soaring buildings reflected the fast-moving Chinese people on the street. No one wanted to slow down for the others, not even the traffic for the pedestrians. My parents were excited when recounting the places they had visited, including the Bird's Nest, the multi-million-dollar

National Stadium that was constantly in the news headlines before the Beijing Olympic Games.

Meanwhile, I learned that kiwi fruit can protect against cancer and honey is good for the immune system. Besides medicines, every method of bettering Mother's life was worth trying. So I looked for kiwis in big supermarkets throughout the city, including the ones that sell imported produce like the Hong Kong supermarket chain, ParknShop, the Japanese chain, Jusco, and the French chain, Carrefour. I seldom went to these supermarkets. There I marveled at the enormous grapefruits, fossil-egg-like avocados and the strange looking dragon fruits. I did not see these fruits when I was a kid before supermarkets came to China.

I looked at item after item on the shelf from aisle to aisle. No kiwis, except kiwi flavor ice-cream or candies. How could it be possible? After all, kiwi, known as Chinese gooseberry or commonly called Macaque peach, originated from China. The fruit was renamed by New Zealand exporters in the 1960s. Since then, "kiwi fruit" had become a global brand. That in fact increased kiwi's value in China simply because people misunderstood that kiwi was an imported fruit.

Normally, I would have hesitated to buy imported goods because their high price often scared me away. I had to pay twice more for fresh organic food. No way. Father always said, "If the same product was made in China and at a more reasonable price, why not support our national brands?" But for the sake of Mother's health, I was willing to buy imported food even though it might cost me an arm and a leg. The ripening season for kiwis was late summer, so there were no fresh kiwis sold in February. I felt lost as they were a thread of hope for me to save Mother. Mr. Liang offered to help. He knew dried kiwis were sold in a neighboring province, Hunan. He asked his friends to get a few packets for Mother.

I also stopped by Macao and Hong Kong to get imported nutritious milk powder and honey for Mother. A couple of relatives recommended them to her. Guangdong province has a long tradition as well as the advantage of trading with the neighboring free market of Hong Kong. Father used to tell me that in the 1960s when the mainland Chinese underwent hunger, poverty and a shortage of essential goods, they would feel in heaven if they received presents—as small as a tin of crackers or a pack of chocolates—from their relatives in Hong Kong. Before international goods became widely available in China, Cantonese people would ask their relatives and friends in Hong Kong to buy products for them. These items ranged from food, cosmetics and books to electronic goods and nonprescription medicine. Today, abundant consumer goods are available in China. Yet, the convenience of traveling and the rising value of Chinese currency encourage mainland Chinese, particularly the new-rich, to pursue the rare, trendy international merchandise in Hong Kong and elsewhere.

* * * * * *

The Chinese New Year arrived a bit late in 2007. It was the Year of the Pig. It fell in late February, a few days after Mother's birthday. Compared to my relatives and friends, my family seldom celebrated this significant Chinese festival elaborately. We did not hang any festive decorations or play any jubilant holiday music. We only had a few traditional foods like red watermelon seeds. A packet or a jar usually contains hundreds of seeds. Cantonese believe the larger the handful you grab, the greater fortune you will make in the New Year. Mother also made *niangao*, the new year cake, whose sound is close to "higher year" in Chinese, meaning raising oneself higher each New Year. It is considered good luck to eat *niangao*, which is made of glutinous rice flour.

At this time of the year, Mother would always replace the fruit plate at the altar with fresh apples and oranges. She also added blooming gladioli before my grandparents' images. Traditionally, Guangzhou residents celebrate the holiday season in the Flower Market during the last three days before the Chinese New Year. So Mother and I would be excited to go there just to immerse ourselves in the atmosphere.

The Flower Market consist of rows of makeshift kiosks in the center of each district. Roads in the area are temporarily closed from vehicles so that people can safely appreciate and purchase myriads of spring flowers, including peony, peach blossom, hyacinth, tulip, azalea, chrysanthemum, cockscomb, kumquats, nipple fruit and dozens of varieties of orchids. A symbol of nobility in Chinese culture, orchids are not cheap in the Flower Market. The common ones, such as boat orchid and moon orchid, may cost hundreds of *yuan*. Although it was Father's job to buy flowers for the New Year, Mother seemed enraptured by the blooming flowers.

147

"Look," she would praise, "how charming are those flowers! I can even smell the fragrance this far away." She was talking about the white daffodils. Layers of onlookers stood around the booth; some of them were potential buyers.

While Mother was attracted by the gorgeous flowers, I was usually curious about the booths selling the festive knick knacks of the zodiac year. Both the vendors and the buyers were mainly young people. This was a good time for high school and college students to make extra money. I remembered in my senior year of high school, my classmates rented a booth in the Flower Market to sell the Year of the Horse souvenirs, from horse air balloons to stuffed toy horses, from red and gold couplets to novelty stationery. The guys, wearing the horse head tiaras, took turns to solicit business in front of the booth. "Come and take a look, auspicious gifts for the Year of the Horse!" they would shout while entertaining the passersby with a large inflatable mallet or showing off the handicraft samples in their hands.

Overwhelmed by the boisterous festivity in celebration of the Year of the Pig, Mother seemed to forget her illness and her grudge against Father. Strolling along the Flower Market kiosks, she smiled and squeezed my arm, as if we were loving sisters.

We visited the Flower Market in daytime to avoid the big crowd in the evenings. The new year music from the public loudspeakers, the haggling, the laughter, the chitchats, the kids' screaming, and the vendors' shouting completely engulfed me. I had to make myself heard by speaking closer to Mother's ear and hollering at the vendors for a bargain. On Chinese New Year's Eve, in particular, the exultation reaches its zenith. The Flower Market would be packed with bulkily-wrapped and joyful people like those in the countdown in New York City's Times Square.

To avoid the crowd and noise, Father stayed at home.

"Every year is the same. It's not necessary to observe the formalities," he would say.

He confessed more than once that he was tired of the complicated ritual. He also suggested that Mother take a break instead of spending hours in the kitchen preparing *niangao* and other holiday goodies.

"The store has everything. The pre-cooked food is just as good," he would say. "As long as you have money, why don't you just buy it?"

148

Mother thought money had soured Father's milk of human kindness. It was important for her to share her home-made cooking with our immediate families to show her genuine good wishes. Had she been in good health, she would have made something for the Year of the Pig. Her steamed water chestnut cake was the best, often receiving compliments from my paternal aunts and uncles.

Every year, we usually had two reunion dinners—one with Father's side of the family, the other with Mother's. And we ate out to avoid the trouble of preparing a big meal and cleaning loads of dishes afterwards. As a matter of fact, eating out for a family reunion has become the Cantonese's first choice. Restaurants in Guangdong are open 24/7 during the holidays. On the contrary, those who are not from Guangdong province—considered by Cantonese standards to be Northerners —traditionally wrap dumplings and cook at home with family for the Chinese New Year. So restaurants in northeastern China, for instance, are usually closed.

The rest of the days of the two-week festival were played by ear. My parents' friends usually came to visit us with presents for the house and Lucky Money for me. Mother would reciprocate with palm-size red envelopes. On the envelopes were gold or silver color paintings and auspicious greeting phrases with such meanings as, "May your career progress step by step" and, "Wish you make big money." Kids love collecting Lucky Money. As I grew older, Mother revealed that as a courtesy she had to give back to the children of our relatives and friends the same amount of money I received. If I received twenty *yuan*, Mother had to reciprocate with a red packet of twenty *yuan* to her friend's child. Father would remind me to remember how much Lucky Money I received from each family and keep him or Mother posted. I definitely had no secret about my Lucky Money with my parents. To avoid "unnecessary spending," as Father put it, he tried to keep away from visiting other homes during the Chinese New Year.

* * * * * *

That year, I accompanied Mother to a reunion dinner with her former colleagues. They used to work in the timber factory with Mother. Some of them were her long-time friends and had watched me grow. I had not seen them for ages. As soon as we met in the restaurant, they stared in disbelief.

"*Wah*," exclaimed Ping Yee, who had short curly hair and a square face. "You've got prettier as you grew older." She perhaps still remembered me wearing dental braces in adolescence.

Embarrassed, I held Mother's arm to the round table, around which seven or so people had already been seated. Women outnumbered men. They were chatting with one another. At times, peals of laughter arose. Although they were not young anymore—a few of them had even become grandparents—they still enjoyed teasing each other like youngsters while reminiscing about the good old days.

"You're a head taller than your *Mama* now," another colleague in a dark-green-dotted blouse said. "Golden Orchid, aren't you happy to have such a good daughter?" She eyed Mother with an appreciative smile. Mother smiled back.

"You've lost some weight," she continued, seemingly noticing the difference in size between Mother and me. "How have you been?"

Mother repeated the same story. "I'm on a strict diet now," she said patiently. "I shall take it easy. This is a chronic disease." She took a sip of boiled water. Her voice was filled with sanguine expectation that she would be healthy again.

Hearing Mother's response, I felt as if a sauce bottle had been overturned in my heart. In Chinese, we have a figure of speech—*Da Fan Le Wu Wei Ping*, overturning a sauce bottle of five flavors. It means when a sauce bottle of life consisting of sweet, sour, bitter, spicy and salty is spilled, all flavors are mixed together, creating a terrible taste. I was too ashamed to look up. I had lied not only to Mother but also to her colleagues—all these people around the table who respected Mother, who helped her, accepted her, cared about her, and loved her like a sister. If Mother had known the truth, she would not have been so stoic; she probably would not even have attended this colleague's reunion. But wasn't it better to let her immerse herself in joyful friendship instead of learning this gathering could be her last?

For a long while I watched my knees brush the edge of the white tablecloth. Internally, I heard mostly gibberish. Only a babble of voices rumbled across my eardrum. In the old days, while Mother was preoccupied with her duties in the factory workshop, I would quietly draw or scribble in a corner.

Mother looked relaxed when listening to others mentioning my youth. Her voice was too mild to overwhelm other conversations, or even be heard by the people sitting opposite her. She used to raise her voice only if needed when working in the factory. I looked at her sideways. Her shoulders were narrow and thin. Her tawny lean hands stretched out of the taupe jacket sleeves, resting on her lap covered by baggy black pants.

Everybody seemed to enjoy themselves. Some men were red-faced from drinking or ranting. After two or so hours, most of the food on the Lazy Susan was consumed. The bill was sorted out, paid from the collective fund to which everyone contributed, including Mother.

"We'll save the change for our next year's gathering," the former accountant said gleefully, arranging the money in a white envelope.

No one objected to her proposal. Mother sat straight, hands on the table. Her lips held the shape of "*ho-ah*," "sure" in Cantonese, after she had said it. *I really wished Mother could come next year, too.* I thought to myself immediately. It was my quick prayer to my imaginary god. *This is too good a group to separate from for Mother. She deserves another gathering.*

The reunion ended with taking group photos. I volunteered to hold the cameras for Mother's colleagues. Women tried to squeeze into a three-seater long sofa while men and a couple of other women stood behind. Beaming happily, Mother sat in the middle, hands on her lap, shoulder to shoulder with her colleagues. They sat tightly like the cloves of a garlic bulb.

* * * * * *

We did not go home right away. Mother wanted to visit her aunt, who pursued gardening as a favorite hobby. I called her *Yee-Po*, grand-aunt in Cantonese. Just like Mother's colleagues, I had not seen *Yee-Po* in many years. Obviously, Mother had been in touch with her.

The last time I visited *Yee-Po* I was still in middle school, and she was living in a dimly-lit house, fronted by a muddy and weedy road. It was nearly impassable at night. This time Mother took me to her new house—a three-story building in the southwestern suburb of Guangzhou. The concrete roads to the new house were clean and wide. Within walking distance spread acres of flower fields. Red, yellow, pink and white blossoms dominated the horizon, farmers busy packaging the blooms in pots for the Chinese New Year sales.

At the age of seventy-four, *Yee-Po* now lived with her oldest daughter, Aunt Fragrance, who was several years younger than Mother. I had not realized how homey Mother felt around *Yee-Po* and how significant *Yee-Po* was in Mother's life. In the following months, Mother visited *Yee-Po* frequently as if *Yee-Po*'s home was as spiritual a sanctuary as Mother's Buddhist temples. Every time we were at her home, Aunt Fragrance would treat us with her tasty *Puerh* tea. With a pretty oval face and a persuasive tongue, she was in the tea business as well as being a tea collector. She could talk about tea for hours, never tiring of the subject. She introduced Mother to drinking tea for good health.

"Tea is much better than water," she said, preparing the tea in a terracotta tea set. "A shower cleanses your body while tea cleanses you within. My mother and I always drink lots of tea the first thing in the morning and after meals." She paused, distracted by pouring boiling hot water into a miniature teapot in which the *Puerh* tea leaves waited. She then poured the hot tea from the teapot over the upside down teacups. This step is called tea cleansing. Both the teacups and the tea leaves need to be cleansed through hot water. In a flash, Aunt Fragrance filled up the teapot a second time with boiled water and covered the lid. "Let the tea sit for a second for better flavor," she continued. "*Puerh* tea, in particular, can help you digest food and lower your blood pressure."

Puerh tea was also called Senior's Tea. The elderly often ordered it at restaurants. Aunt Fragrance proudly introduced us to her tea collection in the cupboard. I was surprised to learn that some of the pressed *Puerh bing,* shaped like a hard iron cake, were worth thousands of *yuan.* In fact, in recent years, the value of high-class *Puerh* tea fluctuated like a stock market index. Chinese tea investors and collectors manipulated the prices, making the demand for *Puerh* tea higher than its supply.

"We bought this Puerh bing for a thousand *yuan,*" Aunt Fragrance said, showing us a rice-bowl sized tea cake. "Now if we sell it, we'll get eight times more money. You can see the real tea cakes all have their birth certificates." By birth certificate, she meant a piece of paper wrapped around the tea cake which showed the name of the tea, the origin, the weight, the year of production and some certified logos.

"My mother will be here shortly," Aunt Fragrance added as if she had seen through Mother's anxious heart. "She's replanting her aloes upstairs."

"You know *Yee-Po* has a garden on the roof?" Mother said softly, her gaze averted from Aunt Fragrance to me. "Later you may ask *Yee-Po* to show you around."

"Yes," Aunt Fragrance chimed in. "She'd love to introduce you to her favorite plants." She continued her tea serving by placing a tea strainer at the mouth of a jug. She gingerly poured the tea from the miniature teapot into the jug. By then, I could smell the steamy fragrance. At last, lifting the glass jug, she filled up our lukewarm teacups with clear brown colored tea.

"Try it," she said to Mother. "This is one of our collections. We only serve it to our potential clients. Your visit makes an exception." She smiled.

As Aunt Fragrance chatted with us, *Yee-Po* showed up, descending from her roof garden. Glowing blissfully, she smiled, a straw hat slung over her back. She only wore a long sleeve blouse in winter. Her black hair was salted with gray. Her shoulders were wider than Mother's. She looked healthily tanned and nimble. Her voice was full of strength, as if she were a soprano holding a key note for a full minute without changing breath.

"There you are," she welcomed Mother and me as she took off the hat. "I'm so glad to see you. We haven't met for quite some time."

"Yeah," Mother eyed *Yee-Po* with glee and said. "We've been out today. We're just dropping in on you since it's been a while."

"How about staying for supper?" *Yee-Po* asked. "A restaurant nearby specializes in delicious roasted chicken. You should give it a try." *Yee-Po* gave me a tempting look.

It is impossible not to talk about food in Guangzhou. The city is known as the "Heaven of Food" in China. Even the travel guidebooks about China usually emphasize the food culture in Guangzhou. Restaurants outnumber scenic spots. To Cantonese, being invited to stay for supper is the most welcoming gesture from the host.

"Do you want to?" Mother asked me quietly, with a zealous gaze.

"Whatever," I said without thinking. "If you want, I don't mind staying. I'll call *Baba*, telling him to take care of his own supper." *I only want to make Mother happy.* I thought. We gave the caretaker a week off work for the Chinese New Year.

Mother nodded and continued to chat with *Yee-Po* and Aunt Fragrance. I went to the balcony to make the phone call. Father did not ask why or comment further but simply wished us to have a good time. Perhaps it was even a relief.

"He's still the same, repairing antique porcelain for others," Mother said as I walked back into the living room.

"Does your husband still drink a lot?" *Yee-Po* asked. She sat on a couch around the tea table. Aunt Fragrance had poured a cup of tea for her mother.

"Yes," Mother said plainly. "Smoke and drink. It's hard for him to change." At times, she scratched her dry skin on her arms or scalp. Father once nagged at this unconscious scratching. A bad habit he thought that could tarnish Mother's personal image in public.

"Does he still work at the old house?" *Yee-Po* asked again.

"No, not any more. He bought a single apartment next door that he made into a workshop. The old house is now empty, ready for the landlady."

"When will you give back the house?"

"Sometime in March. Last month we went back to the old house to burn my parents' portraits."

At the altar at No. 14 hung two framed, black-and-white pictures of my deceased grandparents. When we moved to the apartment, Father had my grandparents' portraits engraved on two square, white, ceramic tiles. He thought the tiles matched better the décor of the apartment than those old, yellowed pictures. I did not know why Mother burned the memorial portraits instead of keeping them. Perhaps it was a tradition to destroy the pictures along with the ghost money and other paper offerings on a last visit to the old house.

"Yes, Fragrance has told me about it. Did you also worship the ancestors?" *Yee-Po* asked after taking a sip of tea. She eyed Mother with an air of a wise elder.

"Yes, with barbeque pork, celery and rice wine," Mother recollected. She looked serious as if she had accomplished a holy assignment. She added, "I found Mother's china bowls in the loft.

It's a shame they were left there." Her firm voice suddenly sounded melancholic.

How could she not be? Over the years, I saw Father discarding loads of used goods, including *Popo*'s effects. In his eyes, everything that did not have immediate value was *trash*. Mother was a hoarder. Her theory was when the time came everything could be of use. She liked keeping *Popo*'s effects and many other daily necessities—mops, slippers, cooking pots, tins, shampoo, dish detergent, cooking oil, toilet paper and even joss sticks and plastic bags. Since I was little, my parents had argued numerous times over this issue. Father often chucked away *trash* when Mother was not at home.

"Dump! Dump! Dump!" Mother flared up when she realized her mementos were gone. "Your father dumps everything without asking. He should've also dumped his fuddled head." "Dump" in English sounds almost the same as the word meaning "dump" in Cantonese.

Knowing Father seldom entered my bedroom, Mother gradually hid her stuff in it—under my bed, my desk, and in my wardrobe. I always felt bad for her when she was scolded even though Father's points were sensible. How could I bear her being harmed again? Especially now, exasperation could be as deadly as her cancer. I cleaned up my bedroom, to make more space for her hoarding.

"It really is a shame not to save the chinaware," Aunt Fragrance interjected. She filled up everyone's teacup with more hot *Puerh* tea. The scent was stronger at the third and fourth refill. The white steam over the teacup soothed my nostrils.

"They certainly have historical value," *Yee-Po* said, eyeing Mother lovingly. "Your mother used to use them for her desserts."

Mother once said *Popo* used to make a living by selling her home-made desserts, including Sweet Soup, such as black sesame soup and papaya soup, and all sorts of cakes like sticky rice cakes and water chestnut cakes. She had her small business in front of No. 14.

* * * * * *

I remembered the day I accompanied Mother to No. 14 for our last visit. It was at 2:30 pm on January 19th, 2007. We were Mother, *Yee-ma*, *Yee-jeong*, Aunt Fragrance and me. In the loft, Mother had found some bowls that belonged to *Popo*. Several of them were Rooster Bowls. On each was etched a red rooster with a big black tail. The wide-brim Rooster Bowls traced back to the early twentieth century during the time of the Republic of China. They were commonly used in ordinary households. That day, Mother used those bowls to worship her ancestors.

Just as Mother told *Yee-Po*, the neighborhood of No. 14 had had a face lift since we left. The narrow alley, the Fifth Big Street, that separated the main house and the kitchen part, was elevated and paved with concrete. The uneven granite stone tiles were gone. The doorsteps in front of each household were gone. The colorful clothes and sheets hanging above the alley were gone. The noise of kids playing in the alley, of gossipers prattling, of birds chirping in bamboo cages, of venders with bikes shouting, "Collecting waste copper, waste iron, used pots, used papers" was all gone. Most of the old neighbors were gone—some had passed away, others had moved elsewhere. Their houses were occupied by migrant workers. To save money, two or three families lived in the same house. I had no idea how a house could accommodate six or eight people. I had felt confined living with my parents at No. 14 when I was an adolescent and there was just three of us.

Today, the alley was flat and white, stretching all the way to the other end of the lane. Since the ground level had risen, walking in the alley, I felt awkwardly tall. I recalled when I was a kid I had to tiptoe to peek through the grid of the metal rods in other neighbors' steel-framed doors. But now my gaze could easily reach the inside of the neighbors' homes. Empty and dry, the alley was quiet like a forlorn village. Doors were closed in the houses of families I used to know.

Instead of the worn red wooden doors, a heavy metal safety door was installed at No. 14. Father told me he had to change the doors after the house was burgled one night. That happened after we had moved to the new apartment and he still used No. 14 as his workshop. Fortunately, he did not lose anything valuable, such as the costly antiques that belonged to his clients. Father said he was lucky that the thieves could not appreciate the value of the antiques; otherwise, he would have gone bankrupt.

After the ground elevation, I thought No. 14 had escaped its fatal destiny of being a house below the "flood level." I was wrong.

In fact, Father was the only person who dealt with the mess after we moved. The downpours usually happened in late spring and summer.

"The ground elevation hasn't protected us much from the flood," Father lamented. "In fact, today more households are suffering from flooding because we're on the same level. The major problem is the sewage system. It's been years since the district government has sent people to improve the drainage."

As a Cantonese saying goes, "When you have headache, you find a cure for your headache; when you have sore feet, you find aid for your sore feet." It means one treats only where the pain is but not the whole problem thoroughly. Father concluded his point with the saying. I saw where that satire came from. The Guangzhou municipal government had spent tons of money on the city's infrastructure before the Asian Games in 2010. Father was surprised that even the low-income areas—mainly the western and northern part of Guangzhou—were in the blueprint of Guangzhou's face-lifting reconstruction. Father was one of many old Cantonese who were disappointed in the local government for caring only about the visible achievements, but not solving the deeply rooted problems of the city.

As Mother opened the door of No. 14, I saw the house had an upside-down appearance, starkly contrasting from the alley. Ugly and loose, the ceiling was peeling like a burnt face, thanks to the leak from the roof. Apparently, Father no longer fixed the roof as often as when we lived there. The water leaked through the roof, drenched the wooden floor of the loft and soaked the ceiling. Rusty water stains had tattooed the ceiling, the wall and the old bookshelf. Every piece of furniture was laden with white dust and reeked of dank mold. The big mirror on the wall was speckled with black mercury dots. Father had used the mirror to reflect the image on the monitor while repairing a TV set. Mother had combed her hair in front of the mirror. I had looked at the mirror frequently to see if any tooth had grown in the black hole in my mouth. The mirror then was so big and high that I had to kneel on Father's stool and lean forward against his desk to reach its upper edge. That was more than fifteen years ago.

While Mother was preparing the ritual, I took photos of the old house. Every nook and cranny was familiar yet distant. I saw myself in the mirror once again. The mirror was not that big any more. I could touch its upper edge just as easily as I could reach the ceiling with my fingertips. Instead of a girl with two pigtails and a silly expression, the person now appearing in the mirror was a young woman, medium height, solid build, a pair of glasses on the bridge of her nose. She still had that long hair but tied back. Her body was fully developed. In her black sweater and jeans, she stood straight in an air of sophistication.

I had changed.

Through the mirror, I saw Mother stooping over and setting the knee-high table.

There were three sets of red chopsticks by each of the three tiny red cups on the table. The red, pinkish and white barbeque pork was on the left whereas the green fresh celery and some tangerines were on the right. *Yee-ma* was not far away, counting the ghost money and dividing the paper offerings into four piles. Her husband, *Yee-jeong*, stood aside, hands folded on his chest. A brown felt hat rested upright on his spiky white hair. His face looked longer when he did not smile. He sometimes gave advice to Mother about how she should worship. Aunt Fragrance was in front of the house, setting up for the burning of the paper offerings. She cut the apples in half and laid them on the ground. She then stuck the lit joss sticks into the apples near a metal pail.

I stayed out of Mother's way, like I was a kid. Not knowing how to help, I would have to wait for her call to bow before my grandparents' pictures. It was always like that in our worshipping to the ancestors. However, on that day, I watched Mother carefully for the first time.

The altar was high up on the wall. Mother had to climb on a ladder to plant the joss sticks and red candles in the incense burner. Mother hid her emotional feelings by preoccupying herself. She meticulously followed every step, from pouring the rice wine into the tiny cups, to kindling the joss sticks, from saying her blessing of, "To have good health and have everyone's dream come true," to removing the framed photographs from the altar. Mother used a rag to dust off the ebony frames, leaving no fingerprints. She loosened the back of the frames and took out the 5R (5"X7") pictures.

Both of my grandparents in the pictures looked young, with sharp dark eyes, high cheekbones, and groomed dark hair. They faced squarely, no smile. What was it before them that had made them solemn? I had never perused their pictures so closely. At the bottom of the pictures were traditional Chinese characters of my grandparents' names and their dates of birth and death.

The dates were recorded in traditional Chinese calendric system which consists of ten Heavenly Stems and twelve Earthly Branches. The ten Heavenly Stems are the elements of an ancient Chinese cyclic character numeral system: *Jia, Yi, Bing, Ding, Wu, Ji, Geng, Xin, Ren, Gui*. They are still in use today, similar to the way the alphabet is used in English. For example, Chinese name Hepatitis Jia, Yi, and Bing instead of the English way of Hepatitis A, B, and C. Chinese say Party Jia, Party Yi, equivalent to Party A and Party B in a contract. The twelve Earthly Branches are those twelve animals in the Chinese zodiac. I used to be proud to recite them aloud in order: rat, ox, tiger, rabbit, dragon, snake, horse, goat, monkey, rooster, dog, pig. These animals represent the years and also the time of a day.

Mother handed me a piece of red paper and a black Sharpie pen. She said, "You have good handwriting. Why don't you copy the dates of your grandparents' birth and death onto the red paper?"

I did not ask why but wrote as instructed. Mother then folded the red paper and gave it to her sister. They planned to keep the paper together with my grandparents' cemetery documents. Cremation is mandatory in Chinese cities. My grandparents' ashes were stored in a cemetery in *Yee-jeong*'s ancestral hometown. Since my mother's side of the family could not afford hundreds of thousands of *yuan* on a grave for the deceased, they rented a locker in the ashes building. Every Ching Ming Festival, they would pay a visit to the cemetery. Over the years, Mother voluntarily paid for the rental. It was three hundred *yuan* each year, much less than the annual administrative fees for the graves.

By the time I came out of the house to see what Aunt Fragrance was burning, Mother had been ready to throw her parents' portraits into the flame. She gingerly held one corner of the photograph while the opposite end was slowly burnt. Eventually, she had to let go both portraits into the glowing inferno.

"I'm sorry, Mom and Dad," *Yee-jeong* croaked as he saw the portraits crinkle and curl and turn to ashes in the fire. "Please forgive us that we can't take you away. If in my next life I have an affluent life, I'll definitely treat you both well."

Standing outside around the pail, Mother and *Yee-ma* gazed upon the portraits turning into unrecognizable black images. Aunt

Fragrance stirred the ashes with a long metal stick to direct the rolling white smoke billowing away from her face.

"Mom and Dad, please rest in peace," Mother murmured, her hands closed before her chest. Her eyes seemed to be watering—either stung by the smoke or by the fact that she had to tear herself away from No. 14 for good.

"I don't know how he thinks. If our house were bigger, I absolutely wouldn't have burnt Mom and Dad's portraits. They'd be welcome to live with us." *Yee-jeong* said resentfully. By then, the portraits had completely burnt out into white ashes.

Although *Yee-jeong* did not identify who that *he* was, I clearly understood he was talking about my father. Perhaps *Yee-jeong* did not want to hurt my feelings. He showed his opinion about Father in a subtle way. He whispered to Aunt Fragrance in front of No. 14 while I was inside the house. I did not know how long *Yee-jeong* and Father had been at odds. They used to be drinking buddies and treated one another like real brothers regardless of the fact they were in-laws at least ten years apart. After the ceremony, Mother invited her sister and brother-in-law and Aunt Fragrance to have supper. Knowing Father would show up at the restaurant, *Yee-jeong* refused.

"I have high blood pressure," he said. "I need to go home to take pills. You all enjoy yourself." After thanking Aunt Fragrance for her help, he took off, leaving *Yee-ma* with us.

* * * * * *

"Yeah, your brother-in-law told me about the chip on his shoulder," Aunt Fragrance said to Mother. We had been at *Yee-Po*'s house for two hours. The conversation remained as hot as the *Puerh* tea.

"He said *Lum Goh* was arrogant and imperious," Aunt Fragrance continued, addressing my father as *Lum Goh*, respectfully using his given name. The afternoon sunshine slanted through the window like a glowing sword thrusting into our eyes. Aunt Fragrance stood and closed the curtain.

"Indeed," Mother responded. "He has changed a lot in recent years. His temper has become peppery. A few times in the past he was on the verge of beating his daughter after drinking his nitwit water." Father's chronic drinking problem was always the focus of Mother's complaints. Mother paused, eyeing everyone around the tea table. She went on, "He always looks down upon my side of the family. He blames my sister and brother-in-law for teaching me superstitious beliefs. If I burn some ghost money for my parents during holidays in the apartment, he'll go berserk as though I'm going to burn down his house. Yes, he's capable of earning money to support the family. But it doesn't mean he can talk down to the family."

Mother reeled off several issues that bothered her, as if she were talking to a live Buddha. In many ways, *Yee-Po* was her goddess. She gave Mother solace, care and advice. After we came back from *Yee-Po*'s house, more than once Mother revealed that she felt extremely relieved. She made similar comments after visiting the temples. I thought, as her daughter, accompanying her to where she could confide and pray and be listened to was the best I could do for her. If she could not freely share her inner world with me, at least I could take her to places that could satisfy her need.

What intrigued me in visiting *Yee-Po*'s was Mother letting down her guard and telling *Yee-Po* and Aunt Fragrance things I did not know. Likewise, they also informed Mother and me. On one of our scores of visits, we saw the second son of our obnoxious old neighbor, The Bitchy Stuff. Aunt Fragrance told us in private that he was also interested in the tea business with her brother.

"His mother is in awful shape now," *Yee-Po* told Mother. "She's in a nursing home in a wheelchair. She can barely move. Many times she just pees and poops in her pants. She's not that far." A euphemistic way for Cantonese to say one is about to die.

My heart sank. Shocked at the news, I found it hard to believe this was the neighbor's destiny. Mother used to say after the neighbor verbally abused her, "What goes around comes around." The Bitchy Stuff got her retribution just as Mother predicted. I wondered what Mother thought. She seemed at peace, patiently listening to *Yee-Po*'s update. Some months later Father told me The Bitchy Stuff must have died. He said before she went to the nursing home, he had witnessed her falling on her doorstep, blood all over her face. "Her life can't last too long," Father said in a tone of sarcasm.

Yee-Po also told Mother and me that another neighbor, Nanny Fong, had passed away. She died of throat cancer because of her chain smoking. Her kind appearance suddenly emerged in my mind. I remembered her soft-spoken voice, gentle smile and her warm touch that quelled my bawling when I was alone at home. It was her mother-like persuasion that strengthened Mother's mind to give Father another chance. It was her discerning appreciation of Father's gifts and skills that encouraged him to work harder in repairing antiques.

"Think about food. That'll make you happy." *Yee-Po*'s words interrupted my thoughts. "You should feel content that you have such a good daughter," she said to Mother. She often encouraged Mother to look on the bright side of her life.

Both *Yee-Po* and Aunt Fragrance knew from Father that Mother had cancer. Like our other relatives and friends, they were also in our "circle of confidence." However, *Yee-Po* was able to talk Mother into doing precautionary things without revealing the truth of her health. As a result, one day, Mother gave me the passwords to all her bank accounts.

"Why do you give me this?" I was stunned at receiving a piece of torn note paper from her. I immediately associated this with the dying people passing on their assets.

"Keep it, just in case," Mother said briefly. She was hospitalized then.

"I hope you don't think your health is on the downhill."

"Nah," Mother replied, scratching her nape. "*Yee-Po* reminded me to do this, just in case I might be ill in bed and need money. This way you can help me to withdraw it."

The stone of concern fell from my heart. *Thank you, Yee-Po, for keeping the secret,* I said to myself. Another time I found a talisman underneath Mother's pillow. It was a piece of raw yellow paper folded in a bizarre triangle. Something was written in red ink on the paper. That must be the spell, I thought. The doodle looked like the unintelligible cursive script. I was afraid I would be cursed if I looked at it for too long. Disturbed, I returned the talisman to where it was. I asked Mother where she got it.

"*Yee-Po* gave me that," she explained in content. "It helps me to sleep better at night."

I prayed Father would not discover it, or else he would scorn Mother for her superstitious stupidity. I had not tested how effective a talisman could be. But I thought Mother's psychological reaction to a blessing was a key. It was like the traditional Chinese medicine. Mother's faith in it enhanced the comfort she had after taking the bitter medicine.

* * * * * *

In early spring, the returning of No. 14 to the landlady's son went smoothly. Mother and I were absent. Father and the landlady's son, now the new owner, chatted for a brief moment in the house; he then returned the keys. According to Father, the owner was an educated man. The conversation was polite and cordial.

Returning the property was a significant event in my family, just as epoch-making as Hong Kong returning to motherland China. The historic issue between my family and the landlady finally came to closure.

As those two wooden doors shut, how many pieces of old furniture were left behind? How many dusty footprints and finger prints of ours remained in the house? How many bowls and dishes that belonged to my grandparents were buried in the loft? How many stories of Mother's, of Father's, of mine had happened in this rundown house? Perhaps on that evening, after Father finally left No. 14 permanently, the mice and the cockroaches had an orgy to celebrate our departure and the newcomers' arrival. Perhaps the beams and girders of the house were now even more ramshackle. Father always said the house was on the verge of collapsing. Thank heaven it did not happen when we lived there.

I took a number of photos on my last visit to No. 14. The photos impressed Father. He said that was the best way to remember the place. He and I both had a whole batch of photos respectively. As for Mother, her way of commemorating No. 14 was to tell me an astounding story about her parents and her sister.

"Your *Yee-ma* left No. 14 as soon as she finished high school," Mother began her recollection on one evening in April. "Alone, I looked after *Popo* and *Gonggong* at home while going to school."

"How old were you when you went to school?" I asked curiously.

"Seven. I went to the same elementary school as you. Back then, the school was much bigger than now. When I was about to go to middle school, the Cultural Revolution broke out. Your *Gonggong* was ill then. So I had to drop out of school to take care of him."

"What about *Popo*?"

"*Popo* was frail, too. She couldn't work much. So I had to substitute for *Gonggong* to work in the timber factory."

That year Mother was only fifteen, one year younger than the legal working age. So she added one year to her birthday when she filled in the employee form.

"What did you do in the factory?"

"At the beginning, I was a porter, carrying sawdust from one place to another. I also loaded a four-meter long timber on a truck. Then I worked in the plywood workshop. They paid me 36.5 *yuan* each month."

The living standard in those days was low. Mother said a spring onion cake cost four *fen* (a hundred *fen* make one *yuan*), and nine *fen* was enough for a bus ride from No. 14 to Haizhu Square, which used to be the downtown before the late 1990s. Today, nothing is worth less than ten *fen*.

"Both *Gonggong* and *Popo* doted on the neighbor's children, who have moved to Hong Kong now. They'd bought the girls candies. I had to do everything in the house. At three o'clock in the morning, *Popo* would wake me to stand in line for pork. In those days, people got up very early and brought their stools along, sitting in line and waiting to buy pork. If I did something wrong with the housework, *Popo* would beat me hard with a wooden stool or bang my head against the wall."

My eyes widened. I was shocked at knowing how relentless *Popo* was. How could *Popo* have such a heart of stone? What kind of a mother was she to treat her own daughter violently? The more I thought about it, the angrier I felt. I placed my hand on Mother's, calming her surge of excitement.

"If I were lucky, Nanny Fong would come to stop *Popo* beating me." Mother paused to allow her words to sink in. My heart quickened as if I had just watched a thriller. How did Mother survive her childhood? Why did she still miss *Popo* badly if she was so mean to her? Where was *Yee-ma*? How come she did not return home to help Mother? Mother read my mind. She continued her story.

"*Yee-ma* met a guy who was a porter in the ice house near our home. *Gonggong* and *Popo* didn't like him. They thought he was stubborn, hot-tempered and rude. But *Yee-ma* fell in love with him and insisted on marrying him. So he became your *Yee-jeong*.

"After they married, *Yee-jeong* sometimes beat and scolded *Yee-ma* and she would return home and cry. The neighbors would come to help make peace." Mother's memories started leaping. She said, "When *Gonggong* was dying, *Yee-ma* wasn't around. It was an evening of torrential rain. The house started leaking. I carried an umbrella inside the house and held it over *Gonggong's* body while *Popo* was looking for help outside. I'll not forget that I saw my father passing away before me.

"After that, *Popo* and I lived together. I was considered as a half-orphan, so I was exempt from having to go to the communal farms. Instead, I worked at *Gonggong's* position in the factory, making money to support *Popo* and me. A few years later, *Popo* had a belly ache. A neighbor helped to send her by bike to the First Municipal Hospital. I was up all night to look after *Popo*. She was constipated. Her doctor taught me how to extract liquid from her nostrils for a sample test. There was no hospital room available, so *Popo* had to stay overnight in the hallway.

"I had to take leave from the factory to take care of *Popo*. She had undergone surgery. After a month's hospitalization, before the second surgery, *Popo* was half drowsy. She asked me, 'Do I have a scar on my belly?' 'Yes,' I said. 'Close your eyes and rest for a while.' Who knows if this sleep is permanent? She was already unconscious.

"*Yee-ma* came to the hospital for a short visit. After I sent her off, I saw *Popo* had already been pushed out of the operating room. I asked the neighboring patient why the surgery finished so early. She said *Popo* was too weak to undergo surgery. The doctor had given her a cardiotonic shot but it still didn't work. 'How many family members do you have?' she asked. 'My sister and me,' I said. 'You should notify your family now,' she said. So I did, calling back *Yee-ma*. By the time we came back to the hospital, *Popo* had gone."

This was the most explicit version of *Popo's* death that I heard. I was thunderstruck at Mother's last word. Her voice was full of regret and sorrow. Her eyes were moist like puddles of water sparkling. Her facial muscles were lax, as if all her nerves were paralyzed by her tragic past. She sat upright on half of the chair, elbows on the armrests.

I was taken by Mother's story. I could not help thinking that I would have to deal with Mother's death the way Mother had dealt with her parents, *alone*. How much courage did she need to face her losses? What should I prepare for the future? It would be my first time to confront death. I quivered at my morbid speculation. Mother's voice again broke my chain of thought.

"After *Popo* died, I lived alone at No.14. *Yee-ma* frequently asked me how many gold rings our mother had left us. I was quite annoyed. Naturally, all the rings belonged to me. *Yee-ma* had married and *Popo* gave the rings to me as dowry. But *Yee-ma* just could not let it go. I took the rings to *Yee-Po* and she weighed them. I gave a lighter one to *Yee-ma*. She still didn't give up. After I was married, she and *Yee-jeong* came to No.14. They lifted up the tiles on the floor and looked for platinum jewelry. When your father came home, he asked what had happened. I pretended I didn't know anything to avoid conflicts.

"*Yee-ma* and *Yee-jeong* never brought any presents when they visited *Popo* and me. I thought my sister was careless and ungrateful. *Popo* used to compare *Yee-ma* to the neighbor's children whom she liked very much. She would say to *Yee-ma*, 'The other children always bring something home. You, return home just with two hands of bananas.'" It is a euphemism in Cantonese to say "to visit with two hands of bananas," meaning to be empty-handed on a visit.

Mother was interrupted by her urge to go to bathroom. By the time she returned she had forgotten where she had left off. She did not continue her story. Perhaps it was too painful for her to reminisce. She retired to bed after taking her medicine and praying before the altar.

Sitting in the living room, I pondered Mother's incredible story. I imagined my grandparents wearing the wide-sleeve baggy cheongsams. *Popo* had a pair of black satin pants like the ones Mother wore. Mother was scrubbing the heavy rags over a washing board, hands all red. *Popo* was insulting her non-stop sideways. The fiercer *Popo* humiliated Mother, the harder Mother scrubbed the clothes. Her body moved back and forth in rhythm like a wobbly doll. Her eyes were red and moist. But she continued her chore without uttering a single word.

I had no idea how to absorb everything overnight—Mother's suffering, *Popo* and *Gonggong*'s indifference, *Yee-ma* and *Yee-jeong*'s greed and Father's disdain. Mother's story was like a gust of wind blowing off my naïve vision of a happy childhood she might have had. How could she let *Yee-ma* and *Yee-jeong* take advantage of her? How could she forgive them, help them, and even trust them more than Father?

166

A few years before, *Yee-ma* had a severe surgery on her spine. Unknown to Father, Mother frequently sneaked to the hospital, then later to *Yee-ma*'s house after she was released. There in bed, *Yee-ma* was all swollen up—her eyes sunken, cheekbones bloated, lips turned black and blue. Moaning in pain as the anesthetic started dissipating, she was immobile. Mother tended to her sister as if she were royalty. She proficiently peeled an apple, sliced it into thin pieces. She then cut it once more into small slips and gingerly fed *Yee-ma*. If *Yee-ma* needed to elevate her feet, Mother would exert all her strength to reel the handle at the end of the metal bed. The veins on her neck turned blue, collar bones shown in her lean shoulders. I would not be surprised that Mother had helped wash *Yee-ma*'s bed pan. I did not witness it. *Yee-ma* had politely requested me to leave before that scene.

In the past, when Father started to bicker at home, Mother often said, "Harmony is invaluable." She then walked away. I began to understand Mother was inspired and influenced by her faith. Leniency is the highest realm in Buddhism. Perhaps she had long realized the essence of a noted Chinese saying—"*A moment of tolerance acquires subsided wind and calm sea; a step of recession gains a boundless sky.*" Perhaps she had comforted herself with such a philosophy of life. She forgave the faults of her parents, her sister and brother-in-law, and even her neighbor, The Bitchy Stuff.

All of a sudden, I felt I had grown older. I seemed to understand Mother deeper, yet, her life story still left me with a series of question marks. *Why does she tell me all this now? Am I old enough to fathom her past? Have I gained her trust? Is it Yee-Po's idea again that Mother is told to pass along the family story to her only descendant?*

Mother would never know how much I appreciated her confidence, how much I marveled at her bravery, tolerance and forgiveness, and how much I felt blessed after comparing her childhood with mine. Alexander Pope once said, "To err is human; to forgive is divine." Perhaps that was why *Yee-jeong* felt sorry when Mother burned her parents' portraits. He might have realized he had done wrong to the family members. I knew I should forgive *Yee-ma*, *Yee-jeong* and Father the way Mother did. But never can I forget.

Chapter 9

The Last Resort

I once asked my father what he believed. He said he believed nothing except fate. At the time, my young life was tediously uneventful. No way could I comprehend what Father meant. When Mother's health issue alerted us, I realized it could be fate that she did not undergo surgery for her cancer.

While my family was looking into the palliative therapy of traditional Chinese medicine for Mother, we were introduced to a journalist who was a friend of Prof. Zeitlin. She wanted to interview my father about his antique repairing. Through word of mouth, she knew about Mother's health condition. Father told me in private after I returned home from work that the reporter recommended her doctor, Dr. Cheng Jianhua, from Guangdong Hospital of Traditional Chinese Medicine. Dr. Cheng was an oncologist, specializing in internal medicine with years of rich clinical experience. He was so well-known that every day dozens of patients visited him, including the reporter.

Father was not sure if it was a good idea to bring Mother to see Dr. Cheng for her first consultation. He was concerned about how to tell the doctor Mother had cancer in her presence. He and I had tried carefully to conceal the fact from her.

After Mother returned home from the hospital, Father and I only discussed her health issue behind the closed door of his workshop. It was usually in the late evening after Mother had retired to bed. Father and I were like two calculating conspirers locked up in the thirty square meter (about three hundred and twenty three square feet) room, reviewing every bit of the frightening truth, and making every critical decision.

"She'll find out she has cancer through our conversation with the doctor," Father said.

"I know," I said with a heavy heart, "but we can't delay the appointment. Mom needs medication." After seconds of thinking, I continued, "Why don't I meet Dr. Cheng alone for the first time and tell him our plan?"

"That's a good idea," Father said after puffing a Double Happiness cigarette. "Bring the CT scan result with you and let me know what he thinks before we take your *Mama* to see him."

Just as planned, I brought Mother's health records and test results from home to see Dr. Cheng by myself. Dr. Cheng agreed to meet me immediately. Wasn't it ironic that the visitor who was supposed to see the doctor was not the patient herself? But Dr. Cheng clearly understood this patient's family's conundrum.

"How long has your mother been diagnosed?" Dr. Cheng asked in a heavily accented Cantonese. His words were laden with indecipherable twangs. I felt embarrassed to ask him to repeat every single time.

"About six months," I replied. "She was admitted to the First Municipal Hospital from last October to December. Then, she was on Western medication at the beginning of the year and we took her to a traditional Chinese medicine hospital for a visit last month." I gave out more information than I was asked for.

"What kind of Western medication did she take?" Dr. Cheng asked, while perusing the test results I brought with me. My gaze fell upon his yellow spotted necktie that stuck out from his white coat. His gold-rimmed square glasses reflected the white fluorescent light on the ceiling. His gray hair shone in the white light in contrast to his few remaining dark hairs.

I told Dr. Cheng the medicine that I remembered and said, "Dr. Zeng from the Municipal Hospital prescribed the medicine to improve her anemia and her malnourished condition."

Dr. Cheng's office fell silent. I glanced at my wristwatch. It was already seven o'clock in the evening. Outside, the office was much quieter than it was during the daytime. I heard no babbles, no bawling, no footfalls and no coughing.

Chinese patients were usually so jittery that they would peek into the consultation room, or even worse, they would stand at the door waiting for their turn. For the sake of the patient's privacy and an undisturbed environment, the doctors had to close the doors after they called in the next patient.

That night, Dr. Cheng was OK about his office door being half open. As he had promised, he was more available in the slow hours of his Wednesday night shift. Compared to the crowded scene in the mornings and afternoons when most of the chairs in the waiting lounge were taken by the agonized patients and their anxious companions, the hospital at night was nothing like that. The unspoiled isolated calm brought a little friendliness of the hospital to me.

"I'll try my best to cooperate with your family," Dr. Cheng uttered as he was absorbed in the computer monitor. "I believe you've done a great job with your family to boost the patient's faith. Based on my experience, the family support is often the best spiritual medicine for a cancer patient. You can tell your family not to worry about taking your mother to see me. In the future, you may leave the patient's health records here. Our computer system also keeps every patient's information and data. That'll save the trouble of having records lost or, in your case, revealing the truth to the patient. I'll write the letters 'Ca' for the word 'cancer.'" Dr. Cheng wrote them on a piece of white paper for clarity. He gave me an affirmative look, as if he had planted a seed of hope in my lonely desperate heart.

"I need to see the patient in person and run some tests before I give you further suggestions," Dr. Cheng continued. "For the time being, you're on the right track to improve her quality of life." His accented statement broke into numerous sound bites replaying in my mind. I did not want to miss a single word.

"How long do you think her life will last?" I could not withhold my urge to ask the question. For months, I had not missed any opportunity to question it whenever I met with a doctor. Dr. Cheng suddenly became my mother's fortune teller. I counted on his words.

"On the good side, it may last eight to ten months," Dr. Cheng said after a careful consideration. He added, "Don't let the time frame scare you. It's not uncommon that some cancer patients outlive the medical presumption. You and your family's supportive effort are crucial."

I thanked Dr. Cheng and agreed to bring Mother to see him soon. He nodded. As I turned around to say goodbye, I saw a light smile on his wrinkled stern face. His yellow necktie looked brighter and the corner of his spectacles glistened.

* * * * * *

I had done this before, reporting what I learned from a doctor to my father. Both of us acted like two bad eggs in a crime movie. This time our rendezvous was in a Chinese restaurant near home. Father did not want any bit of our discussion to flow to Mother's ears.

It was after nine o'clock at night when I returned from Dr. Cheng's appointment. People had started to have their fourth meal of the day—*xiaoye*, midnight snack. But to many Cantonese, mostly men, it was more than a snack. Some ordered entrée dishes like fried noodles with beef and lots of beer, some had *dimsum* and rice porridge, some enjoyed fusion hot pots, and others preferred the kebabs and fried seafood on the street. They drank and ate and talked loudly.

We sat on the second floor of the restaurant with a low ceiling. The noises and the steam from the food were trapped in the claustrophobic-induced space with big sealed windows. Our table was close to the air conditioning ventilator. The spot turned out to be the coolest and also the noisiest. Now nobody could eavesdrop or intercept this father-and-daughter's secret talk.

"Dr. Cheng said Mom's metastatic cancer found in the liver is a severe sign of colon cancer," I said, competing with the hum of the air conditioner behind me. "It's stage IV cancer. He said we should be prepared."

Father was expressionless. All the lines on his faces drooped except his tightly-knitted brows. I saw the Chinese character "川" forming between them again. He said nothing but poured the brandy he brought with him into a glass. Quietly, he tightened the bottle cap, wrapped the bottle with a black plastic bag, and "thud," he plonked down the black solid object on the table. He remained silent.

"Dr. Cheng would like to see Mom in person. She'll need to have some tests done before the doctor decides what to do next. He said traditional Chinese medicine cannot cure her but will palliate her illness," I said, my throat tingled. I leaned forward in the hope that Father could hear me better. I tried to sip tea but it was still tongue-burningly hot.

171

"Dr. Cheng asked us not to worry. Mom won't find out her cancer from him. He'll cooperate with us to improve the quality of her life. He suggests we leave the patient's records with him in the future. And he'll write 'Ca' in the prescription to stand for 'cancer.' He also said we should continue to improve Mom's comfort. That's the best we can do," I spilled out everything important in one breath. My voice was weakened after it had stayed at high pitch for a while.

"What did Dr. Cheng say about how long your mother can live?" Father asked gravely.

"On the good side, eight to ten months but he also says some cancer patients may live longer than the medical presumption."

"Everything you told me tonight is no longer news to me. We just have to do whatever we have to. This is a very long battle," Father paused and sipped his brandy, then he went on, "For you, in particular. You've worked very hard in respect of your mother's illness. I don't want this matter to seriously affect your daily work. I've been through too many rough patches. I'm highly adaptable to hardship. So let me take care of the errands at home. We also have Chan Yee to help out. You can focus on your job."

Father's words sounded like a proposal for changing duties. Perhaps he wanted to take a more proactive role as a lawful husband. Perhaps he wanted to make up for his poor relationship with Mother in her remaining days. He was a worrier. Like Mother, he always worried more about others than himself. I knew him too well. He must have worried that in addition to my full-time job, the family trial would wear me out quickly. He must have wanted me to take a break instead of him. This was the self-devotion of a parent.

But how could I leave Father alone to deal with the worst situation. Although we had hired a new caretaker, Chan Yee, after Kong Yee resigned, I was still uneasy about leaving Mother in someone else's care every day. It must be the Chinese filial piety rooted in my soul. As little kids, we were taught to respect parents and ancestors. I obeyed as told. I joined my parents to pay respects to our ancestors' graves every Ching Ming Festival. I never challenged my parents regardless of how nasty or unreasonable their words were. I tried to help my parents with housework and be a good kid at school and at home. But nothing was like now when Mother was suffering a bout of fatal cancer. A call of repaying my parents' love all these years resounded loud and clear. Filial piety had become my basic instinct. It may be even stronger in an only child. I was not sure.

"I'll take good care of myself as well as you and Mom," I said to Father. He was about to finish eating. I reminded him that we should make an appointment for Mother to see Dr. Cheng soon.

Father agreed and he asked me to go home first. He did not want Mother to notice we met outside if we entered the house at the same time.

* * * * * *

Even the perfect crime would leave traces behind. Although Father and I strictly kept the benign conspiracy, Mother was "not an idiot" as she often said to me after Father chided her. I was often afraid there were some traces we left behind that might make Mother catch us red-handed. When we hired Chan Yee, we did not tell her Mother had cancer for fear she would accidentally let the cat out of the bag. From relatives to friends, from neighbors to doctors, we either did not inform them or had them orally agree to keep mum about Mother having cancer. But that night when Mother rushed to bed after she noticed that I had spotted her leaning behind a half closed door, both Father's and my hearts fluttered.

I was careless not to close the door of Father's workshop. I was discussing the labels on the Chinese patent medicines with Father. After several visits, Dr. Cheng prescribed Mother both the traditional Chinese medicine of dry herbs and also of condensed pills. The former required cooking in soup before use while the latter was taken like Western medicine by mouth daily. However, the labels of the Chinese patent medicine suggested the capsules were good for colon cancer patients and those who had intestinal motility disorders.

"What should we do, *Baba*?" I asked, holding the medicine box in hand.

"Hope she won't read into the description carefully," Father replied after he read the label. "Or if she does wonder, let's tell her that she belongs to the group of the latter part of the description. We can't let her know too much."

As Father's last word fell, the door to Room 303 shut bang.

"Shit!" Father muttered under his breath. He rarely swore in front of me.

173

The last thing I saw was Mother's sparkling eyes disappearing from the dark crack in the door. I had no idea how long she had stood behind the door. I ran immediately after her to the bedroom. She was already lying in bed, mosquito net tucked tightly around the bed, as if it were a fortress closing its gates from enemy invasion.

"Listen to me, Mom." I said.

"No!" Mother rejected hard and hostilely. "I don't want to hear. I don't want to hear."

"Calm down, please," I forced, my fists cold. "Mom, it's nothing like what you heard."

"No, no, no, no, I don't want to hear," Mother cried. I had never seen her so frantic. She covered both ears with her small hands. She kept shaking her head, leaving a deep impression on the pillow. Her wavy dark hair was more disheveled.

"Mom, you're doing fine," I made the biggest lie in my whole life. "Doctor said even though you had *it*, it could be benign. Just like Aunt Sahm's uterine fibroids, after surgery she was fine again." For god's sake, to perfect one lie I had to create more lies and involve more people. I hoped Father's younger brother, Uncle Sahm, and his wife, Aunt Sahm, would forgive me.

"Shut up! Don't bother me! Let me sleep!" Mother sent her ultimatum. She turned her back to me, arms crossed on her chest as if she was enraged. I did not want to impose on her. I knew it was no good to irritate a severe cancer patient.

I left her and returned to Father's workshop. I told him what had happened in the bedroom. He was so disheartened. His weather-beaten face said it all. All of a sudden, I felt my words were so powerless. They could neither convince Mother nor comfort Father. Did I talk too much or did I talk not enough? It was my fault anyway to leave the door open. I screwed up the plan. I caused the pain and unhappiness for everyone. I reprimanded myself a hundred times. That evening was one of my hardest ones.

* * * * * *

After that night, I thought the conspiracy was over. I expected to have a tougher situation in my family since Mother might not trust me anymore. Father relied on me to communicate with Mother. But now he might lose me as his inside person. Yet, the next day Mother appeared like nothing had happened. She did her everyday praying before my grandparents' images on the altar. She took her pills on time and chitchatted with Chan Yee. Father told me he heard Mother singing in the kitchen during the day.

"She seems to be in a good mood," Father said after I came home from work.

"Nothing unusual happened?" I asked in doubt.

"No," he said, "it's like a normal day."

"Did she talk to you?" I was still in disbelief.

"A little like always."

"Oh, that's good. Let's hope it's water under the bridge."

Indeed, no one ever mentioned about what happened the night before. Mother did not ask me at all. She was eager to see Dr. Cheng every other week. She often reminded me of her doctor's appointment far in advance. I did not know how much she knew about her health and I dared not to ask. But I believed her positive attitude resulted from her not knowing about her colon cancer. That was what Father and I believed.

The day to see Dr. Cheng was important to everyone. Besides Father and me, Mr. Liang also accompanied Mother. His presence lightened the frigid air in my family. The long waiting period passed quickly among Mr. Liang's stories—some were legendary, some were real-life, and some were inspirational. Occasionally, Mother even laughed.

Father had asked me to stay at work. But I did not listen. A party of four to visit the doctor, if it was not the biggest, was at least a conspicuous group to walk into the doctor's office. Prof. Zeitlin joined us twice. On those occasions, his appearance aroused more public attention. Prof. Zeitlin wanted to thank Dr. Cheng in person for his friendship and care for my mother. It certainly was good for our rapport with Dr. Cheng. Although he spoke little English, Dr. Cheng was proud to have an American friend visit him. Upon leaving, Dr. Cheng stood up and shook hands with Prof. Zeitlin like old friends. When he did that, it was hard not to cause a scene for such a respectful farewell. The next patients who had already stood outside the office poked their heads in to check what was going on. As we walked out of Dr. Cheng's office, Mother smiled, Mr. Liang smiled, Prof. Zeitlin smiled, and Father bowed and said many thanks. Other waiting patients stared at us with curiosity. I smiled with embarrassment.

I could tell Mother appreciated our company. The more the merrier. She was talkative with Dr. Cheng in his office, revealing details of her diet and daily routines, her discomfort and her reaction to the prescribed medicine. She told no one else in such detail except Dr. Cheng. This was the time I learned more about her health. After the consultation, she was in the company of Mr. Liang. Father and I separated to run errands in the hospital.

Different from the U.S. for example, patients in China filled their prescription in the same hospital after they saw the doctors. So after Dr. Cheng prescribed Mother new medicine, I ran to the cashier to pay the bill while Father stood in line in front of the pharmacy. After I finished the payment I would give Father the receipt as a proof. Waiting for the medicine to be ready often took longer time than checking out. In the past, calculating the medical bill was separate from payment. And the prescription windows for Western medicine differed from those for traditional Chinese medicine. So patients had to run around between windows before they could pick up their medicines.

Today, computers are widely used in hospitals in China. Most work is done by digital machines. With computers, the hospital accountants not only sum up the patients' bills but also collect money from the same window within a short amount of time. If the efficiency declines, the fault is always on the slow computer network. Instead of writing on paper, Dr. Cheng typed the diagnosis and the prescription on his computer. Seconds later, the intelligible printout was ready. I must say I would rather read doctors' typing than their scribbling handwriting. Computers seem to make modern people's handwriting worse.

Mr. Liang tried to relax Mother with conversation while waiting for us. It was good for her not to pick up sad stories from other patients. She hit it off easily with strangers. I remembered more than once when I went out with her by taxi, she ended up chatting with the taxi driver like old buddies. In a fashion store when I tried out clothes, she also would chitchat with the salesgirls or other customers. Our teamwork in the hospital was perfect, saving lots of time.

Dr. Cheng usually prescribed two-week's herbal medicine. So when we left the hospital, both Father and I held two handfuls of bulky plastic bags. On that evening, we often ate out like a little celebration for Mother's good health. We often went to one of the two restaurants. One was just opposite the hospital across the main street; the other was an over one hundred year old Cantonese restaurant called Lian Xiang Lou, meaning "Fragrant Lotus House." But it took about thirty minutes on foot from the hospital. Since it was one of Mother's favorite restaurants in old Guangzhou, the long walk was worthwhile.

One time when Prof. Zeitlin was with us, we decided to walk to Lian Xiang Lou. By Mother's standard, it took only twenty minutes on foot. That was what she told Prof. Zeitlin and I translated for her. Prof. Zeitlin was hesitant about a long walk on a humid early summer day. He came along anyway.

To get to Lian Xiang Lou, we had to pass one of the crowded commercial areas in Guangzhou. Famous for its *qilou* arcade buildings, the Shang Xia Jiu Walking Street was part of the old section of Guangzhou. The three-or-four-story high Chinese arcade houses dated back to over a century ago. However, their architectural style originated in ancient Greece. Introduced by overseas Chinese merchants and colonial traders, the arcades were built tightly side by side, with the ground floor set back halfway into the buildings and the upper floors hanging over the sidewalk, supported by columns. The arcades formed a shaded corridor which kept the shops along the sidewalk and the pedestrians safe from the rain and scorching sun.

The Walking Street teemed with pedestrians all year round. Vehicles were prohibited. Boutiques, delis, restaurants, and department stores lined both sides of the street, extending to the neighboring roads. The retailers went out of their way to drum up business. The sales tactics varied from turning up the disco music to a deafening volume in the stores to hollering sale slogans through bullhorns, or from hanging big advertising placards to distributing flyers to pedestrians. Father seldom shopped here. He said the hustle and bustle caused him a headache. But in those months after Mother saw Dr. Cheng, he yielded to strolling on the Walking Street with all of us. If only Mother understood Father's effort to please her.

Even though Mother was a patient she outwalked everyone. That day she strode through streams of pedestrians on the Walking Street like a light swallow. Father made sure I kept pace with her wherever she went. He and Mr. Liang deliberately walked behind. Prof. Zeitlin lost his momentum halfway and walked with Father in the end. Sweating and puffing, he regretted walking so much but he said Mother's overflowing confidence relieved his concern. He was right. Mother's faith grew exponentially after every doctor's appointment.

* * * * * *

In traditional Chinese medicine, the four basic diagnostic methods are *wang*—inspection, *wen*—listening and smelling, *wen* (different Chinese character)—inquiry, and *qie*—taking pulse and palpation. Inspection means to collect information about diseases through observing the patient's mental state, physical condition, facial expressions and tongue manifestations. This was why it was important for Dr. Cheng to see Mother in person.

Listening to the voices and breath as well as smelling the odors of the patient help the doctor determine the use of drugs. For instance, the sound of cough varies from the causes of dryness to wind invasion, from phlegm to lung injury. Inquiry is used by doctors in both traditional Chinese medicine and Western medicine. Taking the pulse is a routine known to all Chinese patients. Without being asked, Mother laid her arms on the desk after Dr. Cheng asked her a few questions. He placed the middle three fingers on her wrists for a minute. That full minute felt like ten times longer to me because nobody was talking in his office and Dr. Cheng looked highly focused as if the pulsation could speak to his mind.

In ancient times, because medical doctors had low social status, they took the dignitaries' pulses, women in particular, through a thin thread or over their silk handkerchiefs. No physical contact was permitted. When the imperial doctors visited Empress Dowager Cixi, the most powerful woman of royalty in the Qing Dynasty, he could only observe her across a translucent curtain and check her pulse over a handkerchief. Times have changed and the profession of doctor is now highly regarded. Since it takes twice as much time to become a doctor in traditional Chinese medicine as to become a doctor in Western medicine, more medical students in traditional Chinese medicine give up halfway. I assume China has more Western medical doctors than traditional medical doctors. But the demand for traditional medicine remains high. Mother was one of the fans.

Mother made no remark on Dr. Cheng's indecipherable accent. In fact, she often praised Dr. Cheng for his smart appearance

178

because of his necktie. She smiled a lot in his office, sometimes even made jokes about her health. When she smiled, she lit up the room, nearly making me forget she was a patient. Dr. Cheng once took a picture of her with his mobile phone. He might want to take Mother as a positive example for his medical papers. By then we had visited him for four months. Despite the fact her weight declined gradually, Mother's mental state was in perfect shape, better than anyone's expectation.

"Dr. Cheng's medicine is very effective," Mother often praised when she prepared the herbal medicine for cooking.

In the old days, one dose of traditional Chinese medicine was contained in a brown paper bag. Inside the paper bag, all sorts of beans, twigs and cubes were mixed together. You wouldn't know them by name if you were not familiar with their shapes and smell. Today, the herbal pharmacies still use brown paper bags to separate doses. But inside the paper bag are a dozen small sealed packets, containing various kinds of herb. The label on each packet tells you the name of the herb, its amount and its manufacturer. The modern packaging provides transparent information of the components of each dose, demystifying traditional Chinese medicine. I began to learn carefully what medicine Mother was taking before she prepared it.

"Can I help you?" I asked, looking at all the packets spreading over the dining table. Mother meticulously cut open each small packet with a pair of scissors. She then poured the herbs out into a large stainless steel bowl.

"You can help me to write down the names of the herbs," she said gently.

"Sure. But why?"

"So we'll know the differences in Dr. Cheng's prescription every time. See, these are *shanzha*," Mother said, putting several dried Chinese hawthorn berries in her small palm. "They invigorate one's stomach and stimulate the appetite."

"These are *yiren*, they do the same job," Mother continued, pointing to the yellowish grains of Job's tears to me.

A packet of two full length centipedes caught my eye. My gosh! They were dead! But their grotesque appearance remained— elongated, brown body and a Burgundy red head. The dozens of legs on both side of the body and a pair of coiling long tentacles gave me the creeps.

179

"Look, Mom." I held up the packet with my fingertips, as if I wanted to prove to Mother how brave I was to catch the suckers.

"Yes, I know, centipedes," Mother gave a glance and said uninterestingly. "They can clear wind and spasm, dissipate toxins inside one's body."

The wind she was talking about was considered a major cause of illness in traditional Chinese patterns of disharmony. My most direct understanding of the pernicious influence of wind was when I caught a cold. That was when the external chill invaded my body, causing headache, nasal congestion and many other symptoms.

"How do you know so much?" I asked, looking at her with great admiration. Her fragile face broke into a mild grin.

"Having taken the medicine so many times, do you think I'm stupid?"

Speechless, I smiled back. I always thought Mother was street-smart. I hoped she would not figure out what the centipedes were actually for. Mr. Liang told me that centipedes were on the top of the list among the five deadly venoms—scorpions, snakes, geckos, centipedes and toads—in Chinese folk culture. In traditional Chinese medicine, it was a practice to eliminate the toxicant with poisonous agents. It was similar to the idea of setting a thief to catch a thief. And centipedes were effective to restraining cancer cells. That was the main reason why Dr. Cheng included them in his prescription for Mother's herbal medicine.

* * * * * *

I did not think Father had realized how knowledgeable Mother was about the medical value of traditional Chinese medicine. I wondered if she knew that the traditional Chinese medicine that I prepared for her was for the same purpose of slowing the growth of her cancer cells. I simply told her the medicinal soup was for her digestive problem, though. To make my lie convincing, I said the recipe was recommended by a doctor friend of mine.

It happened two months before Mother met Dr. Cheng; I immersed myself in a sea of medical books on cancer treatment, the traditional Chinese medicine therapy in particular. I copied several herbal therapies from the how-to books. I asked Mr. Liang to take me to the traditional Chinese medicine market. With his knowledge of herbal medicine and its market price, I bought bags of herbs including Yellow Essence, Ripe Earth, Goji Berry, Half Branch Lotus, Half Side Lotus, Hundred Flowers Snake Tongue Grass and Ejiao. You may be as amused by these funny names as I was. I could have given their official names but I only translated them literally based on their Chinese characters. It was how I felt when I first read the herbal names from the therapies. They meant nothing to me except for the odd sound when I read them. I could not associate each type of herb by its shape and size. So when I asked for the same amount of Ripe Earth and Half Branch Lotus, Mr. Liang was shocked.

"No, no," he immediately stopped me. "One *jin* Half Branch Lotus is a lot! They're dried twigs and leaves of light weight."

How would I know how much one *jin* weighs, let alone one *jin* of fallen-foliage-like herb? *Jin* is a Chinese unit of measurement. One *jin* equals five hundred grams, a tiny bit more than a pound. Confused, I looked at the weight scale for a numeric answer. The seller had tucked the herb into a half-full black plastic bag. She paused and turned around to check with me. "How much do you want?"

"Uh…" I averted my gaze to Mr. Liang, suggesting that he decide for me.

"Half *jin* this time," he ordered firmly like an experienced merchant. "Now you know where the herbal market is, you can always come back for more," he turned to me and said, as if he was a master passing down his experience to his pupil. In many ways, Mr. Liang is my *shifu*, my master. He taught me how to make *Lo Foh Tong*, the Cantonese Slow-Cooked Soup. He enriched my knowledge of traditional Chinese medicine. I knew through him that both the raven, solid Yellow Essence and Ripe Earth invigorate the circulation of blood. Ejiao, often commercially packaged in hard blocks like chocolate bars, also improves blood supply, especially for women. So do the dates and Goji Berry, shaped like red seeds.

My books on cancer treatment said Half Branch Lotus, Half Side Lotus, and Hundred Flowers Snake Tongue Grass were the most effective herbs. When you are desperate to relieve the discomfort of a cancer patient, every way is worth a try. I followed the instructions in the therapy, mixing the approximate amount of each ingredient together in a specialized pot, adding three bowls of water and setting the flame to high until the medicinal soup boiled. At times I stirred the soup with a chopstick like a witch checking on

181

her recipe. I turned down the flame to medium and cooked for another fifteen to thirty minutes. The pungent smell grew stronger as the soup was about to be done. As I poured the inky liquid into a china bowl, white smoke billowed out of the pot as if the medicine had been cast with some magical spell.

The unpleasant smell told me the medicine was strong and bitter. I was astonished that Mother could drink up the soup completely. She rarely commented on the taste but after she finished my soup, she asked, "Why does the medicine taste so terrible?" I could not tell her the truth or fool her. Betwixt and between, I quoted what she always said to me when I had traditional Chinese medicine.

"The medicine is good for health and bitter for your mouth," I said, passing her a candy. "Take it. It'll sweeten your mouth."

* * * * * *

When you have a cancer patient in your family, you become super sensitive to the subject. Everything you read, you hear and you think is associated with the word "cancer." People you know—close or distant—ask about it in a sympathetic way, as if you were as pathetic as the patient. When the subject is raised, you also find out there are, in fact, many cancer families around you.

I learned through passing friendly regards in the office that a colleague from Crazy English magazines had a father who was a long-time lung cancer patient. My best friend Ivy's paternal grandma had breast cancer. A couple of Father's old classmates died of one or another kind of cancer. And even my older cousin Jacky had nasopharyngeal cancer a few years before. He was fortunate to discover the disease in the early stages and was cured. He was also the most informative person in my family about cancer. He suggested we help Mother apply for the government's Severe Illness Insurance & Benefit Program. The Program would reduce our medical costs significantly.

Thanks to Jacky, we mentioned the Program to Dr. Cheng and received his approval and authorization. Under the special medical insurance program, we only paid ten percent of Mother's medical costs each time. The municipal government covered a substantial sum and the rest was paid by Mother's retirement health benefits. Father kept track of Mother's medical expenses. He told me the government gave medical subsidies to retired people based on the number of years they worked. Since Mother had worked nearly thirty years, she received a considerable sum of benefits after she retired. This Program was part of the municipal medical reform in Guangzhou. The annual reimbursement of the Program to each severe patient reached as high as one hundred and fifty thousand *yuan*.

I always offered to pay for Mother's doctor appointments. It was my proud moment as I could prove my financial independence to my parents. Contemporary Chinese often said, the more money you have, the louder you can speak. Paying Mother's medical bills gave me a sense of empowerment.

The herbal medicine was usually not as expensive as the Western medicine or as the Chinese patent medicine. But when it came to the cure for cancer, Chinese medicinal retailers were capable of telling the most incredible lies. For instance, touted as a cancer panacea, Lingzhi mushroom, or ganoderma, was one of the high-priced Chinese medicines. Numerous advertisements exaggerated the medical value of this huge, glossy fungus. It was said that besides its own anti-cancer properties, Lingzhi could fight against unwanted effects of radiation due to chemotherapy. Together with conventional therapy, its effectiveness in controlling cancer was said to be above fifty percent. Nearly all products made of Lingzhi, whether they were real or fake, cost from several hundred to a couple of thousand *yuan*. Desperate but rational, I paid little attention to these crooks who took advantage of the cancer patients. Dr. Cheng also recommended Lingzhi mushroom. But it was optional. He said only were you able to afford it. He and Mr. Liang both suggested stewed softshell turtles as one of the economical and practical food therapies on cancer treatment. Father made the softshell turtle soup for Mother instead.

* * * * * *

Meanwhile, Father received an unexpected call. It was from Uncle Sahm who proposed a possible solution to save Mother. *Really? Mother can be saved?* A glimmer of hope flashed in my mind. I was also a bit scared. Uncle Sahm was vague about the matter on the phone. So we were asked to meet up in a restaurant on a cool summer evening. From the beginning Father was skeptical of the news. He had warned me not to get my hopes up. He said fatal diseases often gave unscrupulous perpetrators ample opportunities to defraud the patients and their family for money.

We asked Mr. Liang to join us. Unknown to Mother, we met with Uncle Sahm in a Western restaurant inside a park. It was about eight o'clock, another starless night. Our table was in a corner on the patio by the lake. Under the dim light from the lampposts by a huge tree, I could barely see my food and everyone's face. This place was perfect for a tryst. The lit candle on our table looked faint against the reflection in the lake from the bright lights of a stately restaurant on the other shore. Because of its marble architecture, local people nicknamed that restaurant the White House. We all ordered non-alcoholic drinks. Father secretly filled a glass with his own bottle of brandy. Occasionally, a gentle breeze wafted from the lake, lifting a corner of our napkins.

"How's *Yee-Soh* doing?" Uncle Sahm broke the silence.

"So far she's doing not bad," Father said, one hand holding the glass of brandy.

"Her spirit is quite high," Mr. Liang chimed in. "She's been taking traditional Chinese medicine. It looks like she copes well with our original plan." The original plan he mentioned was to give up surgery and to take traditional Chinese medicine therapy.

"How's her diet?" Uncle Sahm asked.

"Dr. Cheng suggests she eat small amounts several times a day," Father said. "We hired a caretaker to take care of her diet. She's about the same age as Golden Orchid, so we hope it'll be easier for them to get along during the day."

"How much do you pay for the caretaker?"

"Eight hundred *yuan* a month, including lunch and one day off each week."

At hearing Father's response, I felt sympathy for Chan Yee. How could she live on such a low wage? Even though I had only worked two years in an office, no promotion yet, my monthly salary was four times more than Chan Yee's. I even had two days-off.

"Can you manage it? If not, I can help you out." Uncle Sahm said as he lit a cigarette. The smoldering end traced his hand gesture like a firefly fluttering in the dark.

"Yes, no problem," Father said without a thought. His glass of brandy was half empty.

Over the years, Uncle Sahm had secretly given money to Father—often thousands of *yuan*—to support our family finances.

Father used to say that among his siblings, he himself lived in the most straitened circumstances. He did not have a respectful and stable profession like his oldest brother, who worked as a high school math teacher with distinction. He did not benefit from social housing like his engineer sister had. Not to mention his living standard was not on a par with his two younger brothers who had their own companies. Father rejected his brother's financial help every time. But after Uncle Sahm insisted, Father grudgingly took it. As a result, he always taught me not to forget those who had helped us and that we must return our gratitude when we can.

"My friend came across this woman in Zhongshan city, under an alias Aunt All-good. She was known to cure severe cancer patients." Uncle Sahm finally came to the subject and said, "Many people went to her and they all highly recommended her after the treatment. I thought she might be of help to *Yee-Soh*."

"How did she treat her clients?" Mr. Liang asked, reflecting the curiosity of all of us.

"No surgery was needed. Patients are required to bring her ten bottles of mineral water. She does something mysterious with her medicine and return the bottles unopened. Patients are supposed to drink them all at home every day. Her ads claim within twenty days the patients will recover."

"I have a feeling that this business is a scam," Father remarked in his weary voice. "I've also read papers about her extraordinary power in rescuing a number of patients in a dire state. But I'm not convinced."

"I thought if you wanted to give a go, I can help pay a hundred thousand *yuan*," Uncle Sahm said and inhaled a puff of nicotine into his lungs. The table was quiet for a minute and the low Kenny G music sounded loud in the background. Uncle Sahm continued, "Apparently, this woman did quite well, owning a villa with an orchard and a luxury sedan. She made so much money that she sent both of her sons to study abroad.

"I mean both she and her husband are farmers to begin with. According to my friend, she has just started this business of curing people over a few years and her overnight success is inconceivable. She claims to have this exceptional gift." Uncle Sahm's attitude began to change. I wondered if he was intimidated by Father's resolute tone.

"That's why the whole business is questionable," Father said as if he had found new evidence to support his point. "If each patient pays her a hundred thousand *yuan*, even though only ten people fall into her trap, she'll be a millionaire. I've read about too many of these swindle stories in papers. If you're lucky, you can get your money back but in most cases, you're both emotionally and financially exhausted."

"It's possible Aunt All-good is a crook, aiming at the gullible and severely ill patients," Mr. Liang said, wiping his mouth with the napkin. "So far, the traditional Chinese medicine therapy has stabilized your *Yee-Soh*'s condition. She's quite cooperative with Dr. Cheng. The most important thing is keeping her outlook positive."

"We also accompanied her to the Buddhist temple nearly every week," I said for the first time that evening. "She always said praying eased her pain and soothed her mind."

"Yeah. It's a good sign that she finds her spiritual sustenance," Father echoed. "I think as long as she's happy we should leave her where she is."

In those few months, instead of criticizing Mother for being a blind follower, Father often spent time with her in the Buddhist temple. He would leave her alone to do the religious ritual while he strolled around the temple, giving a closer look at the ancient architectural design—something good for him to absorb ideas for repairing antique china.

The meeting with Uncle Sahm wound up at about ten o'clock. We rejected Uncle Sahm's proposal. I bet it was an informative evening for him about my mother's illness and our plan. On the other hand, I realized Father was not as distraught as he had admitted. It was hard for anyone to con him. Like he often said, having been in the deceitful antique trading market for so long, he had learned to trick others just as others attempted to trick him. I respected his opinion. Yet, his rejection of Uncle Sahm's proposal shattered the slim hope I had cultivated. I accepted the outcome as Father had warned me earlier. Even so, my one percent of hope still stirred up inside me. What if a miracle really happened?

A miracle did not happen but justice was done. About a month after meeting with Uncle Sahm, Father read the news in the paper that Aunt All-good was arrested by the police on fraud charges. The police found nearly two hundred thousand *yuan* in cash, a dozen debit cards and bank books and three vehicles on the scene.

Exhilarated and calm, Father immediately dialed Uncle Sahm's phone number and told him about the news.

"I'm right about this," Father said on the phone with pride.

* * * * * *

Dr. Cheng's medicine succeeded in whetting Mother's appetite, invigorating her blood circulation, and reducing her gastrointestinal gas. Do not underestimate the gas in the digestive system. Mother said whenever the gas traveled inside her, she felt excruciating pain. But she lived strongly. So strong that sometimes I wondered if she bore too much pain to say it out loud. If she had not told Dr. Cheng, I would not have noticed a new symptom had occurred. Her feet swelled from time to time due to low white blood cell levels. Dr. Cheng prescribed new medicine, and the situation was under control.

Besides frequently visiting places like the hospital, the Buddhist temple, and *Yee-Po*'s house, Mother sometimes ate out as a change from Chan Yee's dull cooking. Crab and yellow catfish were her favorite. We had Dr. Cheng's permission that Mother should eat whatever she liked to improve her comfort. We were still cautious though. But Father said both crab and yellow catfish could be digested easily. It was OK if Mother had more.

Every time I looked at Mother's swollen feet, I felt a twinge. Mother often compared her swollen feet to a pig's trotters. Several blood tests showed Mother's white blood cells levels were drastically low. That meant her cancer cells were hungrier, quickly swallowing the normal blood cells. I learned from my research that protein could improve white blood cell production. High protein found in crabs and yellow catfish, for instance, was exactly what Mother needed at the moment. Watching her chewing on the crab shells and fishbone effortless, my heart was mixed with joy and misery. Mother was *hungry*, too.

To quickly boost Mother's white blood cells levels, we had another solution: to apply a regular intravenous injection of albumin—the water-soluble protein commonly found in blood plasma. However, in recent years, hospitals in mainland China faced a serious shortage of human albumin. Major hospitals in Guangzhou either received half of the normal supply or had zero stock. Thus, only patients recovering from major surgery and other emergency treatments were permitted to receive the drug. In this regard, even

187

Dr. Cheng could not help. We had to resolve the problem on our own.

China's human albumin crisis occurred during the months when Mother was ill. Since it was found a number of hospitals and clinics across the country used fake blood protein in patients' drips, Chinese health authorities had shut down many blood centers that paid people for blood donations to ensure blood quality. The regulation of the blood plasma donation stations significantly reduced the supply of human albumin. Just in Guizhou province alone—a major supplier of blood plasma to the country—four-fifths of the blood plasma stations were closed.

On the other hand, the imbalance between demand and supply caused the price of human albumin to skyrocket. Because I could not find any human albumin in Guangzhou pharmacies, I turned to the Hong Kong market. While those who made the false albumin were making a three hundred percent profit, I had to pay six hundred Hong Kong dollars for an imported 50ml, 10g, and 20% bottle of human albumin solution. If I were not working full time and also had good savings, how could my family afford such an expensive drug?

To reduce my travels to Hong Kong to get the drug in person, I asked Prof. Zeitlin and my cousin in Hong Kong, Graceful Swallow, to help. It was a small success of the CEPA—Close Economic Partnership Arrangement—implemented on the level of ordinary life. The Agreement aims to promote economy and trade between Hong Kong and Macao within mainland China. In my case, Graceful Swallow purchased the albumin solutions and Prof. Zeitlin brought them to mainland China. Both of them graciously offered to pay for the drug. But Father and I refused.

Incidentally, Prof. Zeitlin's daughter was diagnosed with stomach cancer. After he helped me get the human albumin, he had to immediately leave for New York, in time for his daughter's surgery. The news was no doubt devastating to Prof. Zeitlin's family. Yet, his daughter's condition was more promising than my mother's. It was an early discovery of Stage II cancer. With the help of her family, she underwent surgery in the Sloan-Kettering Cancer Center in New York in the summer. I came across the Center's name a few times in my medical research. I thought one might need tons of money and good *guanxi* to be able to schedule a timely operation in this prestigious hospital.

A few weeks later, good news arrived. The surgery was a success and the patient's tumor was removed. Prof. Zeitlin's daughter had to receive chemotherapy for the following months. I could not help comparing the treatment we chose for Mother to that for Prof. Zeitlin's daughter. Basically, cancer led to two different results for two patients. One has lived because of precautionary examination; the other was about to die because she had waited too long to seek treatment. One would feel pain caused by the chemotherapy; the other was suffering slowly from the disease itself. In a short period of time, the one that was under the palliative therapy could eat and travel like a normal person. And yet, the one that survived could look forward to life in the future; the other could only enjoy the present.

It is difficult to watch the one you love suffer from pain. Not to mention when she becomes terminally ill, your emotion is as fragile as her body. Yet, you have to live stronger than the patient because you are her reason to live on, regardless of the length of her life. It was especially so in my family. I gained confidence from seeing Mother doing well while she found comfort from my encouragement. Sometimes I thought we did not choose a palliative therapy for Mother. It was her decision. From the very beginning, she had had unbeatable faith in using herbs. Turning to Dr. Cheng for treatment was Mother's last resort, yet a favorable one.

By the middle of the year, nearly ten months after our bitter journey began, my mindset towards Mother's illness turned into being realistic rather than emotional. Perhaps after numerous hysterical wails, denouncing the unfair destiny, I eventually came to a lull, and shook hands with my inner peace. I did try to cope with my peace of mind. Occasionally, I thought of the flood-ridden childhood home No. 14 and gradually understood why my parents were stoic about their belongings being damaged by the flood. What is done cannot be undone. If you lost everything in a disaster, what else matters? Confronting the gravest complication, I wept with no tears. I screamed with no sound. I had to race with time. I had to race with fate. I had to race with the ongoing bad news. *Let Mom be the happiest person in the world for the rest of her life.* Eyes closed and hands clutched, I prayed quietly to my god. This time I did not anticipate the roaring of a passing plane.

Chapter 10

When the Rock Gets Tougher

It is said that the term "*liu*," namely tumor, first appeared on the oracle bones in the Shang Dynasty (1600 BC-1046 BC). Since then, a number of ancient medical documents have discussed various forms of tumors explicitly, including incision as a treatment. In the Song Dynasty (960 AD-1279 AD), the term "*ai*" for cancer was mentioned in an ancient medical book titled *Wei Ji Bao Shu*, literally *Weiji Treasure Book*. In addition, the Chinese character for rock also refers to the same disease, simply because cancer preserves the same characteristics of a rock: hard, rugged and uneven. Both the characters— "cancer" and "rock"—are pronounced the same in Cantonese, which to some extent, is considered to be closer to classical Chinese in its pronunciation and some grammar.

That summer I thought a lot about the rock inside Mother's body. Every time I thought about it, my heart weighed tons. Her cancer was like an unmovable boulder, blocking the circulation of all fluids and disrupting the nutrition supply in her body. More deadly, it caused constant pain. Mother often awoke to a spasm of belly-kicking, stomach-wrenching pain at night. Her frequent visits to the bathroom deprived her of sleep. If it was not a pang of hunger, it would be the belly ache. She slept fitfully and her temper grew.

For instance, one time when her caretaker Chan Yee was cooking, Mother watched her every move from the living room. She was quite edgy.

"I've told you to dry the wok first before adding oil," Mother said bluntly. "How come you're so dim like a lantern made of ox-hide that I can't illuminate?"

"Yes, yes, I'll remember," Chan Yee said humbly. Standing in front of the gas stove, she was about to throw the prepared vegetable into the boiling wok.

Mother probably had realized her crude language. She quickly said, "Sorry about my hot temper just now. You know, when I'm sick, my mood is out of control."

"Never mind," Chan Yee responded, beaming. "You're aware of my glitches. That means you're not muddled like a sick cat."

Both of them smiled. Moments like this happened almost every day. I thought Mother got along with Chan Yee better than with her previous caretaker. Perhaps because Chan Yee was a forgiving Christian, or perhaps she was more understanding and keen about a patient's need. Stout, caramel skinned, with mid-length hair and a narrow face, Chan Yee shared the same family name and the same Chinese character—orchid—in her given name as Mother's. What a coincidence! A Chinese saying goes, "People with the same surname are close like relatives." Father and I immediately had a good feeling about Chan Yee after we knew her name in the interview. To avoid confusion by calling the caretaker Lan Yee, namely Aunt Orchid, by which many people addressed Mother, we called her Chan Yee instead.

After Kong Yee quit, Mother seemed to be more careful about her attitude to Chan Yee. Father often reminded her to be nice to Chan Yee. He believed Mother's rudeness caused Kong Yee to resign. He even told Mother, "If Chan Yee leaves, I won't look for another caretaker for you."

"Oh shit, like I'd really care," Mother said curtly after Father left the living room one evening.

Another time I overheard Mother speaking on the phone with her co-worker friend. I did not know what they were talking about but I caught Mother using foul language.

"You're shitting me," Mother said in an emphatic voice. "He got retired early, not even to fifty-five, and received damn good benefits from the unit."

"*Aigh*," she sighed and continued, "each umbrella is made differently; each person has a different fate. We were all dumb asses, sweating blood for the factory the whole fricking life. In the end, we still got dumped by *Ah-Yeh*." She referred to the top Party leadership. The nickname originally indicated Chairman Mao.

Mother sputtered her coarse remarks too often in that summer. She might not even notice she had sworn. Her insulting words irritated Father, as if he had tasted chili sauce on a sweltering summer day. One time during supper, Father finally let out, "How come you become so rude, speaking like a hooligan? Can you not swear?"

"This is who I am," Mother retorted, unconsciously scratching her neck and scalp. "I'm not like your girlfriends who talk as sweet as they look. I'm a blue-collar worker, cultureless and ugly. I know shit about your manner."

"See, every time I point out your drawbacks you react so defiantly. How can I communicate with you?"

"Then don't. Go befriend your alcohol and cigarettes." Soon after Mother finished, she walked away from the dining table. She gathered her clothes and went to the bathroom for a shower.

Gazing upon the flashing TV screen, I sat in the living room. While chewing the food, Father snorted heavily. He must be angry. He must be morose. His breath came short and fast, as if he needed an additional outlet to blow off his steam.

In those few months, Father spent most of his time in his workshop. Every night after supper I washed dishes. In winter, the icy water often numbed my fingers to pinkish red. After the shower, Mother would watch TV with me for a while before she headed for bed. It was the only moment I had on a weekday when I could spend time with her alone. It was then Mother began to talk to me about herself. I was not sure if her candid talk was a side effect of her medicine or it came out of her ominous intuition. She became nostalgic and unreserved.

I remembered her watching a TV news report about neighbors keeping an adolescent girl company during a blackout until her parents returned home. Mother conjured up her childhood.

"When I was twelve, my parents both went to work," she said. "My neighbors also invited me to their homes to play while I was waiting for my parents to come home. In the old days, neighbors were helpful and friendly. Times have changed. Today, people don't even know what their neighbors look like, let alone their names."

"Yeah," I echoed, "living in apartment buildings makes it difficult to socialize with other people in the building."

"Living here is comfortable but it's a bit distant from *Gaai See*. The wet market near here doesn't have as many varieties as the one near the old house. You know your damn father always wants to have fresh produce. Even if leftovers are only one-day old, he already shows distaste. Sometimes I buy a little bit more vegetable, so if the weather goes bad the next day, we'll have enough food supply. But he protests against doing that, as if the food will turn toxic overnight."

Mother always came back to the subject about Father.

"It's not the first day you get to know him. Take it easy, Mom." I regretted what I said as soon as I discovered my words only triggered Mother's anger.

"Of course it's not the first day we met. He's totally a different person now, arrogant, unreasonable and full of male chauvinism. He's far from being an innocent and gentle young man like when we first met."

"How did you meet?" I asked.

We no longer paid attention to the ongoing TV show. Its sound became our background music. The flickering images reflected in Mother's eyes. She cleared her mind and began to tell me a story that I had never heard before, a story that Chinese children usually dare not to ask their parents about.

"I lived by myself at No.14 after your *Popo* passed away in 1978. In the daytime I worked at the timber factory, at night I sometimes chatted with Aunt Fragrance since she lived nearby. Then one day, your *Yee-ma* asked me to go out with a guy. This guy was your father. He was introduced by his friend Leung-leung's mother. Both she and your *Yee-ma* knew each other in the kindergarten where they worked." Mother paused for a second and darted her eyes from the TV screen to me and back to the TV.

I nodded to let her know I was listening with rapt attention. I knew the story got interesting because Uncle Leung-leung was Father's oldest classmate and best friend since middle school. He was the one from whom Father secretly picked up the craft of repairing antique china. Knowing that Father competed with him in the business, Uncle Leung-leung was furious and broke the longtime friendship with Father. And then in recent years, they got back in touch but their friendship is not the same.

"Your father could fix home appliances," Mother continued. "Uncle Leung-leung's mother treated him like a son. She knew through *Yee-ma* that I was about the same age as your father, and single. Your father could not find a date after he returned from the communal farm. That's how the matching idea came up. So we met. Uncle Leung-leung's mother paid for the tickets for us to watch a play. We only dated twice before we married. About half a year later, your father proposed. I couldn't make the decision so I took the No.4 bus to *Yee-ma*'s house and discussed it with her."

"What did she think?"

"She said since your father was quite interested in me, and if I was also interested in him, why not tie the knot? Uncle Leung-leung's mother would also appreciate it. I wasn't ready for marriage but *Yee-ma* was my only family, plus both she and *Yee-jeong* approved of it. At last I agreed. Your father was a steel worker then. He was stony broke when we got married. He could not afford my dowry, let alone provide a new home. I spent three hundred *yuan* of my savings on a dowry.

"As soon as your father moved into No.14 to live with me in 1980, he got rid of so many things in the house. Like the metal basin, the wooden bucket, bowls and chairs, he chucked them all." Mother stared morosely at the TV screen, her hands scratching her arms, as if something she said had itched her badly.

"In 1985 when your father was fixing the roof, he missed a step and fell from a ladder by accident. His factory's policy allowed workers to acquire medical insurance if it was a pure accident. So your father reported to his employer that it was you who was playful and did not hold the ladder steady for him. He made you his scapegoat to claim medical compensation from the unit. His leg had a multi-fragmentary fracture. The X-ray showed his bone was broken into a number of pieces. For over half a year he couldn't work. That was when he learned to drink and smoke from his co-worker Chee Ming. He used Chee Ming tending him as an excuse and went to meet Chee Ming's wife.

"When a neighbor told me at first, I didn't believe it. Then one night after supper, I went to the district clinic and saw he and Lucky Lily were together. I got more and more worried. One summer night, I asked you to stay at home and behave in front of the fan while waiting for me. I went to Chee Ming's house and saw your father there. Another night after you slept, knowing you father was at Chee Ming's again, I went to *Yee-ma*'s house and asked her what to do. She told me to suck it up. You were still young I should not let this adult matter affect your childhood."

For many years, I had been waiting for Mother's explanation about her mysterious disappearance on that awful night. I awoke from the scare of losing her, while she went to check on Father and then to *Yee-ma*'s for solace. Everything became crystal clear to me.

"Your father was away from home more often and after he came home, he often dressed me down. Nanny Fong knew about it and persuaded me not to argue with him. I tried to tolerate him. I didn't want to quarrel with your father to avoid gossip from the neighbors. You know, The Bitchy Stuff always looked down upon us..."

Mother's mind skipped. She said, "Your father was injured and his love affair saddened your Granny. I asked Uncle Ju to look at your father's broken leg. Uncle Sahm volunteered to take your father on his motorbike for the medical checkups."

Mother's eyes blinked faster, as if the pictures of the past flashed vividly before her eyes. Her words sank in. I began to understand why Father had mixed feelings toward Uncle Ju. He was an unregistered bonesetter—a practitioner of joint manipulation using traditional Chinese medicine—in a local towel factory. In his late sixties, Uncle Ju was *Yee-jeong*'s brotherly old friend. By seeing him, Father could spend much less money on his broken leg. And with the help of Chinese herbs, Father's leg did gradually recover. However, as he grew older he sometimes limped. He said that was the result of the after effects of the bone trauma. Uncle Ju was more than a bonesetter to *Yee-jeong*'s family. He also gave them medical advice on many other health problems, including suggesting Mother seek help in traditional Chinese medicine for her earlier symptoms of colon cancer. That was what my parents fought about for a long time. Mother refused to take a comprehensive checkup in a general hospital. Instead, she frequently visited the humble clinic near her sister's house. In Father's lexicon, Uncle Ju's knowledge about traditional Chinese medicine was "unprofessional."

Looking at Mother's pale and dry lips, I offered her a cup of water. She took a sip and went on, "Chee Ming was often on business trips and your father took the advantage of seeing his mistress. I had a picture of you, and you looked so lovely in it. I wanted to keep it very much but your father took it and gave it to his mistress. Later, Chee Ming discovered their love affair. He then went straight to our house and had a blazing row. He said he couldn't believe your father was such a scum."

Mother's confession ended on that note. She looked at the clock, it was around nine thirty. She said it was about time to sleep. She covered her mug with a white china lid. The shining jade bracelet hung on her left wrist hit the glass tabletop, sounding familiar and loud. The thump of it pierced into my heart, as if the bracelet was about to break.

I said goodnight to Mother. My mind was overwhelmed by everything she told me. She had shown me the handful of bullets she bit over two decades in order to keep her family together. *How hard has it been for Mom to bear the pain of Father's cheating? Didn't she want to leave us? Why does she tell me about all this now? Has she sensed something?* Perplexed and saddened, I questioned myself for a long time, as if it was the only thing I could do to respond to Mother's reflection.

* * * * * *

Since I was a kid, I had learned to be a peacemaker in my family. I was always partial to Mother though. That was why Father often cried for justice, saying Mother was the good cop and he was the bad cop. However, after I grew up he told me several times that he was pleased I fought for the weak against the strong. I thought I could distinguish between the good and the bad, the righteous and the evil, just as I had done as a kid. But over the love-hate relationship between Father and Mother's sister and brother-in-law, I was totally baffled.

As a young member of the family, I must respect the elderly. After all, as Mother said, *Yee-ma* and *Yee-jeong* were her only elder family. They were like her parents, especially because of the vast age difference. I knew whenever Mother had marriage problems she would go to them for advice. I knew she listened to them wholeheartedly. She would follow what they said. Mother was, as Father put it, "a pure, virtuous traditional Chinese woman." She had not changed.

I could not disregard Father's prejudice about *Yee-ma* and *Yee-jeong*. He always differentiated Mother's side of the family from his own. He labeled *Yee-jeong*'s family Liu Clan and his own family

196

Zhang Clan. His biased comments on my relatives made me feel like I was living in a segregated family.

"This is Liu Clan's influence," he would say if he saw Mother burning ghost money to her dead parents.

"Zhang Clan will never covet the small advantages," he would say when Mother suggested he take his sister to a new restaurant that offered a big discount.

"It's not necessary to do that," Father would say to me when I asked if we should pay a visit to every family member with a box of mooncakes on the Mid-Autumn Festival. "Everyone is educated in Zhang Clan. No one would mind the trivia of a celebration."

After Mother got ill, Father suppressed his Liu-Clan-and-Zhang-Clan talk. But he was more acid when thinking that Mother would rather listen to Uncle Ju and her sister's family about how to deal with her health problems. Knowing Mother's cancer was incurable, he was immersed in rage and expressed to me once, "They are hidden killers. Their ignorance is taking away your mother's life."

At hearing this, I was horrified. Wordless, I felt something choke my throat. My eyes welled up. I noticed Father had a companion that he had not kept at his work desk before—a shot glass of brandy. I did not know how long it had been there. I did not go to his workshop as often as before. I wanted to spend more time with Mother alone. When thinking about not being able to equally share myself with my parents, I wished I could clone myself, several of me, like the Monkey King did.

"What type of siblings are they?" Father snapped. "Golden Orchid has been home for six months. Her sister has *never* come to visit her! She only demanded Golden Orchid to do housework for her. And your mother was so kind that she worked like a slave at your *Yee-ma*'s house."

The more Father lamented, the more furious he was. The brandy must have burned his throat and inflamed his anger. I knew how that felt. I remembered once, in trying to stop him from drinking excessively, I pulled out a glass of equal size to Father's, filled it with brandy and said to him, "If you continue to drink, I'm going to finish your bottle." He did not believe me. So I did what I said. By the second glass, I felt my chest stinging like crazy. My blood was like boiling soup. My ears, my face and throughout my body burned. "Don't be silly," Father said, taking away the bottle from my hand. I took it back and refilled my glass. The third glass made me tear. I was nauseous as hell. I bet my innards must have been fully soaked in alcohol. Embarrassed by my stupid obstinacy, Father finally gave in. As I stood up, I felt a rush of vertigo and nearly stumbled. I could smell my burp of brandy. But it was all worth it.

Father did not cut back his drinking. Instead, he hid his excess drinking from me. Now, watching him drown his sorrows at every meal, I felt the same heart-burning brandy surge in my throat. My persuasion became feeble and useless. Father did remind me that I had not seen *Yee-ma* for months. *What is she doing now? Does she know Mom's health is worsening? Does she remember Mom took good care of her every day when she was immobile? Why doesn't she come to visit Mom?*

* * * * * *

With some effort, we found a small clinic near home to give Mother the albumin intravenous injection. The injection came just in time. It alleviated the swelling on Mother's feet. She felt less pain and pressure on her feet. She could even walk a little. Whenever I thought about how we got Mother to the clinic, it aroused my indignation. I could not get that nurse's snide tone out of my mind. I remembered how I first sobbed as an adult in front of my ailing Mother.

That happened after I got the human albumin solutions from Hong Kong. I brought them to Dr. Cheng's office and asked him to prescribe them for Mother. He checked everything on the package and wrote me a prescription solely for the intravenous injection.

"You bring this prescription to the nurse on the second floor with your mother. She'll know what to do," Dr. Cheng said, passing me a white sheet of paper.

Together with Father and Mr. Liang, the four of us went to the injection center on the second floor. Carrying an overweight handbag on my shoulder, I walked ahead to beat back the crowd. Mr. Liang walked with Mother at her own pace. Father was behind them, making sure everyone was in his sight. We looked like a modern version of the lineup from the classical Chinese epic novel *Journey to the West*. In the novel, Monkey King often walked ahead of his *shifu*. The Buddhist monk, Xuanzang was the second. He sometimes walked side by side with one of his protectors, Sha Wujing. Zhu Bajie, also known as Pigsy, followed behind.

Ironically, one of the Chinese euphemisms for "to die" is "to go to the *xitian*." *Xitian* (pronounced See Tan), literally the West Sky, indicates the direction of India to China where Buddhism originated. It also refers to the pure land in Buddhism. Xuanzang travelled to the West to retrieve Buddhist sutras from India, while my mother was on another kind of journey to the West.

After I got to the reception desk, I gave the prescription to a thirty-something nurse, telling her I had the albumin with me. Looking around, I saw patients on rows of benches, quietly waiting for their intravenous injection to finish. The nurse sat on a cushioned chair on wheels. She rolled her eyes quickly throughout the sheet and said, "Sorry. We can't do it here."

"What do you mean you can't do it?" I was shocked by her reply, eyes popped open wide.

"We don't inject the patients with a non-prescribed drug," the nurse said coldly.

"But I have the doctor's permission. Look at the sheet I gave you."

"I did. Like I said, we don't take the responsibility of injecting the patients with drug from outside sources."

"I'll take all the consequences as long as you give my mother the injection," I pleaded. My heart quickened. I felt a sudden surge of anxiety and anger.

"I said no that's a no."

"Please. Dr. Cheng has approved of this. If you don't believe it, you can call him to confirm. My mother is really in need of the albumin injection."

"What's your doctor's name?"

"Dr. Cheng Jianhua."

The nurse picked up the phone and dialed the extension of Dr. Cheng's office. My mind was all about how to convince the nurse. I did not heed what she said to the doctor. About five minutes later, the nurse put down the phone and looked at me stiffly.

"I spoke to your doctor and also my supervisor. It's the hospital policy. We can't make any exception."

Pissed off, I burst into tears and threatened, "My mother is dying if you don't give her the injection tonight! What will you do if your family is dying? Will you make an exception?"

Words flew out of my mouth like bullets. I did not notice that my parents and Mr. Liang had sat behind me. Mr. Liang immediately came up to calm me.

"I'm sorry, Nurse," Mr. Liang said. "We understand your difficulty. I wonder if you know where the patient can have the albumin injection."

Seeing I was all welled up, the nurse was probably as surprised as my parents were. Her attitude softened a little. She said, "You may try the clinics in your community. They will usually do it."

"OK, *Ng goi!*" Mr. Liang thanked the nurse politely.

I sat for a while next to Mother by the door, trying to buck up. My face must have turned red. I felt as if my body had a fever. Both my eyes and nose were moist.

"It'll be OK," Mother said quietly. "We'll get it done somewhere else."

I thought it should be me to say "it'll be OK" to her and to everybody on my team. Mother's timely comfort picked me up speedily like a flying rocket. I felt sorry for the other patients who had to live with the red tape. Mr. Liang was also fed up with the disgraceful medical ethics. He said bureaucracy was too common in state-run institutions, and not limited to the hospitals. But to smooth things out, one had to suck up to the person who could solve the problems.

"You just graduated from university. You're still a white piece of paper. The more contacts you build in the society, the more you'll learn. Your white paper will be smudged as experience grows," Mr. Liang said to me on the way to the clinic near No. 14, where I used to visit as a little girl.

We followed the nurse's suggestion and asked about the clinic and if Mother could have an injection there. Disappointedly, we were also turned down. The scandal of fake albumin used in hospitals and clinics frightened health workers on a large scale. No one we asked wanted to take the risk of giving Mother an albumin injection, especially if the drug was from an outside source. Every time I looked at Mother's swollen feet, my heart ached more.

"Let's go home first," Father suggested. "You stay with your mother while Mr. Liang and I continue to ask around. It's not necessary to have four people running around town."

"Yes," Mr. Liang echoed, "your mother needs rest. We'll try the private clinics near your home. They're usually quite flexible."

Going to private clinics would be my last choice. I was diffident about the medical practice there because of the frequent medical accidents. These private clinics were usually located in suburban areas, unregistered, tiny and with poor hygiene. Their patients were mostly migrant workers who had low or no medical insurance coverage. Nevertheless, there were some better out-patient clinics with a few more specialized physicians and sound facilities. Those were the kind Father was looking for. As planned, we split into two teams.

After thirty-six hours, in the afternoon of the following day, Mother finally had an albumin injection in a community clinic. Afterwards, she felt relieved as her fat toes were trim again and the hump on the back of her feet was reduced a little. It took a load off Father and me. I welled up once more. But this time I had a rare taste of sweetness. I knew Father did not sleep much the night before. Under his bloodshot eyes were two bags, dark and bulgy.

Internally, I constantly came back to our clinic hunt adventure. How would a patient's life change in those thirty-six hours? How many patients like my mother were also struggling in pain and discomfort while waiting for a shot of albumin? How would the unmoved physicians and nurses feel if they were in the shoes of the patients? Did the government realize the urgency of the albumin supply shortage? Did they understand patients would die because of the procrastination of drug use, and because of a high demand of vital drugs, counterfeit behaviors would be rampant? Would they do something about them?

With Dr. Cheng's prescription, Mother went to the same clinic for an albumin injection a couple of times. When Mother visited Dr. Cheng again, he apologized to us.

"I'm sorry about what happened the other day," he said in his accented Cantonese. By then I had become used to his accent.

"It's OK," Mr. Liang said, "The nurse also has her difficulties."

That was Mr. Liang, slick and sophisticated, always pleasing everyone.

"That nurse was second to the head nurse. She likes pretending she has power," Dr. Cheng said disapprovingly. "I always have trouble talking to her."

"Never mind," Mother said, beaming, "I had the injection in our community clinic. The drug really helped. So did your medicine."

"How do you feel now?" Dr. Cheng inquired, motioning to check Mother's wrist pulse.

Mother placed her wrists one after the other on the desk while Dr. Cheng listened attentively. I stood next to Mother while Mr. Liang preferred standing at the back to observe. Father sat outside, waiting. He said his cigarette smell would annoy Dr. Cheng.

"I feel my belly heavy, especially here," Mother said, touching the part near her heart below her saggy breasts. "Something hard seems to have grown here. When I press it, it hurts."

"How long since it happened?"

"A couple of weeks ago."

"It didn't exist last time when you visited me?"

"No, it wasn't noticeable then."

Dr. Cheng held up a flash light. Mother knew he was about to check her tongue. She opened her mouth like a disciplined child. Inspection of the tongue helped Dr. Cheng understand Mother's condition of *qi* and blood and the nature of pathogenic factors.

"Could you lie down on the bed and let me take a look?"

Dr. Cheng stood up and pulled aside the white curtains behind him. There lay a single treatment table covered with a white bed sheet. Opposite to the table was a hand washing sink. Mother lay down, inhaled and exhaled as instructed. Dr. Cheng lifted Mother's blouse halfway and pressed his fingers down on certain spots of her abdomen. He asked Mother if she felt any discomfort. Mother answered honestly yes or no. The body checkup took less than three minutes. Dr. Cheng seemed to have gathered a sufficient idea about Mother's health condition.

"I'm going to prescribe you basically the same medicine but with a slight change of components and amounts. Besides, you need to do a blood test, an ultrasound scan and a CT scan on different days. You may have your daughter bring the results to me once they're out in the next few days. I'll see you in two weeks as usual," Dr. Cheng said as he was busy typing on the computer.

"Anything we and the patient should pay attention to, like her diet and living habits?" Mr. Liang asked. I looked up at him, seeing only the reflection of the white fluorescent light on his thick black-rimmed glasses.

"Not particularly. The same as what I told you before. As for the swollen feet, you may elevate your legs when you sit. When you sleep, you can also put a pillow under your feet. Don't catch cold as the season changes."

Gratefully, we left Dr. Cheng's office. The entrance was too familiar to me, except it took a bit longer for Mother to pass through the hallway with her lead-filled legs.

* * * * * *

As usual, I muffled my ears with music at work. Especially in the days when I thought I was about to be beaten down by Mother's debilitating health. In the past, I would hang out with my friends after work and meet them on weekends. Now, working in the office was the only time I had to meet my social life.

Perhaps because I am an only child, I take being alone for granted. I enjoy the freedom of independence. I enjoy resolving problems by myself. But I also feel isolated when I need help. Like now, withholding the questions about the family stories I knew, I had no one to talk to. Who would understand me?

The music from the headphones blasted my world. The lyrics overwhelmed me. Christina Aguilera's "*Oh Mother*" reflected my mind. Pink's "*Family Portrait*" cried for my frustration. Again, I loved to be lifted up by Celine Dion's "*That's The Way It Is*." Songs on my playlist spoke to what I was feeling, as if a psychiatrist sang out all my troubles through them. I was sullen. I was sympathetic. I was sentimental. I was sorry. I was moved. Swiftly wiping out the warm teardrops on my cheeks, I replayed the songs over and over again.

One August afternoon, I called Mother around noontime as usual. Her greeting was laden with fatigue.

"How do you feel today?" I asked with great concern.

"Not too good," a feeble voice came from the other end of the line.

"Why?"

"After I finished Dr. Cheng's medicine, I was nauseous. I threw up everything I ate," Mother mustered her energy to finish her briefing.

"How do you feel now?"

"My belly is growling in pain. I'm tired. Let's talk later," Mother said impatiently.

"OK. You rest more. I'll come home as soon as—"

The line went dead.

The rest of the day was fretful. The words "throw up" were snagged in my mind. I was afraid Mother might already have ascites—a condition when fluid accumulates in the peritoneal cavity. Both my research and Dr. Cheng's prognosis said liver cancer would lead to ascites, which would aggravate the patient's liver damage. I heard Mother complain about fatigue and weight loss recently. These were signs of ascites. Thinking of the possible consequences, my heart sank. A wave of horror chilled down my spine.

I could not leave Mother at home without me anymore.

In early September, I made up my mind to quit my job. I walked into the managing editor's office and handed in my resignation letter. In her mid-thirties, Alice Wan was astounded at hearing my decision. She did not read my letter but asked me to sit down on the black leather couch at the corner of her office. She sat across from me over a coffee table.

"I'm terribly sorry for your mother. I deeply understand the difficulty you're going through. But quitting is not a best solution," Alice said warmly as if she was talking to her little sister.

"I want to spend more time with my mother. Her condition deteriorates," I said as my eyes began to moisten. "I find it hard to focus at work. I frequently have to take leave from work to accompany her to the doctor's appointments. Concerning all these factors, I propose to resign and I hope you will approve."

"Yes. I know how you feel. In the past, we have also had colleagues' requests for resignation because of family catastrophes. But I really want you to give it a second thought. Your mother is ill and has been on medical therapy, your family must be in need of money more now than at any other time. If you quit now, your family will lose a major financial support.

"On the other hand, on behalf of the entire staff I really appreciate your contribution to the firm. If you need more time to spend with your mother, I'll absolutely support you and give you my permission. I'll notify the administrative office and we can work out a flexible working schedule for you. Any time you need to be away for an emergency during office hours, don't hesitate to notify me and I'll approve your leave. Please rethink what I said and come to see me again if you really want to quit," Alice spoke everything in one breath. She seemed to be more prepared than me.

Speechless, I agreed to think twice and left her office. Mother had known I had tried to quit my job. That evening, I repeated Alice's words to Mother. She was at ease.

"If your boss wants you to stay, you stay," Mother said, scratching her arms and neck from time to time. "These days getting a job isn't easy. Getting a job you like is even harder. Your company is not far from home and your schedule will be flexible. You can come home anytime you want."

"Don't you want me to stay home with you?"

"Yes, but your career is more important. Don't be like *Mama*. I got unemployed young. You work and earn your own money so you won't need to depend on your man. Men aren't reliable."

I figured Mother was about to return to the subject of Father. I interjected, "Have you taken pills yet?"

"Yes, after my supper. My chronic disease takes time to recover. It's not necessary for you to quit your job for my health. I know you're a good girl. You take me out and you give me monthly spending money. I've saved it. I was like you, when I worked I used to give *Popo* thirty *yuan* every month. I kept ten *yuan* for myself."

"So ten *yuan* was enough for you for a month?"

"Yeah. I scrimped and saved. It cost eight *fen* for a canteen dish. The dish wasn't bad. In summer, I received two *yuan* per day for the high temperature allowance. Before you were born, I worked three shifts. Afterwards, I did only one shift and I could also take a nap. I remember there were many mice in the workshop. In the 1980s, I was promoted as a monitor in the workshop. I got 50.8 *yuan* each month." Mother thought for a second and said, "You're an educated university graduate. You deserve to get a better job. *Mama* is cultureless. So I had to live on my manual labor."

Mother's words resonated with me. Father often thought Mother's life was not as bitter as his because she had not experienced a *zhiqing* life. But in my eyes, Mother had a different kind of hardship. Her young life was impoverished, pathetic, despised, bullied. Her self-esteem was trampled, in all her life, in all her complexity. After talking to her about my job, I no longer felt alone. I had Mother to share my life. So did she with me.

"OK, I'll stay at my job with one request," I said. "You must keep me posted every day about your health."

Mother murmured yes and left her seat. I watched her retreating figure getting smaller and smaller. And yet, her image in my mind grew bigger and bigger.

* * * * * *

One day in my lunch hour, I dialed *Yee-ma*'s home phone number. I wanted to ask her to visit Mother. As routine, she inquired about Mother's health.

"She's not doing too well lately," I said hesitantly, after a brief moment of self-debate about whether I should respond superficially or whether I should tell the truth.

"She's exhausted and fidgety. She's taking ten pills a day in addition to the herbal medicine," I said seriously.

"Yes, I also noticed that she looked much thinner when we met in a restaurant a couple of weeks ago."

I summoned my courage and said, "I don't know how long she can hang on. Could you please come to visit her more often? I bet she'll be thrilled to chat with her sister when she's feeling down."

There was a minute of silence on the other end of the phone.

"I think we should cherish the moment to be with her. She won't be living too long," I said. As the last word fell, I was caught up in sorrow. I felt a warm blush rise to my cheeks. Snuffling, I held the phone tightly against my flushed ears.

"OK," *Yee-ma* said in a tone of embarrassment. "You know, after my spinal surgery, I'm not as mobile as before. Although I can walk I can't bend down. I'll try my best to visit your Mother often. She's always praised you to me. If you have any difficulty, don't hesitate to call Wai Syu for help."

After saying goodbye, we both hung up the phone hard and fast. *Yee-ma*'s words lingered on my mind for the rest of the day. I had no idea how often she had asked her only son, Wai Syu, to be her substitute of presence. Her son often ran errands for her as if he was her personal assistant.

In his forties, tall and slim, my cousin Wai Syu was the closest member from *Yee-ma*'s family to mine. He often came to our apartment for supper and went out for *xiaoye* with Father and Mr. Liang. He was the bridge of communication between Father and *Yee-ma*'s family as I was between my parents.

I did not tell my parents about my phone call with *Yee-ma*. I just hoped the call would bring *Yee-ma*'s attention to Mother. It did. A few days later, Mother asked me to accompany her to a Chinese restaurant near our home. She said *Yee-ma* was waiting for her there. As we walked into the restaurant, the roar of noise from patrons' conversation, the clink of dishes and the TVs' blaring engulfed us. We found *Yee-ma* sitting at a big round table with other retired people.

"There you are," *Yee-ma* said, pulling up an extra chair from the next table for me. Apparently, she did not expect my appearance.

Mother greeted *Yee-ma* as she sat on the empty reserved seat. I sat next to her.

"Would you like to order some *dimsum*?" *Yee-ma* asked while filling up both Mother's and my cups with hot tea. *Yee-ma*'s voice was quickly submerged in the noises.

"I've eaten," Mother replied and then turned to me and said, "You may go to get some food."

"Maybe later, let me first have a cup of tea," I said.

"How do you feel?" *Yee-ma* asked Mother. She cupped her mouth with her hand in the hope that her voice could pass to Mother's ears.

"So-so," Mother said briefly, as if the noises had absorbed her energy. She blew off the steam over her teacup before taking a sip.

"I met your mother here several times," *Yee-ma* turned to me and said. "Uncle Ju sometimes comes here for morning tea, too. But I don't see him today."

"Yeah, if you arrive here before eight o'clock in the morning, your tea is free of charge," Mother said, looking at *Yee-ma* with her sleepy eyes. "We're going to the Hualin Buddhist Temple after this."

I thought Mother was too tired to talk but it turned out she probably did not want to discuss much about her health. She probably preferred to keep her distress to herself.

"Good. If you can walk, take the chance to relax in the outdoors with your daughter. It's better than staying at home. Graceful Swallow went to Nengren Temple in Jiangxi province recently. She prayed for this bracelet for you. It's been blessed," *Yee-ma* said, giving Mother a bracelet of shining pink beads.

Mother thanked *Yee-ma* and put on the bracelet. It matched her jade bracelet on the left wrist. Both were glinted with luster. What's more noticeable, Mother beamed in happiness as if a magical charm had rejuvenated her. I had missed her happy look for a while. She even smiled less when she visited Dr. Cheng.

"You're so close to our home. Why don't you come in to visit us?" I asked *Yee-ma*.

"It's too much trouble. I don't want to make your father uncomfortable for my visit."

I said nothing. I knew it was a polite way of saying my father was unhappy to see her, and as a matter of fact, her husband, too. So she invited Mother out to meet once in a while just as secretly as Father and I had our own information exchange outside Mother's hearing range.

* * * * * *

After meeting with *Yee-ma*, Mother and I continued to visit the Hualin Temple as our weekend routine. The Temple was built in the 6th century. Like most of the worshippers who came here, Mother did not care much about the historical aspect. Her sole purpose was to communicate with her God through her prayer. She first lit a bunch of joss sticks, then faced the entrance of the main hall, she held the joss sticks and bowed. She murmured something from her trembling lips. After she planted the joss sticks into a two-meter tall big censer, she strode across the knee-high threshold and entered the main hall, where five hundred golden arhats statues sat in various postures and moods.

I was particularly impressed by the Laughing Buddha statue in the center. Bald and fat, the robe-clad Laughing Buddha sat with one leg propping his arm, on which he was carrying prayer beads; with the other leg lying horizontally before his potbelly. Everyone who passed by him adored his heartening smile. On both sides of the statue was a couplet that read: "Big belly can tolerate the most intolerable matters; grinning all the time to laugh at the absurd people in the world."

Since smoking was prohibited inside the Temple, worshippers only could bring in unlit joss sticks. Wherever Mother prayed she laid a couple of bunches of joss sticks on the altar. Standing in front of a Buddha statue, Mother bowed, prayed, kneeled, bowed again, prayed and finally stood up from a square hassock. She was so devout and focused. I did not want to disturb her, only observing her at a distance like a bodyguard. Surrounded by a low drone of Buddhist music and the prayer by the monks and other worshippers, I had no idea what Mother was murmuring about. But I guessed she was probably reciting the prayer she learned from books or from *Yee-ma*.

At this time and place, Mother seemed to have found where she belonged. No fear, no anger, no tension, no pain, no sorrow, no hunger, no worry, no enemy, no poverty, no gossip, no comparison, no violence, no suspicion, no criticism, no misunderstanding, and no isolation. Mother always stopped me from killing a moth. She said it was an incarnation of *Popo* visiting us. Gazing upon the glowing Buddha statues like she would watch a moth fluttering in our house, Mother felt blissfully protected.

* * * * * *

It seemed every part of the present life could trigger Mother's memory of the past. She reminisced about the time when a clear stream flowed in the neighborhood of No. 14. "The water was so clear that we saw fish at the bottom," she said, "When the water rose, we sailed paper boats on it."

Her memory also flashed back to her marriage with Father, which she talked about the most. "...He often had a binge outside with his friends," Mother recalled, shivering from a high body temperature one day. She said, "After he got home, he was so drunk, he puked right on the floor and babbled deliriously. I was away one night and you cleaned up all his shit. You were only seven." She gulped and let her words sink in. She continued, "He often yelled at me when he had drunk so much nitwit water. I didn't want to quarrel with him because The Bitchy Stuff would be so happy to hear our argument, and she would spread the gossip as speedily as a fly transmitting disease."

Another day in the middle of Mother's recollection, I asked her if she regretted marrying Father.

"Yes," she said after she thought for a second, and then she added, "I did after some time when his temper started to change."

I should have followed that vein and asked more questions. But I did not. She did not feel well and I was quite depressed. I hated to say it but I saw my parents' marriage was a mistake, a huge mistake that was too late to correct. I remembered I once asked Father before if he would divorce Mother.

"No," he said, his back to me, "At my age, I don't plan to. I'll fulfill what a husband should do."

I was an adult then. I understood what love was. At least I knew better than when I was four years old, having no clue about Father actually dating Lucky Lily in the park. Tagging me along with him was only a foil. What I did not understand was how selfless my parents' love was to bind two unmatched people together. Perhaps it was not love. It was commitment. Both of my parents stayed together solely out of obligation. Perhaps this was what made traditional Chinese marriage unique. This was what made me—as their only child—even more indebted to my parents. How could I say they were not the Lost Generation? They lost a second chance. If they wanted to seek another love, they gave it up because of me.

I remember when I was a kid I compared my parents' marriage with the one between Prince Charles and Princess Diana. I was just learning to read. While reading news about the royal couple, I frequently came across a four-character Chinese phrase—*Mao He Sheng Li*, meaning united in appearance but divided in minds. As I was doing homework at a desk with a glass top, underneath of which was my parents' black-and-white wedding photo, I constantly observed it and wondered if they were also *Mao He Sheng Li* like the royal couple; seeing them lovingly leaning against one another for that particular photograph, I did not think the phrase fitted. But hearing them frequently bickering in the house, I thought there was no better phrase than that to describe my parents' marriage, ever.

Having been exposed to Western culture for some years, I often thought Westerners seemed to take marriage much more lightly than the Chinese. When I heard my Western acquaintances say they had married twice or thrice, the first time I was shocked; the second time I was still shocked, the third time I chuckled, the fourth I acted normal, and the fifth and more I finally took the fact for granted. I learned from the current news that the divorce rate in America was fifty percent. That meant, only half of the married couples in the country would live together the way my parents chose to. There was no right or wrong about their decision. The more I pondered, the more I believed so. For the sake of their well-being, it would be sensible for my parents to separate. As a saying goes, "It is better a little loss than a long sorrow." But for the sake of their child's well-being, they stayed together. It would be cruel for me to live in a single parent family. My parents certainly understood that. They must have thought it out, through and through. In the end, they made a sacrifice of their respective happiness for *me*.

On this note, I shall forgive Father's cheating on Mother. It was his inappropriate way of pursuing free love. I shall overlook Mother's coarse speech. It was her unique way of expressing herself. I understood now that her submissive nature and her devotion to Buddhism were her ways of seeking peace and harmony. Knowing the bits and pieces of my parents' past, I gradually awoke to the realization that their affection for one another might have died a long time ago, but their duty as husband and wife, and as parents, was what kept their marriage alive.

Chapter 11

The Road to *Hengfu*

One late September evening, from our darkened living room, before I saw Mother sitting in the shadows, I heard her familiar frail voice.

"How I wish you could come home more often to keep me company."

She sat on a big hard mahogany chair with a carved symmetrical Chinese floral pattern. In her worn pajamas, her cotton pants hung to her knees.

"I do come home to see you right from my work," I reminded her.

"I know. If only you could sleep with me."

"What happened? Did you have bad dreams at night?" I asked, surprised by Mother's unusual wish.

"Nothing. Just sometimes I feel extremely lonely at night. Then thoughts about my parents emerge in my mind. It'd be nice if another person can sleep with me."

I had no clue about where Mother's loneliness came from. I could have suggested Mother sleep with Father again. But her loathing for Father was deep. She complained about his drawbacks more than she praised his merits. It would be better for me not to mention Father in my quality time with Mother.

"If you wish, I'd be happy to sleep with you tonight." I said it almost without thinking.

"*Ho-ah*. Let *Mama* tell you a bedtime story."

"A bedtime story?"

"Yes. One that can make you fall fast asleep."

Curious and touched, I quickly got ready for bed while Mother did her evening praying. After she offered the lit joss sticks to the ancestors, she turned off the electronic incense burner. The red shadow disappeared instantly, leaving only a soft orange light on. The living room turned dimmer and drearier.

I entered my bedroom, and noticed some dark thumb-size insects moored on the mosquito net. Looking closer, they were *moths*! They looked like corpses hung on the net, still and stiff. I shuddered. Where did these moths come from? I was uneasy about a dozen pair of eyes staring at me in bed. I rolled up a piece of newspaper. Just as I raised my arm, Mother walked in and stopped me.

"Leave them alone," she called. "*Popo* and her friends are visiting us."

"No. There're too many, and they're very distracting and ugly," I said.

"Let it be. Once the light is off, you won't see them."

I did not want to contradict Mother so I gave up the thought. I crawled up to the side of the bed against the wall while Mother slept on the other side, giving her easy access to the bathroom. She said not a single night passed that she did not get up to go to the bathroom. Lying in bed facing Mother, I was as nervous as a newly-wed bride about to sleep with her husband for the first night. It had been so long since I slept with Mother. I slept with my parents until I was almost four. Thinking back, sleeping with Mother then might have been destiny. Otherwise, I would not have been able to protect her from Father's unreasonable reproaching after his drinking spree. More embarrassingly to say, if I had not slept with Mother at four, she would not have been able to change my diapers in time at night. I was told I still wet the bed at that age. Mother was so concerned that she often made walnut soup for me. It was said that the kidney-shaped walnuts are effective to stop kids from wetting the bed.

"So what's your bedtime story?" I asked after Mother turned off the bed lamp. My surroundings began to take shape as my eyes adjusted to the darkness.

"Once upon a time," Mother began, "there was a turtle living in the mountain. One day, a rabbit came to visit him."

"Are you telling me the Rabbit and the Turtle?" I interjected.

"No, don't be too smart. Just listen patiently," Mother said in a didactic tone.

A shaft of mellow light flooded in through the window by the bed. It was bright enough that I could see Mother lying on her back, her arm resting on her forehead.

Mother continued, "The Rabbit asked the Turtle, 'Uncle Turtle, may I borrow your bucket to get water from the river?' 'Certainly,' the Turtle said, 'let me go and get you the bucket.' He then turned around to his house…"

As I was listening, tears slid down to my ear, warm and quiet. It was not the story but the way Mother told it that stirred my emotions. I barely remembered if Mother told me bedtime stories in the past. If she did, her stories must have had the magical power that put the childish me to sleep instantly. But as a grownup, I found that magical power was Mother's aura of existence. I believed the young me could feel it even though I was in slumber. Otherwise, when I was four, after Mother left me alone in bed, I would not have awoken to fear. That sense of security a mother gives to her child was exactly what my mother was seeking through reminiscing about her past.

That night Mother's storytelling voice transported me back to my childhood. I felt little again. But instead of feeling the sense of security from her tale, I was nervous and sad. The darkness in the bedroom haunted me. I could not close my eyes but watched Mother all the time. Her voice was familiar yet fading. The aura of her existence was faint. I was so afraid of losing her right away that I reached out to her. I wanted to touch her rough dry skin once more. I wanted to sense the warmth of her body against mine. When my hand landed on her body, I was aghast at finding her small waist. It was as if it was made of straw. Her jutting pelvis disturbingly pressed against my fleshy arm.

Mother did not put away my hand from her body like she used to. She might feel as safe in my embrace as she would have felt in her lover's arms. My mind was overwhelmed with the unusual bliss that I could be so close to her physically. I kept telling myself: *feel it carefully, enjoy it, or I won't have another chance.* I no longer followed closely Mother's rabbit and turtle story. I felt as if she was uttering meaningless sounds, similar to her whisper of a comforting prayer. Her voice warmed my shivering soul. Perhaps Mother also realized that it was a special occasion—we could sleep together like the old days when I was little. The precious moment allowed us to relive together the supposedly sweet experience of my childhood. Mother was so into her storytelling. She did not notice I had been looking at her in the dark, with a throbbing pain in my heart.

214

"...The Rabbit gave the Turtle a big carrot as a gratitude present. From then on, they became very good friends," Mother said, raking through her unkempt wavy hair.

"That's it?" I asked naïvely in disguise of my sorrow. I swiftly wiped the rolling tears and my running nose with my thumb.

"Yeah. Finished."

"I thought there was more," I said, slightly dissatisfied. Mother would not know I was absent-minded all along. I completely missed the story climax.

"No more. I'm tired now."

"OK, let's sleep. Good night," I said as I covered Mother's body with a thin blanket.

"No, I don't need it." Mother pulled the blanket off.

"Take it. You'll feel chilly after midnight. Dr. Cheng said you should not catch a cold."

In the name of Dr. Cheng my words became more persuasive. I covered the blanket over Mother's body again, she did not resist. The bedroom fell into deadly silence, making the hum of the air-conditioner from the living room louder. Being watched by dozens of moths, I closed my eyes as my mind repeated the same thought: *This is the last time I sleep with Mom. If only I could turn back time.*

* * * * * *

In one more month, three quarters of the year would have gone. The Autumn Tiger had returned. Like in the summer, the air conditioner continued to hum its song throughout the night in my house. Cantonese people were wearing their tank tops, short pants and miniskirts longer than Northerners. From September on until the end of the month, urban people were usually as busy as the harvesting farmers. They were preparing a month earlier for their annual week-long vacation during China's October 1st National Day Golden Week. Some people would decide to travel at home or abroad, some wanted to visit their rural hometowns, some chose to reunite with family and friends in restaurants, some would long for the car shows and real estate open house events in that week, while some others could not wait to test drive their private cars.

After a hard debate with myself, I traveled on the National Day vacation. Making that decision was not easy. Since I knew Mother had cancer and her life was shortening, I was inclined to see

215

everything I did as my last in her lifetime. I talked to Mother a few times about my thoughts of travelling. Every time she assured me she would be all right without me and I should take the chance to relax. I stupidly listened to her and made my last travel in Mother's life to Inner Mongolia. Only when I was far away from home did I realize how indispensable I was to Mother. Thinking of her was like a tumor in my head, sickening and steady. Although I called her every day, sometimes several times a day, I still felt a void inside me that I never could fill. Among the many times I talked to Mother on the phone within five days, there was one occasion she called me. That was when I found out she did not do as well as she had assured me prior to my trip.

"Hi Mom, how do you feel today?" I answered the phone as soon as I saw the caller ID. My ring tone of the Beatles' "Yesterday" was cut off in the first few notes.

"Terrible. I have a constant pain in my abdomen. My feet are swollen like a pig's trotters again. I can barely walk. My foot pain is killing me."

My heart sank quicker than the sand dunes in the Inner Mongolia desert. Mother used to joke that I cried so easily I should become an actress. She was probably right, especially now. Her debilitating health made it easy for me to well up, something I did not do in the presence of my parents. At hearing her groan on the phone, my sight was blurry. The yurts in the distance emerged in multiple watery shadows.

"Did you take medicine?" I asked although I knew the question was useless.

"Yes. My belly was extremely upset today," Mother said in agony.

"I know. I know. Hang in there. Perhaps you should lie in bed, elevate your feet with a pillow, and try to catch some sleep. It may help." Having said it, I hated myself terribly for saying this nonsense.

"*Mama* cannot be around with you like I used to be. You must take good care of yourself," Mother said softly.

"Yes, I will," I said bravely. I gulped, tears gushed out like a broken fire hydrant. *Why does Mother say these things? Has she found out about her disease when I am not at home?*

"Mom, don't think too much. I'll be with you very soon." I mustered all the calm to say it. I could taste the saltiness from my running nose.

"I have to eat now," Mother said feebly.

I said goodbye to her. As I hung up, I felt my mobile phone weighed like a heavy magnet sucking my clammy palm. A sense of guilt engulfed my heart. I should not have travelled this far. *Why am I so foolish? You know Mom will never get better. You also know she trusts you the most in the house. Not Chan Yee, not Father, but you—her only daughter.* A disapproving voice repeated in my head. I could not stop it. I remembered I had promised Mother that I would take her to Thailand for a Buddhist pilgrimage, like the tour *Yee-ma* took with her second daughter, Graceful Swallow. It would be her first overseas trip in her life. But here I was, sitting in my hotel room in Hohhot, regurgitating Mother's last-wish-like words, I felt sick to think that it was impossible for Mother to travel to Thailand. She could not make it for her swollen feet and worsening health. I had failed her. I had failed myself.

Looking at my return ticket, it was the day after tomorrow; I could not wait for the day to come sooner. Feeling as if I was trapped, I rested my head on my elbow and bawled.

I am a bastard. I yelled at myself inside.

* * * * * *

Within two weeks, the moths perched on the mosquito net multiplied. I killed a few while Mother was not around. But they seemed to know the way to come back. They were like mini bats hung on the net. I was baffled why so many moths were in my bedroom. If Mother said they were her parents and their friends coming to visit her, I was more inclined to believe they were the dark angels that came to accompany Mother to finish the path of her life.

I became sensitive to every unusual phenomenon in my life. I suspected even an ordinary object could be sending me a sign from the psychic world. Like on one gloomy day in September, I was on a bus to somewhere. A van with half open windows sped past my bus. I saw the passengers in the van were mournful, heads down and hands holding white handkerchiefs and blotting their faces. As the van accelerated, white papers flew out of the windows. The van was a hearse.

Unlike in the West, dead people in China, especially in the cities, are required by law to be cremated. So after the funeral, the corpse would be sent directly from the funeral home to the crematorium next door. In other words, the hearse in China is not used for transporting a coffin but for carrying the bereaved family to and from the funeral. Rich families would pool their private cars while the not-so-rich usually chipped in to hire a van or a bus for the service.

It is common practice in Guangzhou that after one dies, the family throws out the white slips of paper on the way to the funeral home and to the deceased's home on the way back. Made from coarse rice paper, the narrow white slips are a type of ghost money. People believe that by scattering the ghost money on the road, the deceased's spirit will follow the vehicle, and will have sufficient spending money on the way to heaven.

The passing funeral van was an ominous sign. *What are the odds that a funeral coach passes by me?* Rarely, except that I was less superstitious before than now. *Is that van sending me a message that it is also about time Mother said her farewell to me? Will I be one of those sobbing passengers in the van pretty soon?* Looking out of the window, I never saw a sky so grim, so much like Father's taut face. The traffic on the road sounded like a depressing dirge. The ghost money flying out from the hearse windows looked like white paper planes gliding in the air. They lost their momentum and landed on the concrete highway, then rolled up again as vehicles zipped by. Could the deceased's spirit catch up with the van or would he or she be left out with the littering trash on the roadside?

* * * * * *

Mother's new test results were worse than her previous tests. The last time Mother had her appointment with Dr. Cheng she was too frail to walk. Father waited with her downstairs in our apartment building while I ran to the closest intersection to hail a cab. In her favorite orange polka dot blouse and black pants, Mother looked heart-wrenchingly gaunt. Anguish and loss glinted in her eyes. Her feet were so swollen that she had to loosen the straps of her sandals.

When she saw Dr. Cheng, she was not talkative. Prior to this meeting, Dr. Cheng and I had a private meeting to discuss Mother's condition. Mr. Liang was there, too. According to Dr. Cheng, Mother's liver tumor had grown. Because she had severe anemia and her white blood cell count had dropped to 2,600 from a normal low of 3,500 white blood cells per microliter, Dr. Cheng said that Mother needed to be hospitalized as soon as possible.

"I have a student working in the Second Provincial Chinese Medicine," Dr. Cheng said to Mother at her regular doctor's appointment, "I can arrange for you to stay there and it'll be easy for me to follow your case through my student."

"The Second Provincial Chinese Medicine" is short for Guangdong Second Provincial Traditional Chinese Medicine Hospital. It is located on Hengfu Road, one of the popular trodden paths for newly-weds in Guangzhou because of its auspicious name. The Chinese character for *heng* means everlasting while the character for *fu* means happiness. Therefore, it is a common scene that a fleet of luxury cars festooned with flowers and ribbons rolled along the Everlasting Happiness Road. They always attract the envious eyes of the pedestrians.

"Are there any hospital beds available?" Father inquired.

"Yes, the accommodation there is more available than here," Dr. Cheng said. "The wards in this hospital are always occupied. You may have to go to the branch hospital for a vacant bed. That's further than the Second Provincial Chinese Medicine. Once you've decided, I can contact my student."

"What do you think?" Father asked Mother, fixing his gaze on her.

Father rarely asked for Mother's opinion. I placed my arm around her narrow shoulders to give her support.

"You decide," Mother said listlessly.

"My student is called Li Zhiming. He's one of my best students. I sometimes visit the Second Provincial Chinese Medicine to exchange medical experience. So I'll be able to visit you on my way as well."

"OK, please check with Dr. Li to see if we can check in today," Father said gravely. Perhaps he and I thought the same thing: *Mother is going back to the hospital. But this time she may never come home.*

Dr. Cheng fetched out his mobile phone from his pocket and called his student. The conversation only took five minutes, and then Dr. Cheng confirmed to us that Mother could be admitted to the hospital later that afternoon.

"We still have several bottles of albumin solution left. Can my mother have the intravenous injection there?" I asked.

"Yes," Dr. Cheng said, "take them with you. Dr. Li will know what to do. I'll transfer the patient's health records to him. And I'll keep in touch with Dr. Li. So please don't worry."

Before we left, Father and I shook hands with Dr. Cheng in an unspoken farewell. I was apprehensive about how often Dr. Cheng would visit Mother and how much he would heed Mother's declining health. After all, technically, Mother was no longer his patient once she was admitted to another hospital.

* * * * * *

We went home and had Mother pack her duffle bag with some necessities. Father had a brief conversation with Chan Yee in his workshop. I guessed he was telling her it was her last day working in our house. He must have paid her two hundred *yuan* more in addition to her salary. Father had told me that he had a soft spot for those who served him. Indeed, he often tipped the waitresses when he ate out, although tipping was not a part of Chinese tradition. Mother often teased him, saying Father was more generous to strangers than to his wife.

Chan Yee came out of Father's workshop and bundled up the used newspapers, getting ready for a recycle sale. In Guangzhou, households can sell their collections of used plastic goods, used papers and metal to the local disposal recycle sites. They can get money back based on the weight of the items.

"I'll bring back the change to Mr. Zhang after I sell the used paper," Chan Yee said to Mother.

"Keep it yourself," Mother said, as she kindled the joss sticks before the images of her parents.

"No, I shall return the money to you. Such a big bundle can be worth a lot."

"Just keep the money. You'll need it for your ailing husband," Mother said with compassion.

220

I did not know Chan Yee's husband was ill until Father told me later. Her grownup daughter was the breadwinner and her younger son was still in school. Since her husband was not able to work, Chan Yee hoped that her earnings from caretaking could make ends meet, or at least help out her daughter.

"Thank you so much," Chan Yee said. "A good man deserves happy returns. My Lord will be with you."

While Mother was praying to our ancestors with her hands clutching a tuft of joss sticks, I asked Chan Yee if she also prayed at home.

"Yes, but we don't burn incense. We pray with our hearts," Chan Yee said, patting on her left chest with her stubby fingers.

I thanked Chan Yee for taking care of Mother as she walked out of our apartment. Mother had already planted the joss sticks on the balcony. Threads of white smoke coiled up from the incense burner, as if they carried Mother's prayers to heaven. Sitting on the big hard mahogany chair, Mother was ready to leave for the hospital, a new but familiar habitat. She impatiently scratched her scalp and arm. Every time she put down her left arm, her jade bracelet banged the solid armrest. The thump of it was out of sync with my heart beat.

By now, Mother was experienced in packing her bag for admission to the hospital. Besides a plastic basin and her slippers, she also brought half a dozen rolls of toilet paper and a stainless steel lunch box. She said it would save her money to bring them from home instead of buying new from the hospital store. Mother's bulky basin contained her gargle mug, toothpaste and leather shoes. Holding the basin in my arms, I felt like a newcomer in a penitentiary. Melancholy descended upon me.

* * * * * *

In the cab, Mother rested her head on my shoulder, as if telling me she was too tired to see the world outside the window. She liked a window seat as much as I do.

Her room was on the sixth floor with two female roommates. Her bed was in the center, neither close to the window nor to the hallway. The room was smaller than the one that she had stayed in before. One major defect was that there was no bathroom attached. So if Mother needed to shower or use the toilet, she had to stagger to the end of the hallway where the public bathroom was located.

Mother changed into a faded patient gown and sat on her bed, filled with anticipation. A twenty-something nurse came to Mother's bed and measured her blood pressure. As she held Mother's small hand, she said in astonishment, "your palm is pale."

"I have a tough life," Mother said dryly. I noticed she had taken off her favorite jade bracelet.

The nurse smiled and continued with her work. She asked Mother to lie down and deftly wrapped the army green cuff around Mother's arm. She put on the stethoscope and inflated the cuff. Seconds later, the reading came out.

"Your blood pressure is low. Just relax. Dr. Li will be with you soon," the nurse said as she released the cuff from Mother's arm.

Mother closed her eyes, one of her arms resting on her forehead, the other pressing her belly, as if it would alleviate the pain. Her legs stretched out, forming a Chinese character— " 人 " —human. While waiting for Dr. Li's appearance, I asked Mother about her jade bracelet. She asked me to take it from the night stand.

"Can you take it back home for me? It'll be in the way while I have my injections."

I wrapped the bracelet with toilet paper and carefully put it into my pocketbook. Wearing a pair of thin dark-rimmed spectacles, Dr. Li walked in as quietly as Mother breathed.

"*Nin Hao Ma?*" How are you? Dr. Li asked, shaking hands with Father, who sat on a chair next to Mother's bed, and with me, leaning against Mother's night stand.

"She feels listless and her feet are swollen in pain," I said, gazing at Mother.

She blinked slowly, trying to prop up her body.

"Stay put. I can see you this way," Dr. Li said, and he motioned to Mother to lie down.

He walked near Mother, put his hand over her forehead and checked her wrist pulse. His fingers were long and lean like a pianist's hands. He lifted Mother's patient gown halfway, asked her to breathe in and out while he used both of his hands to feel the movement of her abdomen. It reminded me of how Dr. Cheng inspected Mother's body with his hands. Like *Shifu*, like apprentice.

"Tell me when it hurts," Dr. Li said while pushing his hands lower to Mother's colon.

"*Aah!*" Mother cried. "It hurts when you press it."

"I see," Dr. Li removed his hands from Mother's belly and pulled down her hem. He gently touched Mother's swollen feet. He thought for a moment and said, "Dr. Cheng has told me about your condition. He said you had some albumin solution left. I can ask the nurse to give you one injection now."

"Yes, here," I said. I immediately handed him all the boxes which included the catheters and syringes. I felt as if I had committed a crime of hoarding the authentic albumin solution.

"Give them to the nurse at the nursing station," Dr. Li instructed.

I followed his words and handed the albumin solution to the nurse whom I had just met in Mother's room. She took the bottles out of the boxes and placed labels on them before putting them in the fridge. I walked back to Mother's room and heard Dr. Li's voice.

"Besides having the albumin injection every other day, I'm going to prescribe for you some medicine and other drugs for intravenous injections. Our hospital can cook medicinal soup for in-patients. So I'll have the paramedics prepare the traditional Chinese medicine for you. Get some rest now. I'll check in with you tomorrow," Dr. Li said, pushing up his glasses on the bridge of his nose. He left the room quietly.

Mother felt drowsy for the rest of the day. Her injections seemed to be non-stop. It was like that in the days to come. Words between my parents and me were scarce. They communicated mostly through action and facial expressions. The grimace of pain that appeared on either of my parents' faces weighed heavier than before. Father insisted on staying overnight in the hospital. Only one family member was allowed to stay overnight with the patient. The patients' family member could sleep only on the rental beach chairs.

Mother's roommate by the window often went home at night. Her house was nearby and she was about to be discharged. So Father could sleep on a shaky beach chair between Mother's bed and her roommate's vacant one, with his feet elevated on a wooden chair. But how could that compare with a comfortable bed at home? I tried to persuade Father to change shifts with me. He always hurried me to leave at night, saying I had to get enough sleep before going to work the next day. Seeing my parents both sleeping in the hospital for different reasons, I felt like I was that little me again who sat at the edge of the loft watching them shovel the floodwater out of No. 14 alone. I was not helping at all. My heart ached even more.

* * * * * *

Besides the on-duty nurses and doctors, there was another group of people, mainly women, living with the patients. They were the trained paramedics. Many came from the same hometown in rural China. They were hired by families to care for severely ill patients. Chores were not limited to feeding the immobile and accompanying those in wheelchairs to take a stroll, but also included cleaning the bedridden patients, changing their diapers and dressing them. The difficulty of the job scared off local people. As Father put it, while the Cantonese complained about the migrant workers who had taken their jobs, nobody wanted the dirty work. And that made the demand for paramedics in urban hospitals fairly high. We knew it was a pressing matter that Mother would also need a paramedic. That would slightly relieve Father's stress of watching over Mother for a long day.

"If she likes my company, its OK," Father said to me one day. "But my presence is so unpleasant to her. I don't want to impose on her. Plus, if we have a paramedic, I can spare some time during the day to repair antique porcelain."

Father had his point. His absence might be the best way to make peace with Mother. In the hospital, she complained more often about Father's bad breath.

"His breath stinks," Mother lamented when Father was not around. "I was often awakened during the night by his smell of cigarette."

"He was trying to keep you company." I tried to say good words for Father.

"Who needs his crocodile tears? He sleeps more soundly than I do. Even a fire will not wake him up, let alone watching over me."

Mother's harsh words came out of her loathing. She became rebellious in a way that was more apparent now. Perhaps the medication affected her mood.

"Don't fret," I comforted. "I'll change shifts with *Baba* and I'll stay with you on weekends, all right?"

Mother nodded agreeably. Just as I was about to stay overnight in the hospital, Father hired a paramedic. We called her Xiao Liu, little Liu. She was in her mid-thirties. I cannot forget her round face with ruddy cheeks, sesame eyes, and thin lips. She spoke fast with a Sichuan lilt, but not as heavy an accent as her compatriot who took

224

care of Mother's roommate. I could barely decipher what Xiao Liu's fellow villager said, although she was a kind woman in her late forties. She introduced us to Xiao Liu.

A paramedic on average tended two to three patients. If the family was willing to pay more, she could give 24/7 care to only one patient. According to Xiao Liu, her co-workers on the sixth floor envied her higher wages and considered her a poor caretaker. As a result, Xiao Liu received fewer requests from patients' families. I thought the story sounded like a feud among the working girls in the brothels in old China.

"I appreciate that you hire me," Xiao Liu said when she came to Mother's room. "I hope you don't mind that I'm still committed to another patient. Her room is on the same floor. She's pretty much capable of self-care. I just need to check on her from time to time to make sure she's OK."

"Can you spend as much time as you can during the day while my daughter and I are not around?" Father asked solemnly.

"Yes, yes, consider it done. I'll stay in this room with your wife most of the time."

I left the whole matter to Father. I did not recall how much he paid her but it was affordable. Xiao Liu helped Mother get meals, walked with her to the bathroom and ran errands. Mother had no complaint about her, although I doubted there was much interaction between them during the day. Mother was like a tame horse tethered to the intravenous pole, except for supper time when Xiao Liu and her fellow villager brought in rice boxes smelling of pungent hot pepper for themselves. The notoriously famous red pepper from Sichuan province sent the scent of the tongue-burning spice throughout the room. Even a half-dead patient would have sprung off the bed. Usually at this time, Mother had completed her daily injection and I came to see her after work. She would leave the room to get away from that nose-running smell. She was nervous about a long wait for a shower so she showered early while others were eating.

The sixth floor was quite busy at dusk because people would come to visit the patients; some patients would stroll as exercise after supper. The paramedics did their own business if their employers did not need their help. The canteen server would deliver the third meal of the day with a metal pushcart. A cacophony echoed through the hallway of chatters, chuckles, high heels' clip-clops, slippers' shuffle, sneakers' squeak, metal clangs, running water, moans and groans, and the muffled traffic sound from Hengfu Road.

The women's public bathroom included two stalls for a shower and two toilets. Although the paramedics were not supposed to share the shower facilities with the patients, if they needed to stay overnight in the hospital, they showered there anyway. Father and I tried hard to press the head nurse and Dr. Li to change the room for Mother. But every time we got the same response: the few rooms with bathrooms were for severe patients in a critical condition. Xiao Liu told us privately that the room at the end of the hallway had a bathroom. There was only one patient in that double bed room. It was said the patient was a high-ranked military officer. He commuted to the hospital for his regular chemotherapy. Because he did not want to share the room with others, the hospital reserved the entire room just for him.

It was no news to me that soldiers and their immediate families have privileges when receiving medical treatment in state-own hospitals. In the past, it would be fine that they queue jump in front of me to register and pick up medicine. But today when Mother was in a no better shape than that military officer who hogged an equipped room, I could not bear it. What had he done for the country and the people that a whole room was reserved for himself? If it was because he was a man and he could not have a female roommate like Mother, there must be a severely ill man on the sixth floor who could stay in that room, too.

Standing outside the bathroom while waiting for Mother to finish her shower, I often read the posters on the bulletin near the elevators. I wondered if Mother knew this floor was specialized for cancer patients. The posters gave an overview of the situation before and after surgery on cancer and advice on how to maintain diets while undergoing chemotherapy. *Has Mother paid any attention to the contents of the bulletin?* The thought flitted through my mind. But I was not as frightful as I had been before. For a moment I thought I was numb to the literature about cancer. I had read so much in the past months. If Mother wanted to learn the truth, she could have learned it from the description on her pill bottles. She could have pressed her relatives and even her sister for the facts. She could have been aware of the patients around her, many of whom were also suffering from cancer. I remembered one time I saw a bald-headed young man lying on the extra bed in the hallway. He had just had chemotherapy. His bright eyes blinked a shimmer of hope. The smile on his pale face brightened his worn, black-striped, white patient gown. I learned that the young man was in his late twenties, and because of his young age, he reacted well to chemotherapy. He was released from the hospital shortly afterwards.

But how many patients on the sixth floor would be as fortunate as this young man? Confined in this one-building hospital, in-patients were dressed in the same faded black-striped, white gown. Like prisoners, their routines were systematic: breakfast at seven, doctors and nurses on their bedside rounds at eight, medical treatment the rest of the day, lunch at noon and then a siesta, finish medical treatment by late afternoon, supper at five, shower or change at six, chitchat and watch TV at seven, bedtime at nine. The hallway light shut at eleven. In between these routines, nurses came to the rooms to check patients' blood pressure, and apply new intravenous bags. The paramedics helped take care of the needy. Close friends and family took turns to pay their visits. The in-patients were like prison inmates, each hoping for release and new life. But some never achieved that hope.

For example, the woman in the bed by the window recovered speedily after surgery and chemotherapy. In less than a week after Mother was admitted, the woman was discharged. On the contrary, the old lady sleeping next to Mother by the door was immobile. She could hardly eat. Her food was semi-liquid, most likely rice porridge. Mother told me her neighbor could barely speak because she was asleep most of the time. Mother learned from her neighbor's daughter that her mother's debilitating health was beyond the capability of a nursing home. She was sent to the hospital, and her daughter hired a full-time caretaker for her mother. The daughter confessed she was too busy with her life to tend her mother. That would not be my excuse of leaving my mother to someone else's full care, not even to Father's after what was about to happen.

* * * * * *

Xiao Liu did not work long for us. She resigned after one weekend. So Father returned to his "night guard" duty, accompanying Mother overnight in the hospital for four nights before he hired a new paramedic.

Her name was Lei Chunhong. Chunhong means spring flowers. As her name suggested, she was warm and pleasant. We called her Lei Yee, Aunt Lei. In her early-forties, she was more slender than I but was much stronger. She could singlehandedly lift up Mother. Her black, medium-heeled shoes revealed partly her flesh-colored silk socks, suggesting that she had adapted to the down-to-earth taste of urban fashion in Guangzhou. Her dark, wavy, long hair was tied back with a butterfly barrette that matched her age. Because of her sweet and petite oval face, she could be mistaken as being from Suzhou and Hangzhou, which boasted of being the cradle of beautiful Chinese women. Lei Yee was in fact from Hunan province, which was one of the key provinces sending the most migrant workers to Guangdong province. She had lived in Guangzhou for about fifteen years. She understood Cantonese but she was shy to speak it. We communicated with her in Mandarin.

"I'll change shifts with you to accompany Golden Orchid overnight," Father said to Lei Yee in a businesslike tone.

"Fine," Lei Yee said, beaming. "Actually I can sleep over in the hospital all the evenings. You and your daughter work too hard during the day. You should get better rest at night."

"No, no. That's too hard on you. You also have a long day in the hospital. Let's change shifts. And on the weekends, my daughter can stay overnight here." Father eyed me for affirmation.

At last, we all agreed that on weekdays Father and Lei Yee took turns to accompany Mother overnight, and I replaced them on the weekends. Mother developed high temperatures, and after the fever subsided she felt nauseous. She talked less and less. When Dr. Cheng came to visit her once en route to his medical meeting on the sixth floor, Mother broke into a mild grin, as if she wanted to tell Dr. Cheng her hospitalization did not do her any good. Dr. Cheng did not say much either, except giving Mother a one-sentence pep talk, "Take it easy and rest more." He then left.

On a Wednesday night in late October when Father stayed overnight in the hospital, Mother walked to the bathroom as usual after midnight, and she fell. An egg-sized lump grew on her forehead. Her lusterless thick lips were bruised from bumping against the railing along the hallway.

"What happened to my *Mama*?" I was appalled at Mother's wounded look the next day when I visited her. She was half-asleep, lying still in bed as if she had ignored the world.

"Your father was so guilty about it," Lei Yee said to me. "It happened last night when your mother went to the bathroom. Your father gave her a hand as she was woozy. But she adamantly rejected it and insisted on walking by herself. Your father followed behind her though. Just a few steps before the bathroom, your mother slipped and fell. Her head must have hit a hard object. A couple of patients in the room near where she fell heard a heavy thud in the middle of the night. Your father blamed himself harshly for not catching her in time." Lee Yee allowed her words to sink in and went on, "I told him not to be so self-critical. It wasn't totally his fault. He even sobbed about this matter this morning when I changed his shift."

I was speechless. I felt as if my heart was torn into hundreds of pieces. The feeling was like overturning a sauce bottle of five flavors. I kept thinking of a *what if*. What if I were staying with Mother the night before, would this accident have been prevented? Looking at Mother's lumpy forehead and bruised lips, my eyes began to mist and I blinked back tears. I held her small pale hand, reminding her that I was here in the hospital. Her hand was warm and I could hear her deep breath. She wiggled her hand as if she wanted to shun away from the people she knew. I let it loose. She made a noise acknowledging my presence. Her eyes remained closed.

"How's she doing today?" I asked quietly.

"Not too good. She's been in bed all day except for using the bathroom. She had not eaten any food. Basically, she only lives on the fluids injected into her body." Lei Yee said.

"Does Dr. Li know about her fall?"

"Yes. He came to check on her this morning and had the nurse apply some medicine on the bruises on her face."

"Did he say anything else?"

"Not much. But he said he had requested a room with a bathroom for her. So she'll be transferred to a new room any time soon."

Didn't this request come too late? Did Dr. Li feel guilty as Father did? Had the accident frightened the on-duty nurses? Had they now learned a lesson the hard way from their negligence of a patient's need? The next day Mother was transferred to the room which the military officer used to occupy. The head nurse told us that the previous patient was discharged and the room had become available. What a lie!

* * * * * *

Moving into the room that we longed for did not bring ease to Mother. I regretted that I had missed the hardest part of the day while Father and Lei Yee were with Mother. The minute I stepped into the new room after work, I saw Mother struggling fiercely to get away from Father's grip like a mental patient going berserk. She screamed and yelled in raw language while trying to pull off the catheter from her hand. Drenched with sweat at the brim of her dark hair, Lei Yee helped Father to calm Mother down.

"I don't want this shit!" Mother cried, trying to reach the catheter while Father was stopping her. "Get your hands off me! Get your fucking hands off me!" Mother fought against Father's masculine strength like a furious mare. Her hair was unkempt, patient gown disheveled and her feet bare.

"Please calm down and stay still until you finish this bottle of injection," Lei Yee said, holding up the intravenous bottle above Mother's height to prevent her blood from flowing back into the catheter. I noticed Lei Yee was slightly taller than Mother.

"Calm your shit," Mother muttered in Mandarin. Her abrasive words even offended me. I unloaded my pocketbook and tried to help.

"Mom, please listen to us. Come on, be a good girl. Let's finish the injection," I pleaded, getting on my knees before her.

"Get out of my face. I need to go to the bathroom," Mother sputtered as if she was talking to a stranger.

"Hey, you know who I am?"

"Who the hell? Don't block my way to the bathroom." Mother seemed to have lost her sanity, forcing herself to the doorway.

"Look at me, look at me, Mom." I raised my voice and stared into her listless eyes. "I'm your daughter. I beg you to lie down and complete the injection. Please, please, I kowtow to you." I bowed frantically to prove my heartfelt sincerity. As I said those words, my insides constricted with despair. How could Mother have become so irrational? Was she aware of her unruly behavior? She must have not been. She was delirious and could not recognize people. She talked dirty. She looked shitty. She threw a tantrum like a spoiled kid. Things changed too fast, too suddenly. Did that concussion from Mother's fall cause her fit?

"She's been like this since this afternoon after we moved to this room," Father said exhaustedly. His voice was husky. A gulp of water might be exactly what he needed. "She's not cooperative today. She refuses to eat, to take medicine and now refuses to have the intravenous injection." Father briefed me in the short moment of truce when Mother sat on the bedside, hands hanging limply and mouth mumbling, "I want to go to the bathroom."

"OK, OK. Let me take you to the bathroom. But please have your injection with you." Lei Yee tried to compromise. She held Mother's arm with one hand, and the intravenous bottle with the other. Father tried to help with the intravenous bottle but Lei Yee said she could handle it.

We followed Mother to the bathroom. I asked Father to send a doctor here while I watched Mother. A standard sit-on toilet stood in the center of the bathroom. On the right was a shower. On the left a small sink and a mirror hung above on the wall. The bathroom was big enough for Lei Yee to stand next to Mother while I stood at the doorway. We could not close the door. Just as Mother sat down on the toilet, she pulled out the injection port from her hand. Oodles of blood burst from her purple vein, splashing on her dull black-striped patient gown. Those spots of blood on her hem and on the floor reminded me of the tiny red dots of blood in her excrement that I saw nearly a year before. But the red smudges before my eyes appeared to be much louder and larger.

"No—" I cried in panic. "Don't do that!"

"I don't need this shit!" Mother swore.

Lei Yee quickly lifted Mother and pulled up her pants while I held up the intravenous bottle. Lei Yee carried Mother out from the bathroom to the bed. In came a doctor and a nurse, followed by Father. As soon as Lei Yee secured Mother in bed, the nurse applied medicine to stop the overflowing blood on Mother's hand. The doctor touched her lumpy forehead to check her body temperature. He also checked Mother's heartbeat and her eyes. He then deftly injected a dose of drug in Mother's arm. I assumed it must be a tranquilizer as Mother quickly became drowsy. The doctor suggested that the nurse reapply the intravenous fluid to Mother. In addition, she placed a set of prongs into Mother's nostrils and adjusted the tubing to fit behind Mother's ears. That was called an oxygen nasal cannula. I understood Mother's condition was dire once it was put on her.

"She's stabilized for the time being," the doctor said. "If anything unusual happens during the night, let me know. I'll be on duty tonight. I'll notify Dr. Li about her status first thing tomorrow morning."

"*Xie xie*, doctor," I thanked the doctor as he and the nurse retreated from the room. Father nodded to show his gratitude. Lei Yee had already returned to her work of cleaning the mess in the bathroom.

"It's late. Why don't you get something to eat and go home?" Father said in a voice of persuasion.

"I'll be fine. You look tired. Let me stay with *Mama* tonight."

"No, let me stay," Lei Yee responded after she heard our conversation. "Anyway, tonight is my turn."

"No, you've done a lot today. Without your help, I don't know I can deal with the situation," Father said, implying his subtle thanks.

"I'm trained to take care of the patients. I can handle it. Please leave this to me and get a good night's sleep at home tonight," Lei Yee said positively as she wiped off a strand of loose hair on her face with the back of her hand.

"All right. I'll come here to change your shift early tomorrow morning. Please don't hesitate to call me if you need help or an emergency happens during the night," Father said after a second thought.

"Don't worry. You may come back after your breakfast. It's usually a slow day on the weekend. You won't miss anything in the morning even though you come a bit late."

"OK. I'll see you tomorrow."

I also said goodnight to Lei Yee as I followed Father to walk out of the door.

* * * * * *

We did not go straight home. Instead, we went to a diner near the hospital for a quick bite. It was one of the few restaurants in the neighborhood that served Cantonese food. I did not know the diner had become Father's canteen during his visits to the hospital. The owner was so friendly to him that he allowed Father to store his brandy at his place. Whenever his frequent patron came, he would politely bring the bottle and a glass to the table where Father sat.

"*Nihao*, Mr. Zhang," the owner greeted as he saw Father and me walking in.

"Two please," Father said.

After the owner seated us, he went to get Father's brandy and a glass. Shortly, he returned and said, "You're late for supper tonight. Is she your daughter?"

"Yes," Father said while glancing through the menu. "I want two simple dishes: one sautéed water spinach in preserved tofu sauce and one steamed perch with spring onions."

"Sure. I'll be right back." The owner took our order and quickly disappeared from our sight.

At eight o'clock in the evening, the diner was nearly empty, except for only three parties, including us. Like many other restaurants in the vicinity of a hospital, the diner also had a prosperous takeaway business to supply the hospital staff, the patients and their visitors. It was indeed a hole in the wall but the food was good. No wonder the diner attracted someone like Father who was fastidious about food.

Our dishes were served in no time. Father and I ate without saying one word. We were like two strangers sharing the same table. Perhaps Father was as distraught as I was, slowly recovering from the frantic moment in the hospital. His short deep breath was in rhythm with his chewing and slurping. I did not stop raking the rice into my mouth. The sound of my bamboo chopsticks poking the bottom of the china bowl resonated in my eardrums. I knew if I had a mouthful, I would not feel too bad about not starting a conversation.

But in that instant, the silence stung me as if I were sitting on pins and needles. Perhaps I was afraid that if I did not say something I would never have the chance. Perhaps I was afraid to find out how much I had missed Mother as silence seeped in. In the past, even though my parents bickered at supper time, their inharmonious noises reminded me that at least we were still living under the same roof.

Mother's health deteriorated fast and without notice. I cringed at the thought that Father's lonely life would be near. In fact, since we knew Mother had cancer, Father had been in a lonely life. He lost himself in work and drowned his sorrows in his workshop. But it was his choice. I guessed it was just a matter of time. Like only children, from our childhood to adulthood, we were used to being alone.

As I gazed towards the dishes, they were half empty. I had finished my meal. Father was raking his bowl of rice into his mouth after drinking his brandy. He was a slow drinker and he was also a deep thinker. I imagined what happened in the past three days must have haunted him. He looked fatigued and morose. I passed him a napkin to break the ice.

"Here's a napkin," I said. "Lei Yee has told me about the accident of *Mama*'s falling. Please don't blame yourself. I could have stayed with her that night."

"Let bygones be bygones. It's not worth dwelling on the past." Father finished his meal, too. He wiped his mouth with the napkin I gave him. He asked for the check.

"I'll keep *Mama* company tomorrow. So you can stay home and get some rest."

"OK. Let me know what Dr. Li says if you see him."

"Yes. It's late. Let's take a cab home, shall we? I'll pay for the fare."

"No. Taking bus is fine. I don't want you to splurge on me. If we were with your mother, we would take a taxi. But just you and me, let's take bus. I have enough change."

Father fumbled in his back pocket and took out a wad of *renminbi* notes with a small face value. It cost two *yuan* to take a one-way bus in Guangzhou and we needed to transfer to another bus before getting home. So a thirty-minute cab ride from home to the hospital would take about an hour and half by bus.

We crossed Hengfu Road to catch the bus in the opposite direction. The rush-hour traffic had gone. Instead, the occasional passing taxi cab rumbled through the night. About three to four blocks away there was the nightlife district in the vicinity of the Garden Hotel. I remembered I took Mother to the five-star hotel to see the biggest Christmas tree in her lifetime the year before. I remembered how small she was in front of that three-story high tree. Gazing upon the plain hospital building across the road, I was saddened to say to myself that Mother was unconscious inside that building.

Father stood by the sign that showed the bus route information. He lit a cigarette and gave a hard drag on it. A wisp of cigarette smoke appeared. He hid his left hand in his pocket, and held the cigarette between his right fingers in a delicate way that neither the night breeze nor people around him could touch it. As autumn slipped into winter, the chilly evening like this was most likely to cause people to rush home. The biting wind unfazed Father yet it made me tremble. I fell into my contemplation.

I remembered a few days before I stood at the same bus stop waiting for my bus, I saw those white slips of ghost money dancing in circles with the dried dead leaves on Hengfu Road. When cars zipped by, the ghost money suddenly got the momentum to fly further until it disappeared out of my sight. Were those white slips a harbinger of something ominous about to happen? What about the black butterfly that fluttered outside my balcony window for the last several mornings? Was it also an omen? Were those moths in my bedroom relatives of that black butterfly? Perhaps the butterfly was an incarnation of a happy afterlife, deriving from an ugly metamorphosis. Would Mother be going somewhere like that?

The bus finally arrived. As Father and I got on the bus, the hospital building was soon out of my peripheral vision. I thought to myself that if the tranquilizer worked, tonight was probably the first time Mother could sleep through the night in a very long time.

Chapter 12
Waiting

When one's life is in danger, every second counts. I remember vividly how I counted those seconds by Mother's bedside in her ephemeral life. Only several days later did I know it was the last weekend I would spend with her.

After her rough first day settling in the special care room, Mother had been in and out of sanity. Although her eyes were closed, she seemed to know what was going on around her. At least she knew her room had a sit-on toilet. Whenever she had the urge, she would attempt to get up. Yet, the convenient facilities had come too late. She was tethered to many catheters and ducts, some of which were connected to a new apparatus—the electrocardiogram (ECG) monitor. The gadget read Mother's heartbeat and pulse in real time, as if the readings were the messages from her confused brain, signaling to all of us she was still kicking despite the fact she looked dormant.

The nurses suggested we get Mother adult diapers to reduce her movement of getting off the bed. At the beginning Mother defiantly resisted using diapers. She might look frail all day but when Lei Yee wrapped a diaper around her waist, she yanked it with all her strength. Her lips quivered. She must have sworn under her breath. I could not decipher her speech. She looked upset, sometimes even in pain, as if she was being molested. I doubted she heard Lei Yee's comforting words. Lying in bed, Mother just refused to pee in her diaper-wrapped pants. But she was too weak to get up. She would then murmur, "I need to go to the bathroom."

"Come on, you can pee right here without walking to the bathroom," Lei Yee suggested.

"Take me to the bathroom," Mother said, her eyes remained closed.

"No, you can't get off the bed now. You have an IV and a monitor on."

"Bathroom, take me to the bathroom," Mother pleaded. She was on the verge of crying like a child who played her last tactic to reach her purpose.

Softened by her beseeching look, I offered to take her to the bathroom. As I stood by her bedside, she spread her arms to me like a child who wanted her mom to hug her. In my twenty-four years of living, I had never seen Mother so childlike. She was desperate to be carried away from that constricted bed.

That moment when Mother opened her arms to me is frozen in my memory. We were so close—within arm's reach, and yet we were so far. In the company of the beep from the ECG monitor, Mother's hug was a call for rescue. An impulse to grab her feeble body off the bed and take her away from this place crossed my mind. It was unbearable to see her suffer this way, given the circumstance that she was ordered to pee in her pants. What a humiliation. She was not incontinent like an infant. For her, resorting to the adult diapers was a sign of her failure to care for herself, of her privacy being deprived, of her dignity being tarnished. Mother did not stop struggling. She must have recognized my aura—a distinct code between mother and daughter—as I have felt hers.

"All right. Take it slow," Lei Yee said as she helped to remove the electrodes on Mother's body and wrists. She probably had an epiphany that she was dealing with a patient with a strong will.

"Xiao Zhang, could you help take the IV bag? I'll carry your mother to the bathroom," Lei Yee instructed. I knew she was trained to handle this situation, including holding a severe patient properly, which I could not do.

"OK. I'll follow you."

I stood on the other side of the bed, taking off the intravenous bag from the metal pole and raising it up above my head. A clear tube carrying amber fluid into Mother's arm dangled from the bag. Suddenly, Lei Yee was like a hunk filled with miraculous strength. She put her arms under Mother's legs and back, scooped her up from the bed and carried her to the toilet. She secured Mother's position on the toilet seat, guarding her with both of her hands on Mother's shoulders. Mother lowered her head with messy hair. I could hardly see her face. Her hands were like bamboo shoots hanging vertically on her sides. She looked like an invaluable Buddha statue that was about to collapse any minute.

As the trickling sound in the toilet petered out, Lei Yee knew it was time to carry the patient back to bed. She gently informed Mother what we were about to do. She then summoned all her energy to sweep up Mother's feet. After a couple of steps, she gingerly laid Mother's body on the bed, as if her patient was made of glass. Swiftly, Lei Yee secured the electrodes, pulled down Mother's patient gown, and covered her body with a white sheet. Mother was at peace again.

"You're amazing," I said to Lei Yee, hanging the intravenous bag on the pole by the bedside.

With the brim of her hair drenched, Lei Yee heaved a sigh and said, "Your mother is even more amazing. I know she's in pain but she's reluctant to utter a sound."

"Yes, she's a strong woman," I said with admiration. I motioned Lei Yee to sit down to take a break.

"Before she changed to this room, she often talked to me about you." Lei Yee sat on the side of a vacant bed and continued, "She said you often took her out for good meals and gave her spending money to enjoy life. She's proud of you. As a mother myself, I can tell she misses you a lot. But she doesn't want to interrupt your work. Several times I asked her to give you a call when she felt uncomfortable. She often said it was not a good idea. She thought her discomfort would go away quickly."

At hearing Lei Yee's words, my eyes were swimming with tears. I blinked fast to hold them back. *All these years, Mom has never changed.* I said to myself. In the past, even though she needed a shoulder to cry on, she would rather sob alone. She never asked for anyone's sympathy. After she healed her wound privately the way women in old China tended their bound feet, she always bounced back resiliently from her downs. Her tolerance humbled me.

As the days became more dire, I began to think Mother probably had sensed what fate lay before her. Perhaps she was trying to protect Father and me from feeling sorry for her. She would rather keep what she knew in her heart. Wouldn't it be the most ironic farce? Father and I had kept her illness from her, while she might have concealed the truth that she already knew. I laughed at my stupidity. Would Mother really hide a secret from us? Could she? Yes, she would, as she had decided not to tell me about her discomfort for fear she would interrupt my work. Yes, she could, as she did not tell us her symptoms early on. We learned them only afterwards from the doctors. For the sake of not worrying us and disturbing our normal life, Mother could seal her lips.

A pang of horror descended on me. I believed my heartbeat outpaced the ECG monitor reading. That rhythmic beep disrupted my chain of thought.

In early afternoon, a nurse came in to check on the intravenous fluid and the ECG monitor. She asked me about Mother's bowel movement. I reported honestly that Mother insisted on using the toilet.

"Please try to persuade the patient to use diapers," the nurse said, taking notes. "It does more harm than good if she gets off the bed."

"Yes, I understand," I said. "But she doesn't cooperate. We can do nothing about it."

"It's hard the first time for everyone. But she'll get used to it."

"How? She struggles if we don't let her to go to the bathroom. I'm afraid she may even refuse to poop as a protest," I said in frustration. Everything the nurses suggested sounded easier said than done.

"Please work harder. We all want to make the best for the patient. Ask your paramedic to help you. She's one of the experienced ones," the nurse said as she walked briskly towards the door.

The room returned to silence, except for the pulsating beep. For three days Mother had not consumed any food. Nor did she poop. On one of his bedside rounds, Dr. Li said if Mother did not have a bowel movement by the end of the day, she would need manual stool removal. I was quite concerned about the process. It was so difficult to talk her into using the diaper.

I sat in a wooden chair, looking squarely at Mother in bed and at the constant progression of waves on the monitor screen. I had never felt time passing so slowly, as if each second was divided into hundreds of segments, and each segment was broken into numerous mini units. I thought I could read. But I could not fix my gaze on a newspaper. My mind was as blank as the bed sheet. I heard my breathing loud and clear.

* * * * * *

I had no idea how long I had been alone in the room with Mother. The next time I looked at my watch was in early evening. Lei Yee was getting ready to clean Mother's body. Since Mother was unconscious, the bathroom was meaningless to her. But the room did give us privacy as Mother was the only occupant. After we closed the door, Lei Yee undressed Mother, wiped her body with a warm towel, sprinkled on some baby powder, and put on a clean patient's gown. Mother was like an infant being taken care of. This was probably the second time I saw Mother naked. I vaguely recalled she had showered with me once when I was a baby. But Mother's fifty-three-year-old body was like a withered leaf, far from being as attractive and curvy as she was in her thirties. Her skin was tawny and coarse. Her breasts seemed to have been leveled by her illness, making her chest bones more pronounced. An A cup size of bra might be even too large for her. She wore much less at this stage—no bra and no panties, only one sheer layer of the patient gown. Underneath it was a bulky adult diaper. Lei Yee deftly changed Mother without my assistance.

"Your mother is heavier now than before," Lei Yee said while her hands were busy.

"Why?" I asked, having failed to turn Mother on her side.

"You're lifting mostly dead weight when she's unconscious. You need to be trained to do so."

"I saw you carrying her to the bathroom earlier, though."

"She wasn't as heavy as now. At least she wanted me to carry her. So she cooperated. "

No wonder it felt like a big damp loaf when I tried to push Mother over from her back. I felt ashamed that I did not have the strength to carry her. If it were not because of Lei Yee, my weekend with Mother would have been a disaster.

My gaze fell on the lump on Mother's forehead. It had subsided a bit but still looked like a quail's egg, black and blue. The wound on her lips began to form a maroon scab.

"I should have stayed with *Mama*. I didn't persuade my father hard enough that night." A wave of guilt surged inside me.

"Let it be," Lei Yee comforted. "It's already happened. Your father still blames himself. I asked him not to. You should move on and buck up. Even though your mother is unconscious, I bet she's content that you're with her now."

A moment later, Dr. Li walked in. My conversation with Lei Yee came to a full stop.

"How's your mother doing today?" Dr. Li asked.

"She's asleep most of the day although she did wake up dreamily asking for the bathroom."

"The nurse who was on duty also told me about that. How many times has she peed today?"

"Twice," Lei Yee said, looking at her notebook. She had been recording Mother's bowel movements. To complete her report, she added, "Once in early morning, the other time at noon."

"How about her stool?"

"None," Lei Yee said disappointedly, glancing over her notebook. "Not since she came to this room."

Dr. Li also took his notes after reading the patient's record card hanging at the end of the bed. He put on his stethoscope and listened to Mother's heart activity. He checked her pulse on her wrist and examined her feet. They were not as swollen as they had been.

"I think it's time to give the patient the manual disimpaction," Dr. Li said after a careful calculation. "It may cause the patient discomfort but if we don't do so, the patient's life will be in danger."

"OK. Thanks, Dr. Li," I said blandly. At this moment, besides agreeing with Dr. Li, I lost my hope of finding a new solution. I did not know when Mother would come to her senses. Nor did Dr. Li know. He said Mother's fall complicated her condition but was not the cause of her stubborn reaction. That night, he repeated to me Mother's future was uncertain. What sort of diagnosis was that? I thought Dr. Li was like Moses leading his patients and their family to a promised land. But now even the doctor was unsure what was going to happen. Facing the uncertainty, I had to play it by ear.

Shortly after Dr. Li left the room, a tall nurse came in with a medical apparatus in her rubber-gloved hands. She was going to insert a thin soft tube into Mother's anus to induce the faeces. It was my first time to witness such cruelty. Holding the tube in hand, she was like a white angel about to slaughter a human being. My heart hammered against my chest like a moth in a lamp. I wished I were not there. Surprisingly, Mother's face showed no agony. She was like a vegetable. The ECG monitor was pulsating with that familiar beep. Somehow that sound gave me a sense of assurance. The whole procedure did not take long. The tall nurse looked a bit disappointed for she could not get out too much waste from Mother's body.

"She did not eat for three days, only living on the IV fluids," Lei Yee said, as if she was asking the nurse to have mercy on Mother.

"Yes. I figure," the tall nurse said coldly. "She's fine now. Please continue to keep track of her bowel movements."

"Yes, I will," Lei Yee said. She helped straighten Mother's clothes and the bed sheet.

"Oh, make sure that the set of prongs are in her nostrils," the tall nurse said while adjusting the oxygen nasal cannula in Mother's nose.

"I did. But she pulled it off her face," Lei Yee said. "She rebuffed anything on her, including the IV catheter and the monitor electrodes."

"Her mood fluctuates. Try to watch over her closely. I'm on night shift tonight. If you need assistance, call the nursing station," the tall nurse said as she wrapped up her gear and left the room.

* * * * * *

That was precisely what I did that night—watching over Mother closely. It was my night shift by Mother's bedside. Lei Yee left for home in the evening. She told me not to worry about Mother's bathroom problem because Mother was wearing a diaper. If a problem arose, I could call her or the on-duty doctor and nurses. She lived within walking distance of the hospital.

The fluorescent light in the hallway went out at eleven. The sixth floor instantly quietened down. I nearly forgot there was a world swirling outside Mother's room. My curiosity led me to the doorway. That night was my first time to stay over in the hospital. Standing at one end of the hallway where Mother's room was, I saw a long straight path roll out beneath my feet. It came to an end at the turn to the stairwell and the elevator. About halfway, the tile floor reflected the working light from the nursing station. It was the brightest spot. Yet, the hallway was not in complete darkness. Several dim night lights were spaced out at the bottom of the wall along the hallway.

242

My mind was transported back to the night when Mother fell. I wanted to retrace the path she took to the public bathroom. But as I looked to the other end of the hallway again, the frigid dark corner gave me goose bumps. I dropped that idea. Perhaps when Mother was groggy, she was not aware of how creepy this place could be. Perhaps the on-duty nurse was as chicken-hearted as I was and mistook my parents for two unpleasant ghosts. Without the daytime commotion as a distraction, the hallway at night was tinged with a sense of desolation. It was a long way to walk alone anyway. Suddenly, the dreadful coughing sound of a man echoed in the hallway. Shivering with surprise, I returned to the room.

I switched on the lamp above the vacant bed and put out the fluorescent light. The room immediately felt homely. If only Mother was awake, we could watch TV together. But now the TV set was just as meaningless to her as the toilet in the room. She was sleeping soundly as she had never slept for the past months. I moved the wooden chair by her bedside, sat down and held her small left hand. The lump on her forehead was not noticeable from this angle. Her sallow face was the most relaxed I had seen for days. Her jowl was long gone. It was nearly a sharp curve from her chin to her neck. Her friends used to joke with her that her double chins were a symbol of happiness. Did it mean her happiness was gone? Her full lips were still there, a bit dry though. Lei Yee taught me how to apply lip balm on her lips. I tried to moisten her lips without hurting the scabs.

The beep from the ECG monitor continued to pace my heartbeat. Holding Mother's hand, my prayer for her sang in my mind unbidden. *Why does Mom become like this? Is it a punishment for her? Is it the best way to alleviate her pain? Please my dear god, tell me what to do. Will I talk to her again? Will she at least wake up to say goodbye to me? I don't want to say goodbye to her yet. Please make her feel good. Please let me suffer for her. Please give me some faith to go through these days…*Sniffing and snuffling, I pulled out the napkin from my pocket and wiped my damp face. I should not let Mother hear my sobbing. I checked the time. It was only half an hour after midnight. That evening was damn long.

I was restless. I did not plan to close my eyes anyway. I was afraid of what Father had said before—an emergency always catches us off guard. Being Mother's guardian angel, I must be responsible and vigilant. I made sure Mother was tucked in under her sheet, the prongs were in her nostrils, and her feet were elevated on a small pillow. It was a small yellow pillow with a cartoon lion's face on the top. I brought it from my office. In my sedentary job, I used it to support my lower back.

Lei Yee told me that I had to turn Mother regularly to improve her blood circulation. She said patients who were confined to bed were more likely to contract bedsores, also known as pressure ulcers. I learned her words by heart. So I broke down my *long* night into several two-hour periods. I wondered which was Mother's preferred sleeping position: on her back, or on her sides. She sometimes scratched her scalp and rubbed her feet against the sheet, as if her dream made her fidget. I held her knees close to my heart to calm her. She stopped. Then probably fifteen minutes later, she flailed her arms and jerked again. Was her dream frightening? I shooshed her gently like what Mother used to do when I was spooked by my bad dreams. I told her lightly, "Mom, I'm here. Don't be afraid. I'm here."

Sitting on the bedside and stroking Mother's feet, I felt my heart thump. I also needed someone to tell me not to be afraid. The windows were mostly closed except a slit for a draught. I saw darkness looming outside. There was a deathly hush out there. My body temperature dropped as quickly as the night frost permeated in the air. I remembered those nights when I was in high school. I often stayed up to study in the hope of getting good grades to make my parents proud. I had sat in this drop-dead silence and felt the dark before dawn. But now I felt strange and uneasy at this hour of the day, which used to be my favorite. I repeated my prayer to gain strength.

There was no flying plane roaring at this hour. Instead, I heard the whistle of an oncoming train. I forgot there were railroad tracks nearby. Some trains that came to Guangzhou had to pass by the hospital. The rumbling train transported me to my childhood in No. 14. We lived not far from railroad tracks. Father used to take me to pick up rocks between the tracks. Mother used to ride her bike with me on the back seat crossing the pedestrian overpass above the tracks. *Where is that family now?* I thought.

* * * * * *

After a long fall night, I waited anxiously for the first ray of light. The sun rose about an hour after the train passed. At six thirty, the mundane routine of an in-patient life began. The early risers were the paramedics. They had to wash off before tending their clients. I thought I would have panda eyes—dark rings circling my eyes from lack of sleep. Instead, I had a pair of bloodshot eyes.

Since Mother did not eat her meals, I took her food. Saturday's breakfast was two white dough buns and a carton box of milk. While I was munching on a bun, Lei Yee showed up in another set of clothes. She brought in her breakfast.

"*Zaoshang Hao*," Good morning. She greeted in Mandarin, "You got up early."

"*Zao*," I said with a mouthful. After a gulp of my food, I said, "You come early, too. I thought you would be here by nine. It's only seven."

"I know you had a long day yesterday. You should take a break. Or you'll get sick."

"I'm fine. I'm young, got lots of energy," I said, trying to disguise my fatigue. I could feel my head weigh on my neck. My hands and feet were still icy cold from last night.

Lei Yee opened the windows before she sat down to finish her breakfast. The din of the urban traffic wafted in from outside. Hengfu Road seemed to have no day off. It was busier on weekends, partly because more couples were getting married. At eight-ish, Dr. Li made his bedside rounds. He looked groomed and fresh. He did his routine checkup on Mother and passed me a slip of paper—an official notice for the family of severely ill patients.

"Your mother's coma is caused by her poor functioning liver," Dr. Li said seriously, as if he had slept on my questions about Mother. "Medically, we call it hepatic coma. Her symptoms suggest she may live for another two to three days." Dr. Li paused to allow his words to sink in. He looked at the notice and said, "Here is just a notice to inform the family about the patient's status. You and her close family should be prepared for the worst."

"I see." It took me a while to utter words. I held the notice with both hands to stabilize my trembling nerve. Every Chinese character on the notice looked strange to me except Mother's name: Golden Orchid. It was only three lines of text. But the way the characters came together to form a meaning sent shivers down my spine. At the bottom of the paper was a blank space for a signature.

"Can I show this notice to my father?" I asked. My lips trembled.

"Yes, you may," Dr. Li said. "After you sign it, please return it to any nurse at the station. I'm about to get off my shift. But if you have any questions please call me. The on-duty doctors and nurses will also help you."

I nodded. I did not know when Dr. Li left the room or where Lei Yee was. I did not care. In that instant, I just wanted to shut myself away from the reality. *How can I tell Baba about this? He'll be here any minute. How will he take in the news?* I lowered my head, as if I were an ostrich looking for a hole on the ground to hide. My throat was choked. The food I swallowed minutes before regurgitated. The acid lingered in my mouth, reeking of a foul smell.

Father came in time, after I had dried my glasses with a tissue. I showed him the notice and repeated Dr. Li's words. His stoical acceptance surprised me. All my worries were dissipated after he signed the notice and said, "It's expected."

"I'll notify the Zhangs. If you want, you can tell *Yee-ma* and the others," Father said, giving me the signed notice. He then said, "*Goo-ma* and Uncle Sahm will come to visit today. If you're tired, I can host them."

"It doesn't matter. I'll stay till they come," I said. My head weighed even heavier.

* * * * * *

Days before when Mother was conscious, I met Father's eldest brother, my *Baa-fu*, in Mother's room. He was my cousin Jacky's father. Given the fact that he was concerned that his son's cancer could reoccur, *Baa-fu* was most sympathetic about my family situation. My American teacher, Frank, also visited Mother a couple of times. Their body language seemed to convey meaning better than my translation. One time after Frank's visit, he told me that Mother gave him a hand gesture of a "No" and of shuffling poker cards. He got the idea that Mother was sending him a message—she could no longer play cards with him.

She had been in bed for more than thirty-six hours. Thank heaven she was still breathing. But her sleep deepened second by second. When Lei Yee checked on Mother's diaper again, she spotted dampness. Mother's subconscious mind had commanded her to pee in her diaper *finally*. No more fuss. No more struggling. Was that a worse sign?

The word "hepatic coma" hung in my mind, isolated from the rest of words I heard during the day. I surfed the web for the definition of the term. My heart sank as I found out most of Mother's symptoms meet the description—irritability, confusion, indecipherable speech, tremor, jerking movement of the limbs, and lethargy. It made sense that Dr. Li had stopped the use of albumin solution. The consumption of protein would increase the risk of hepatic coma. Seemingly, death was the ultimate consequence.

The time bomb set twelve months before in my head was about to explode.

A nurse came in to make her noontime rounds. After she examined Mother's eyes with a flash light, she meticulously added two square gauze pads on them. I did not know the purpose of the gauze pads. In late afternoon, *Goo-ma*, Father's elder sister, came to visit Mother. In her early sixties, she had the closest resemblance to Granny—high cheekbones, narrow chin and piercing eyes. She came with her husband, *Goo-jeong*, who I believed came to see Mother for the first time. Father was at about the same height as *Goo-ma*. Both of them were shrouded in a solemn air.

"How's she doing?" *Goo-ma* asked, approaching Mother's bedside.

"She's in a coma," I said impatiently. Deep down I detested this moment. Was this visit necessary? Why didn't she come earlier when Mother was conscious? If Father's so-called Zhang Clan was as united as he boasted, why didn't his side of the family visit Mother more often? I felt as if Mother's vehement protest against Father's judgment had taken control of my emotion.

"How long has she been like this?" *Goo-ma* asked, sounding ignorant.

"Four days from the day she fell."

"Golden Orchid," *Goo-ma* held Mother's hand and said, "I'm your sister-in-law. We're here to visit you." Mother remained like Sleeping Beauty. "How are you?" *Goo-ma* spoke into Mother's ear.

"She hears us, doesn't she?" *Goo-ma* asked me.

"I don't know" I said. I saw Father sitting on the wooden chair, looking as anxious as *Goo-jeong* who stood by him. They both hoped that Mother would utter a sound.

247

Goo-ma noticed the gauze pads on Mother's eyes. She was curious and asked what they were for. Again, I replied "I don't know." She then gingerly lifted one pad and there she saw the whites of Mother's eye. Petrified, she immediately put the pad down.

"Later when Uncle Sahm comes to visit, please don't let him see your mother's eyes," *Goo-ma* said as she walked away from Mother's bed. "Or it'll remind him of the look on Granny's face before she died."

I recalled Father told me before that Uncle Sahm found it difficult to tear himself away from his grief over Granny's passing. I also remembered at Granny's funeral ten years before, Mother was the daughter-in-law who wailed the loudest. At every Ching Ming Festival, Mother was also the most hard-working family member at Granny's grave in preparation for the memorial ceremony. She wiped the gravestone with a wet towel, pulled out the weeds around the grave, placed three sets of cups and chopsticks before the gravestone, assembled the ghost money in order, and helped burn the paper offerings to our ancestors. However, her effort provoked Father's inappreciative remark. He once said to Mother, "Your superstition has gone too far! Look, no one in Zhang Clan can compete with your knowledge of burning the incense and worshiping the gods. You're always in the vanguard of what to do every year when we sweep the grave." As always, Father's criticism only alienated Mother from him.

Goo-ma stayed briefly in the room and left with her husband. I guessed she visited Mother before Uncle Sahm on purpose so that the room would not be overcrowded. About half an hour after she left, Uncle Sahm and his wife arrived. Their fashion taste never disappointed me. Uncle Sahm wore an indigo polo shirt and a pair of casual pants that matched the color of his shirt. After all, he was a businessman on holiday. I had not seen his wife for a while. Aunt Sahm's hairstyle was different from the last time I saw her. Her permed dark hair was at the right length to cover her ears, kissing the edge of her dark turtleneck sweater. Father once said Uncle Sahm and his wife were a perfect match among all his siblings and their spouses, including him and Mother. I could not agree more.

"Hi, *Yee Gor*." As Uncle Sahm walked in he greeted Father. "How is *Yee-soh*?"

"She's been in a coma," Father said in a low voice.

Uncle Sahm and his wife stood next to the vacant bed for a while. Both of them looked in the same direction—Mother's face. They must have spotted the gauze pads on Mother's eyes, the lump on her forehead, and the scab on her lips. Uncle Sahm looked around at the objects around Mother's bed—the ECG monitor on her left, the oxygen valve on the wall above her head, a couple of intravenous bags strung on a metal pole on her right. Mother was inert and wooden, as if there was a world between us. Uncle Sahm walked around the bed to get a closer look at Mother.

"Has she awakened?" he asked.

"No. She was somewhat delirious after a fall on Wednesday early morning. The doctor said it's a hepatic coma. She has only two or three days." I mustered my courage to announce the fact as calmly as possible.

The silence in the room made each beep of the ECG monitor disturbingly loud. The absence of speech lasted long enough that the clear beep bounced back and forth between walls, resonating in my eardrums.

"How much are the medical fees? Can I help you out?" Uncle Sahm asked mildly, eyeing Father.

"Manageable. Golden Orchid is in a medical program for severe patients. And our daughter has helped a lot financially. We can pay the bill. Don't worry about it." Father seemed to feel embarrassed about Uncle Sahm's question. He probably thought it was shameful for a man if he could not afford his wife's medical expenses. It was a man's ego as Mother had said in the past.

"We'd better get going. If you need anything, don't hesitate to call me," Uncle Sahm said.

"How about I walk you out?" Father offered.

"OK," Uncle Sahm said, motioning his wife to the doorway.

Father followed both of them.

As I saw them leave, I heaved a sigh. Finally, Mother and I were left alone. The familiar silence delighted me. It was not that I did not welcome visitors to see Mother. It was not a good time. Having known Father was there that night when Mother fell onto the floor, my feelings for him changed. I was not sure if I was angry. But I did not want Father to get too involved with Mother's life or death. I wanted him to keep a distance from her. Perhaps my snub of him came out of my instinct to protect Mother, for which I was well-trained since childhood.

However, this was a difficult time. It needed family to stand together and show our solidarity. Lei Yee had told me several times that Father was full of guilt about Mother's accident. I believed that. He was extremely reticent the last few days. He was expressionless like Mother but he was conscious and mobile. Mother's illness had tortured him day and night, if not physically, at least mentally. It would be cruel to Father if I left him alone to drown his sorrows. He needed to be recognized as part of our solidarity. He needed to be loved.

* * * * * *

My close friend Ivy also visited Mother in the hospital. She was about a year older than me. So I always thought her experience was one year ahead of me. When I was a senior in high school, she was the freshman in college. She told me about her wonderful college life. When I was a senior in college, she had been working in her first year. She told me about how stressful her job was. But now I felt I was more mature than she was. No doubt that I knew better than her about how to take care of a dying parent. I could tell her how painful it was to see someone I love dearly dying.

Before Ivy left, she gave my mother a red packet containing a one hundred *yuan* note. She said the money was a gift to buy nutritious food for Mother.

On the same day, Ivy's parents, Uncle Cheong and his wife together with Uncle Yu and his wife, visited Mother. Rarely did Mother make friends with the wives of Father's friends. But she got along well with these two wives of Father's close friends. These three women could share the one thing that they had in common: they all have an only daughter of about the same age. There were almost no secrets about their daughters among them. They must have also shared their complaints about their husbands. I remembered Father once warned Mother not to talk too much about her woes to his friends' wives.

"You know, your complaints will affect other couples' relationship." Father said. Although his voice sounded conversational, his words projected a warning. He was miffed that Uncle Yu had an argument with his wife after she chatted with Mother on the phone about their husbands. Perhaps because of that warning, Mother was more private about her feelings, not even telling anyone about her abdominal pain when her friends came to my house for a visit. They and their husbands visited my ailing Mother more often than my relatives. I was moved by their material and spiritual support.

"Your Mother has a lot of guests this weekend," Lei Yee said, beaming. She showed up in Mother's room after the guests left.

Indeed, I was swamped with socializing the uninvited but friendly people in Mother's room. I was oblivious to Lei Yee, who worked like a bee around Mother's bed. Knowing Lei Yee and I were capable of receiving guests and tending Mother, Father often went out of the room—most likely standing or sitting near the elevator entrance where smoking was permitted. We also took turns to go to bathroom or grab a bite. We made sure either one of us stayed in the room with Mother in the following few days.

"I'm sorry that you have to work on weekends," I said to Lei Yee. "I wish the visits could be spaced out a bit."

"Haven't you heard of a saying?" Lei Yee said, "*Urban people are so busy that they don't have the time to get sick, let alone seeing a doctor.* I bet your relatives have to work during the week. Weekends are the only time at their disposal. Our job is quite the opposite. The hospital is always understaffed on weekends. So we're very busy at this time of the week."

While Lei Yee and I were chatting, *Yee-ma* and her husband and their oldest daughter, Soaring Swallow, appeared at the doorway. I had not seen Soaring Swallow for a long time. We usually met once a year at the Chinese New Year dinner. She looked tanned and weary. Her job as a shoe vendor must have worn her out. She and her husband opened a store in the campus market of the Sun Yat-sen University. They worked long hours seven days a week, twelve months a year.

I had not told *Yee-ma* and her family about Mother's fall. What wind brought her uninvited to the hospital? She looked about the same as when I saw her last in the restaurant. Wearing an azure blouse, she waddled with her stiff body. Soaring Swallow held her mother's arm to support her.

"We've just been to the Guangxiao Temple. I thought since we're out, why not come to see your mother. How is she?" *Yee-ma* asked, getting closer to Mother.

I could not remember how many times I repeated Mother's critical status. Each time I said it, my tongue burned and my heart felt like it had been stabbed. My feelings for *Yee-ma* were more difficult to describe than mine for Father. They were more than simple anger or loathing. I felt as if that sauce bottle of life had been overturned in my heart.

"We've been thinking about your mother," Soaring Swallow said. "We prayed for her at the temple. I'm told *Ah-yee* is very sick. We're devastated. My Ma has been sleepless because of that." Soaring Swallow called my mother *Ah-yee*, a family title for one's mother's younger sister.

"Golden Orchid, it's me. Your sister comes to see you," *Yee-ma* spoke to Mother, clasping a ball of creased tissue in her hand.

Perhaps *Yee-ma* had noticed Mother's lump on her forehead and the scab on the lips. She choked up. She covered her half-open mouth with the white tissue. In the meantime, Mother got excited. The beep of the ECG monitor sounded crisp and short. Her heart rate went up to a hundred and fifty beats per minute (BMP), beyond the normal range of sixty to a hundred BMP. Frightened, I threw myself by Mother's side and embraced her. I patted her arms, repeating "Mom, it'll be fine" to her ear. I came to realize *Goo-ma*'s suspicion was correct—Mother could hear us.

"Perhaps you should not get too close to her," Lei Yee suggested to *Yee-ma*, trying to separate them.

Yee-ma did not listen, she croaked, "Golden Orchid, I'm so sorry for you. It saddens me that you're so sick like this. You don't deserve this…"

As *Yee-ma* continued to talk and weep at the same time, Mother got more emotional. Unconscious, she tried to say something but was incapable. She looked frustrated, as if she had suffered a stroke that deprived of her speech. Anxiety got to her. She jerked and yanked and kicked. Her face was contorted in pain. The gauze pads fell off her eyes, revealing the whites. She uttered several heart-wrenching "*uh*" sounds. The reading on the ECG monitor showed big choppy red waves. The number of her heart rate climbed up to a bit over two hundred BMP, a bad sign, an awful sign. The rapid beep was like an outcry from Mother's disordered brain over *Yee-ma*'s belated visit.

Lei Yee stepped up and held down Mother's shoulders as Mother attempted to get up in her sleep. *Yee-jeong* rose to his feet from the chair, feeling as nervous as anybody who stood in the room. Lei Yee adjusted the gauze pads on Mother's eyes. But that could not disguise Mother's sheer miserable look. She was murmuring. The words on the tip of her tongue were like fish bones choking her relentlessly.

"I'm sorry but I think it's better for you to leave her at the moment," Lei Yee said to *Yee-ma*. "The patient is overexcited and her status is very unstable. She needs to calm down instantly."

Soaring Swallow pulled her mother's arm. *Yee-ma*'s eyes welled up. Her eyes and cheeks were pinkish red. She turned around and walked with *Yee-jeong* to the doorway. I briefly said goodbye to all of them while patting Mother's body gently, as if she was a crying baby in a crib.

Lei Yee inserted a tablet into Mother's mouth with water. Gradually, Mother calmed down. She returned to her marathon slumber. The ECG number declined to the normal rate. The rhythmic pattern of green waves reappeared. The beep was in sync with my watch again. I was relieved a little.

"Your mother must have a strong feeling for her sister," Lei Yee said.

"Yes," I sighed and said. "How do you know?"

"Her strong reaction says it all."

"I thought she was in a coma and couldn't respond to anyone."

"Not quite. It's the air, the biological sensor, the exterior sounds—everything is possible to trigger a coma patient's subconscious mind. I've seen this situation before with other patients."

Lei Yee thought for a second and let her words sink in. She went on, "Your mother and her sister are blood related. Believe it or not, she can feel her sister's presence. Her eruption of excitement comes out of this kinship connection."

"I'm her daughter. I wonder if she can feel my presence," I said.

"You're different. You come to the hospital every day. She knows you're here with her. She has already been familiar with you. But her sister doesn't come to see her too often. That's why she has an unusual reaction," Lei Yee explained.

Her words sent a ripple of dread down my spine. Having no siblings, I could not understand how love could lock two sisters' hearts, and how that same kind of blood flowed through two lives, sending signals to search for the other. What would Mother want to say to *Yee-ma* the most? Did she want to tell her how much she missed her sister? Was she choked up with words of joy, or of wrath?

Did she want to ask the same question as me—*why the hell are you here now?*

Seconds slipped away. I did not know what time of the day it was. By the time my mind came back to reality, I realized Father had reappeared in the room. He asked me to go home to change my clothes and catch up on some sleep. Perhaps my bloodshot eyes had given away the fact that I had stayed up the night before. I agreed to go home only if he let me stay overnight in the hospital again. He was reluctant. He thought the whole night shift would make me collapse. I assured him I could handle the night shift better than he could. Perhaps his lingering fear of hurting Mother again overcame his masculinity. He backed off as I wished. I left the hospital after thirty-two hours and I planned to come back later to change shifts with Father.

I waited for the elevator to arrive at the sixth floor. As the metal doors glided open, two young robust men in dark plain clothes pushed a gurney out of the car. Both of them wore a pair of black rubber gloves, like the ones on a fishmonger's hands. One man had bushy hair; the other had a long face. They did not look at me at all as if I were invisible. Somehow their deadpan faces caught my attention. I nearly missed the elevator.

I was the only passenger. My mind flashed across those two pairs of fierce-looking eyes. Who were those two men? They looked more like gangsters who were about to rob a bank than like medical workers. Suddenly, I felt the elevator was cloaked in creepy cold air. Shafts of fear descended on me.

Seconds later, a sound of *ding* alerted me. An assuring thud of the car shook off the scary images in my mind. I had safely arrived onto the ground floor. My quickened heartbeat slowed down as the elevator doors opened again. The hustle and bustle of Hengfu Road re-energized me. I felt as if I were a prisoner released from the penitentiary. Yet, my incarcerated time was not done yet. I was on a parole. After another six hours, I shall be back. Never mind. It was still good to hear the urban sounds again.

Chapter 13

Bai-shi

It was three days before Halloween in 2007. The real nip in the air grew stronger in subtropical Guangzhou. Because of the crisp cool breeze, people were reluctant to stand near drafty windows. The sun was radiant in a clear high sky. Its glaring rays of light seemed to be a bit too much, whitening the green curtain in Mother's room to a splodge of lime green.

Mother continued with her marathon coma, showing no signs of giving up. After one hundred and eight hours, her heart rate fluctuated between forty-five and sixty-something BMP. The beep of the ECG monitor spoke for the silence between Lei Yee and me. Father had just left after his youngest brother, Uncle Sei, who paid a visit to Mother. Since he squeezed the time from his hectic business agenda, he ought to receive accolades for his presence. Mother used to joke that Uncle Sei was busier than the Prime Minister, so busy that he did not even have time for his family life. Wasn't that also true for many money-oriented Chinese?

I sat on the wooden chair, gazing at Mother with a hollow echo in my mind. I had overheard that a male patient on the same floor had passed away the day before. Quietly and swiftly, the news was like a malignant tumor spreading among the paramedics' mouths. I did not know that patient but I figured out which room he used to occupy. Now vacant, the room was opposite the one where Mother used to stay. I remembered seeing Dr. Cheng go in and out of that room when he came to the hospital for a medical meeting. He must have known that male patient fairly well, perhaps better than he knew Mother. I also recalled hearing a young woman sobbing when I passed by that room a few nights before. Leaning against the back of the chair, I brooded over what would come next.

The tune of the Beatles' "Yesterday" suddenly blasted. It was my mobile phone ringing. Panicked, I immediately silenced the phone and walked out of the room to answer it. I was afraid that the unexpected ringtone would interrupt Mother's seemingly stable brain activity. The caller ID showed the name Frank.

"Hello," I answered the phone in English.

"Hi," my American teacher said. "I don't want to disturb you. But I'd like to know how your mother is doing and how about you? You sounded very sad on the phone yesterday."

"Thanks for asking," I said, turning around to check Mother. "She's still in a deep coma. My dad and my uncle were here a few minutes ago. Sorry that I have you worried."

As I conversed with Frank, Lei Yee cried, "Xiao Zhang, come and see! Your mother is having a seizure. Together with her highly-strung voice came the rapid sound of the ECG monitor from the room. Cutting off the line, I scrambled to Mother's bedside. I halted, shocked at what was happening before me. Mother's out-of-control heartbeat seemed to have jolted her. She jerked fiercely, as if high voltage zapped through her body. Her mouth opened wide, breathing in all the air it could take. Her gasp raced with the beep of the ECG monitor, overlapping one another. The readings went skyrocketing high. They were so quick and so red that I thought the monitor would explode from malfunction.

"Quick, call the doctor!" Lei Yee shouted, pressing Mother down in bed. The authority of her words kept me from retreating into the shock that had paralyzed me.

I turned around and ran like Forrest Gump towards the nursing station.

"Plea-plea-se," I stuttered, "my *Ma*—my *Mama*, she's in danger! Send the doctor in immediately!"

The on-duty nurse must have sensed the urgency from my pale face. She stood up and said, "Got it! I'll call the doctor right away! Go stay with the patient." The scrape of her chair against the floor as she turned away sent a chill down my spine.

I ran back to the room. Lei Yee was gripping Mother's shoulders down as Mother struggled to get up but her strength failed her. Short of breath, Mother looked like a drowning child. I felt as if I had lost my memory. Everything that was familiar—Mother, Lei Yee, the white bed sheet, the metal single bed, the intravenous pole, the ECG monitor, the beep of its sound, the wooden chair, the sit-on toilet, the antiseptic odor that permeated in the room—suddenly became strange. I looked away to the windows shaded by the green curtain. The afternoon sunshine was relentless. It penetrated the nooks and crannies of the windows as a strong breeze kicked open the green curtain.

"Call your father now," Lei Yee said. Like a robot being commanded, I stiffly picked up my mobile phone and dialed Father's phone number. Each pending *Dooooooo* ring sounded like a span of a thousand years. Father finally answered the phone.

"Come back to the hospital," I said bluntly, omitting the usual respect a daughter should show to her father. "*Mama*'s life is in danger."

"Yes, I'll be there shortly," Father said. He sounded terrifyingly calm. We both hung up the phone at the same time.

Just as I was calling Father, a bespectacled doctor strode in, followed by two nurses who pushed a cart of first-aid drugs and tools. I retreated to the doorway to give room for the influx of people and equipment. The doctor must have noticed the flashing red alarm on the ECG monitor as he approached Mother. Assisted by the first nurse, he held down Mother's arm with one hand, accepted a drug-loaded syringe with the other. Quietly, he injected the drug into Mother's arm without the slightest hesitation. I stood by the door like a mute watchdog. The two standing nurses blocked half of my sight. I could only see partly what was happening in the room. But I was too scared to crane my neck to find out more.

Father showed up in the blink of an eye, as if he sprung from a magician's hat. He told me when I called him he was waiting for the bus. The look of horror on his face was all I could remember. He saw the doctor and the nurses were preoccupied with the procedure of rescuing Mother. He stepped aside, watching the commotion in the room at a distance.

Outside Mother's room was a row of windows at the end of the hallway. Not far from them was an exit to the stairwell. Standing close to those windows, I felt the warmth on my back as the sunshine flooded in. Its warmth heated up my anxiety. I kept peeking inside. The three white-clad angels surrounded Mother, as if they were performing a sacred ritual on a dying body. I averted my gaze to the hallway. A couple of paramedics seemed to have noticed something was happening on the sixth floor. They came out of other rooms and looked in my direction. I avoided their stare.

Minutes went by. I heard whispers between the doctor and his assistants. Another few minutes nibbled away. A nurse rushed out, as if she had forgotten something. Stricken by despair, Father and I both crowded the doorway. The doctor motioned us to come closer.

"I think it's time for you to call her immediate relatives now," the doctor announced, his white sleeves folded halfway to his elbow. "The patient doesn't have much time left."

As the doctor's words slowly seeped into me, the nurse who just ran out returned. In her hands was a white chest, on the top of which was emblazoned a red cross. Father had stepped out of the room, making phone calls. As the nurse who stood next to the doctor opened the chest, I saw a dozen glass vials tidily standing shoulder to shoulder, as if they were miniature soldiers waiting for their command. With the doctor's instruction, the nurse swiftly took out one of them and extracted its small dose of drug with a syringe. Slowly pressing out the air from the syringe, she injected the needle in Mother's body—near her heart. Mother's story about how *Popo* passed away after receiving a shot on the surgery bed occurred in my mind. My heart quickened like it was experiencing a free fall. Would Mother's life end the same way? My question was answered in no time. The drug effectively slowed Mother's heart rate to a safe range. The red alarm on the ECG monitor was released. While the nurses were pushing the first-aid cart out of the room, I heard Father growling under his breath.

"Shit," Father sputtered, "the whole family is alike."

"What happened?" I turned to Father and asked.

"Nobody answers the phone in your *Yee-ma*'s house, or at Soaring Swallow's," Father said angrily.

"Let me try," I said. "You call Wai Syu and Mr. Liang."

I knew Father had lost his cool to talk to *Yee-ma* anyway. Her son, Wai Syu, and Mr. Liang were probably the only two close members that mattered to Father. I fetched his mini directory and dialed my cousin Soaring Swallow's husband's mobile phone number. The phone rang a few times. It finally got through. My cousin-in-law answered the phone.

"Is Soaring Swallow next to you?" I asked without saying hello.

"Yes, hold on." My cousin-in-law passed the phone to his wife.

As soon as I heard Soaring Swallow's voice, I spitted out, "Please come to the hospital right away. My mother is dying." The last word rang in my ears with a deafening echo, as if I had struck a gong too hard. I gulped to clear my ear pressure, then said, "I can't reach *Yee-ma* and *Yee-jeong*. Can you help me inform them as well?"

"My Ma is here in the store with me," Soaring Swallow said tensely. "And my *Ba* is probably out for an afternoon stroll. But I'll reach him and we'll be there soon."

I hung up the phone and told Father that *Yee-ma* and her family were on their way to the hospital. Father also told me her son and Mr. Liang were coming. He walked into Mother's room to see her. The doctor and the nurses had gone. Lei Yee was washing Mother with a towel, as if she wanted Mother to present her best at the farewell. I came to Mother's bedside and held her small hand. It was lukewarm and partly scrunched like a bird's claw. She lay on her back straight and stiff. Her feet were slightly parted, pointing outwards. I leaned close to her head, whispering to her ear, "Mom, I love you." I wondered how much courage I had to muster to say those three words. It was rare for a Chinese to express feelings so directly, let alone saying "I love you." But I knew if I had not said it, I would never had the chance.

I saw a sparkle of excitement in Mother's half-open eyes. The doctor had removed the gauze pads from her eyes. Her iris was hidden underneath her eyelids. She seemed to look upwards, revealing the whites saturated in water. Her tawny face looked more pallid as if it were made of frosted glass. All the time I was with her, her chest hardly heaved, suggesting her breathing was faint and fragile.

I was so focused on Mother that I did not notice Father standing behind me. *Yee-jeong* and Wai Syu had arrived. Father greeted them briefly. As I heard their voices, I stood up and stepped back.

"My mother and sister are on their way by taxi," Wai Syu said to Father.

"Yes, they'll be here shortly," *Yee-jeong* chimed in. Perhaps because of *Yee-jeong*'s high-blood pressure, his bloodshot eyes looked even more noticeable on his reddening face.

I had never seen Wai Syu well up. His eyes were red, too. Father went to the bathroom to let out his emotion behind the door. Suddenly, a disturbing long beep squealed. A straight line went across the screen of the ECG monitor. That line was like an eternal dash, indicating so many words unsaid, things undone, and people unseen. Mother left me, left all of us just like that—quietly and peacefully. Perhaps she was too weary to wait any longer. Perhaps she thought it was better this way—while Father was away and *Yee-ma* had not arrived—to bid her farewell. Perhaps she saw her parents waving to her to join them on the other side of another world.

Appalled, I stood as stiffly as Mother lay in bed. The bespectacled doctor reappeared in the room immediately. He listened to Mother's heart with the stethoscope again. He pulled open Mother's eyes with his fingers, examining her pupils with a flash light. Father must have heard the long beep. He came out of the bathroom just as the doctor announced Mother's death.

"I'm sorry. The patient's death is confirmed at 2:06 pm," the doctor said solemnly after checking his watch. "Please send one of her immediate family to the nursing station to complete the release procedure." By that, he meant a family member needed to discuss with a nurse how long the corpse was to be kept in the morgue. The family also needed to pay off the medical expenses and obtain a signed medical certificate of death.

"Doctor, could you please give us a few more minutes?" Wai Syu asked. "My mother and sister are about to arrive."

The doctor nodded and said, "Don't take too long. The orderlies will come soon to take care of the body." He turned and left.

Father stood in front of the bathroom. Tears of sadness erupted from his eyes. His weather-beaten face looked like a creased paper towel, strained and soaked. Lei Yee motioned to me to go comfort Father. She also looked sad but remained calm, as if she was sending me a message—*Be strong. Don't cry.*

Surprisingly, I shed no tears.

I had questioned myself every day how would I face this moment when Mother passed away. I had expected to wail the loudest like Mother did at Granny's funeral. I had prepared myself to become a wreck, unable to support Father. But nothing happened the way I imagined. I thought crying was as contagious as laughter. I thought I would be moved to tears after seeing Father's, Wai Syu's and *Yee-jeong*'s reddish, moist eyes.

My eyes were dry like a desert.

Even though I squeezed my eyes hard, they were dehydrated. Something was wrong with me. The more I saw how bereft Father was, the calmer I felt. As a famous Chinese proverb says, "Things will develop in the opposite direction when they become extreme."

Perhaps I had reached the climax of misery. The abnormal composure was my only reaction to Mother's death.

* * * * * *

Yee-ma and Soaring Swallow finally showed up. Like the other day, *Yee-ma* was overwhelmed with sorrow. She wept and murmured in front of Mother's bed, praying beads in her hands. I reckoned she was saying her Buddhist prayer for Mother. It was her ritual to bid farewell. After a few minutes, she gave me a small, brown, paper pack.

"This is from *Baat Goo-Po*," *Yee-ma* said to me. "She got it through her Buddhist congregation. Unwrap it and sprinkle the *zhusha* on your mother's forehead."

I did as I was told. What *Yee-ma* handed to me was the fine powder of cinnabar, a mineral with a reddish brown color. It was said cinnabar could expel evil spirits. *Why doesn't Yee-ma do it herself? Wouldn't it be more sincere and appropriate if she sprinkles the zhusha on her sister's forehead? Is she frightened that Mother might revive and have a fit like the other day? Is she scared to touch a dead body?* A wave of questions swept over me.

I held Mother's hand once more. It was cold and hardened. The aura of her existence had perished, like a shooting star. Only an empty body remained. I thought my morbid fear of death would make me faint. I was only inches away from a corpse. But I did not faint. Sobered, I pecked on Mother's forehead and whispered to her, "Mom, I love you." I let go my hand and salted the vermilion *zhusha* on her forehead, hands and feet.

Thinking back, I would not have that courage to finish *Yee-ma*'s ritual if the dead body before me were not my mother. It was the family love that strengthened me to make the extraordinary effort. It was also the family love that hindered me to make vital decisions. Had I agreed to have Mother use a colostomy bag or undergo surgery and chemotherapy, would her life have been any easier?

"Xiao Zhang," Lei Yee jolted me out of my conflicting soliloquy. "It's time you and your relatives leave the room. The orderlies are on their way to remove your mother's body. Let me change her clothes now."

I looked to the doorway. Father and Wai Syu were in the hallway, surrounded by several women paramedics. Following *Yee-*

ma and the other family members, I walked out of the room. The paramedics crowded around me immediately like a swarm of desperate paparazzi. But they were not looking for a scoop. They all offered to help out cleaning the room. Bombarded by their eagerness, I let them in. They raided in like hungry wolves. The door closed behind me.

Yee-ma and the others waited outside by a row of windows. I told Father I would take care of Mother's release affairs. He and Wai Syu walked away to the other end of the hallway for a smoke. Seeing Wai Syu wrapping his arm over Father's shoulders and both of them diminishing in my sight, my sorrow was mixed with relief. At least someone was with Father, giving him that sort of comfort I could not understand—the male mentality.

* * * * * *

At the nursing station, I spoke to one of the nurses who just now tried to rescue Mother. She leaned against the counter, and took notes while asking me questions.

"What's the name of the patient?"

"Golden Orchid."

"What's her date of birth?"

"February 15, 1954."

"What's your relationship with the patient?"

"I'm her daughter," I answered matter-of-factly.

"What time did she pass away?"

"At 2:06 p.m.," I said after a thought.

"How long do you want the body be kept?"

"I don't know. How long can I have it kept?"

"It varies," the nurse said, looking at me in amazement, as if I were too immature to deal with this sophisticated adult matter.

I returned my gaze to her, suggesting she carry on.

"We usually have the body embalmed for two to three days."

"That's it?" I questioned. "Any longer period? We haven't decided a date for the funeral yet."

"Well," the nurse paused for a second and said, "seven days is the longest. Or you have to pay extra money for more days."

I felt as if I was transported to the day when I signed the surgery waiver before Mother was permitted to be discharged. I had to make a decision for my family again. But I did not have the answer to the nurse's question. I only knew I would not go for the option of paying more.

"OK. Seven days then," I said firmly.

"Sure. Dr. Li isn't here today. He has to sign the death certificate. And without the death certificate, you can't prove to the cashier that the patient is released. So why don't you come back tomorrow to get the paperwork and pay the bill?"

"You mean I can leave now?"

"Yes. And bring back this receipt tomorrow," the nurse said, handing me a long breakdown of Mother's medical expenses. It was like a medical diary, recording the everyday medication and the costs. Holding my breath, I looked at the bottom for the sum— 14,909.04 *yuan* for eighteen days of hospitalization. It would be an astronomical number for my family if I did not have a full-time job. But like Father said, it was manageable. I released my breath.

By the time I returned to Mother's room, she had been dressed in her plain clothes. The half dozen paramedics who I just let in reached their hands to me on their way out. I did not know what they wanted. Lei Yee prompted me, "By custom, you should give them red packets."

I came to realize why these women were so fervent to help out. They disgusted me more than the professional beggars around the bus stop on Hengfu Road.

"I don't have any red packets. Can I give you bare cash?" I said, my hand reaching into my handbag for my wallet. I could not wait to get rid of these greedy charlatans.

"Here," I said, handing out a wad of ten *yuan* notes, as if I had become a wealthy philanthropist.

The crowd dissipated. I gave a note of twenty *yuan* to Lei Yee. She refused. I insisted and said, "You deserve this money more than anyone. My father and I are very grateful to you."

"No," Lei Yee said. "Your father often paid me extra in addition to my wages. I'm the one who is grateful to you for supporting my family. You should save this money for your mother's funeral." She paused a moment and added, "Even though she's not around you now, you know she's always proud to have you as her daughter."

Lei Yee's eyes welled up. She held my hand and pushed the money back to me. I did not push back. At this moment, two men strode in rashly, parking a gurney parallel to Mother's bed. They looked familiar to me. They wore a pair of big black gloves. Their dark plain clothes looked the same as...A ripple of horror passed through me. Gosh! They were the two fierce-looking men at the elevator! So, they were corpse scavengers! The other day they must have been here on the sixth floor to remove Mother's male neighbor's dead body. How stupid I was. I did not realize my encounter with them at the elevator was an omen of Mother's death.

The two young men seemed to know their job only too well. Swiftly, they wrapped Mother's dead body with a human-sized black tarpaulin bag. Long Face jumped on the bed and lifted one end of the bag. Bushy Hair lifted up the other end. Together, they moved the cumbersome bag onto the gurney as easy as brushing their teeth. With one pushing and the other pulling the gurney, they disappeared like a swirl of wind. The bed was now empty. On the white bed sheet were several overlapping gray footprints. Tissues and papers scattered on the floor. The room looked like a shop being looted.

"Now, take home the things that you want," Lei Yee said. "We'll have the cleaners clean the room thoroughly later."

Father and Wai Syu came back to the room just in time. We emptied the night stand and took away the useful stuff that belonged to Mother. It was believed that the effects of the deceased bring bad luck. I did not know that until *Yee-jeong* reminded me.

"Leave them here. You can get these things in the store easily," he said, seeing me folding Mother's towels.

"I know," I said, annoyed by his supervision. He would not understand how much Mother's effects could help me remember her and give me solace for the days to come.

We roughly packed up a few things, leaving Mother's personal items behind. I secretly tucked the small yellow pillow into my handbag. I remembered Mother used to rest her feet on that pillow which had a cartoon lion's smiling face.

Before I left the room, I said goodbye to Lei Yee. I gave her a hug, as if she embodied the warmth of my mother.

* * * * * *

I will never forget that day—October 29, 2007. Father, Wai Syu and I scrambled into a cab in front of the hospital. Holding my bulky handbag tightly in my arm, I looked at the one-building hospital that we had just exited. The setting sun gilded the building's whitewashed façade, on which danced the shadows of the hustle and bustle on Hengfu Road. The noise on the street sounded like jubilation of Mother's new life in heaven. I made a little prayer. *May Mom rest in peace. May Mom have found her Hengfu, her everlasting happiness.*

For a long time, I did not avert my gaze until the building vanished from my sight.

* * * * * *

Having discussed with *Yee-ma*, *Yee-jeong* and Mr. Liang, Father and I set the date—three days after Mother's death—for her funeral. In Chinese, we call funerals *Bai-shi*, white events. White connotes mourning and grief, whereas red represents happiness and celebration. As a result, weddings are also called *Hong-shi*, red events. By Chinese custom, if one family has a *Bai-shi*, the family members are not allowed to attend any *Hong-shi* for a month or perhaps longer. It is believed that the bereaved members will bring bad luck to the newly-weds. For that reason, Father's nephew could not attend Mother's funeral. His wife was pregnant, which was also considered a *Hong-shi*.

With the help of Mr. Liang, Father and I went about the city to arrange Mother's funeral. We aimed to make it simple to accord with Mother's simple lifestyle. For the first time, I experienced the nitty gritty of a Chinese funeral. All businesses in China seemed to be specialized, including planning a funeral. Like organizing a *Hong-shi*, one could throw hundreds of thousands of *yuan* for a *Bai-shi*. At the funeral home office, we got a booklet in which were listed various packages at different price ranges. We picked the most economical one that included a paper coffin, basic makeup, a shroud, flowers, rental for a ceremony room with simple décor, and a master of ceremonies. We also bought a big white cloth, some ghost money and paper offerings, a black photo frame, a black armband for Father and a hairpin with an indigo ribbon for me. We needed to wear them because we were the immediate bereaved family. Mr. Liang told me in old China, the bereaved children had to put on white capes and white clothes from head to toe at the funeral.

Father asked me to look for a close-up photo of Mother. I rummaged through dozens of pictures taken in the past twelve months and found a few of them for him to choose from. Each of these photos conjured up my memory of Mother's happy time. Father picked a unique one to enlarge as a black-and-white portrait at Mother's funeral.

That picture was taken in Father's ancestral hometown— Xingxing county in Guangdong province. It was in March when the three of us together with Mr. Liang went there for a brief visit. Except for Father, none of us had been to his home town. Mother had been looking forward to another outing since our successful trip to Shaoguan on New Year's Day. The change of scenery in fact relaxed her and strengthened her optimism for life.

I remembered we met Father's eighty-year-old aunt and her family. The four generations lived in a bright three-story townhouse adjacent to acres of rice paddy fields. In the center of the house was a color poster of Chairman Mao. As a city girl, I thought worshipping Mao was already out of fashion. But it was a belief in some Chinese villages that Mao was considered a powerful figure that could expel evil spirits. So Mao's posters were like Chinese door gods' images, often hung in the center and front, facing the doorway. Besides growing rice and other crops, Father's cousin showed us his chicken farm within walking distance. He said today's chicken feed could increase a chick's growth significantly. Within three months his little chicks became roosters and hens. Pointing at his almost empty cages, he said with a grin, revealing his yellow cigarette teeth, "You're out of luck. I just sold a batch of chickens in town a few days ago."

On the sandy path from the house to the chicken farm, Mother smiled as brightly as the sun in spring, radiating the knee-high verdant crops on both sides of the path. Walking side by side with Father's aged aunt, Mother revealed the most natural and innocent expression.

Ka-cha! My finger released the shutter. Mother did not notice that I took a candid shot of her. She wore her favorite orange polka dot blouse and a pair of black pants. Her newly-trimmed hair was short and dark, shining in the sun.

"Normally, it's inappropriate to have a memorial picture of the deceased person smiling with a half-open mouth," Father commented in his workshop, holding that photo. "But your mother looks most relaxed and natural when she smiles like that."

"I think we should show the best of her," I said. "Let the sweet memory last in everyone's mind."

It was easy to persuade Father this time. He took that picture and had the image etched on a porcelain tile. Together with my grandparents' images, Mother's picture was placed in the center on the altar in our house. At last, she could be reunited with her parents.

* * * * * *

At the wake, we had incessant visitors to our house starting in the late afternoon. I had never received so many guests in one day, not even during Chinese New Year. Besides my relatives who were expected to come, the managing editor, Alice Wan, and a colleague on behalf of my company, also paid a visit to my house. Uncle Cheong and his siblings' family also visited us. I was amazed at how Mother's death could draw a number of familiar people together again under one roof. The atmosphere was warm and reflective. For my family, such a reunion was as rare as a warm embrace between my parents. Why couldn't this moment have happened more often when the deceased was alive?

Father converted the TV stand into a makeshift altar for our mourning. He covered the stand with a big white cloth and placed Mother's portrait in the middle, flanked by white ginger lily— Mother's favorite. Before the portrait were an incense burner, a bundle of joss sticks, a plate of pears, a box of candies and some coins. The pronunciation of "pear"—"li" in Chinese shares the same sound with the character "separation"; the pears connote our separation with Mother. Candies bring sweetness. After mourning Mother which was considered a bitter experience, the guest took a candy and a coin as reward. It reminded me of the times after I had drunk the traditional Chinese medicine, Mother often handed me a candy.

Everyone who came that night contributed some money for Mother's *Bai-shi*. I was told to mark down their names and their contribution so in the future when these families had *Bai-shi*, I would reciprocate.

Traditionally, the money donated to the bereaved is usually a round figure with an extra one *yuan*. I did not know the reason until *Yee-jeong* explained to me. While I was taking notes, he handed me two hundred and one *yuan* and said, "This is from *Yee-ma* and me."

"Why is there one *yuan* extra?" I asked.

"So the *Bai-shi* happens only once. No more," he said emphatically, as if I should not have asked him such an obvious question.

Indeed, nobody would want to experience another *Bai-shi*, especially to the superstitious people like *Yee-jeong*. Chinese people worship double happiness but not double sadness. By custom, the bereaved family gives one *yuan* and a candy to the funeral attendees as appreciation. Or you can take it this way. If the money donated to the bereaved is a round figure, there will be a number nine in the last digit after the subtraction of one *yuan*. Number nine signifies eternity. Who would want a *Bai-shi* to last permanently?

That Chinese people have a fixation with auspicious numbers bewilders me. Good things should come double. Gifts for the *Hong-shi* are in pairs. The lucky money on Chinese New Year is always a round figure. The pricing on consumer goods, food, and many other things is often associated with the numbers six and eight. They both connote a wish of making a pile of money.

Overnight, I did feel rich. I collected nearly four thousand *yuan*, including five hundred *yuan* from my company as an employee benefit. The money covered the flower wreaths and a reunion dinner. It is customary that after the funeral the bereaved family invite all the guests for a dinner.

Unexpectedly, I received a phone call from Aunt Fragrance. I had not seen her for several weeks. Mother was too ill to pay visits to *Yee-Po* and her.

"Just wanted to remind you to bring an extra bag of your mother's clothes and shoes to the funeral tomorrow," Aunt Fragrance wasted no time and said directly. "My mother said it's a Buddhist belief that the body should be cremated together with the clothes. So when your mother gets to heaven, she'll have plenty of clothes to wear."

"OK. Will do," I said, perplexed by her words.

"You don't need to bring too many pieces. But select a few sets of your mother's favorite clothes of all seasons. So she won't be frigid in winter," Aunt Fragrance added. "My mother won't attend the funeral but I'll be there. See you tomorrow."

After the phone call, I searched Mother's wardrobe and chose several decent blouses and pairs of pants. Her new and old clothing were apart distinctly. To my surprise, Mother had many new clothes unworn. They looked fresh and bright. The old ones must have been her favorite as their colors were mostly faded.

"Your *Mama* is a thorough hoarder," Father walked in the bedroom and said. He must be aware of Mother's collection of unworn clothes.

"She's like you. As long as the old ones were wearable, she didn't want to put on something new," I said, bundling a bag of clothes together.

Father did not say anything but his face was filled with regret.

"Bring this bracelet," he said, giving me Mother's jade bracelet.

"You sure you want it to be cremated, too?" I asked in surprise. The jade bracelet was silky smooth and shining, suggesting Mother had worn it for a long time from the day she got it from Father as a present.

"Yes," Father replied as if he had mulled it over. "I know it's your mother's favorite. I want it to be with her forever."

He left the room quickly as if he did not want me to see a fit of emotion overflowing on his face. I wrapped the bracelet carefully and tucked it between the clothes in the bag.

* * * * * *

Like Father and Mr. Liang said, I was inexperienced in planning a *Bai-shi*. The last time I was at a funeral was when Granny passed away ten years before. The procedure was vague in my memory. I only remembered hearing a peal of wailing and dirge at the ceremony and we had a vegetarian dinner afterwards.

Now, ten years later, I returned to the funeral home. The place looked more modern and spacious than I remembered. Wide corridors, walls of manicured pine trees, clean and bright, it was like a park but cloaked in an air of solemn silence. In the main building, ceremony rooms lined up one after another and floor by floor. It looked like a classroom building to me.

As the bereaved family, we had to arrive early to make sure everything was ready. I was like a toddler of *Bai-shi* planning. The whole day I followed Father and Mr. Liang and did what I was told. We left the bag of Mother's clothes to an office worker. I learned that the undertakers dressed Mother and applied makeup to her prior to the funeral. After signing in, the suit-clad office worker led us to the ceremony room. It was on the ground floor. The décor looked just as we had seen it in the funeral home booklet.

The elegiac couplet was hung on either side of a glass platform that led to the viewing of Mother's body. The wording of the elegiac couplet was in the form of ancient Chinese literature. Similar to Japanese Haiku, its pithy and balanced characteristics were evidence of the concept of "less is more." I selected the couplet that was appropriate for the death of a mother. Its general idea was: her virtue is hard to forget, her grace is remembered forever. The centerpiece was an eye-level high flower basket under my name. The red roses formed a heart shape surrounded with yellow chrysanthemum. It was my dedication for Mother's greatest love. On both sides of the room were the flower wreaths contributed by our relatives and friends, most of whom attended Mother's funeral.

"I just got the notice," the office worker said to us after talking to the walkie-talkie in her hand. "The makeup is done. You may view from the glass platform. When the ceremony begins, we'll elevate the body from the vault."

Father and Mr. Liang walked near the glass platform and looked down. I followed suit. We were probably three-story high from the vault. Apparently, this modern building had a huge basement which served as a secret passage from the funeral home to the crematorium. The mechanical noise wafted from down under. The vault was well-lit with a concrete floor. It was like a big workshop underground, unseen by the public's eyes.

Stunned, I saw Mother lying in a coffin, shrouded with a gold blanket, on which was embroidered ancient Chinese characters. The gold blanket covered her hands and feet. So I was not sure if she was wearing the jade bracelet that we had requested to put on her. Her body seemed to have shrunk to a size I could not remember. Like a swaddled infant, she was in deep sleep but with no movement. I felt as if my heart fell into the hole beneath the glass shield. I had not seen her for three days. I ached. What about three weeks, three years or thirty years from now? Perhaps the white light from the underground plant was too bright. It dimmed the color of Mother's face. She looked darker than I remembered, as if the undertaker had smudged mud on her face. The dot of rouge on her lips enhanced her unnatural expression. Mother rarely applied makeup on her face. This was probably her first and the last.

"What do you think?" the office worker asked, adjusting her black business suit. "If you're dissatisfied, I can forward your message to my colleague to modify it."

After a careful observation, Father said, "She has a lump on her forehead. I wonder if you can modify the bruise close to her skin complexion."

"Yes, no problem. Anything else?"

"No. I don't think so," Father said and removed himself from the glass shield.

I also gave a hard look at Mother's forehead. Her lump remained there, but not as bulging. I could not spot it right away.

"What about the room? Is everything OK?" the office worker asked Father.

"Yes," he replied after a glimpse of the entire room.

"So please allow me to go over the procedure with you now," the office worker said, pointing us to a waiting room next door. "You and your daughter will be waiting in that room while the guests enter here."

A wooden door led to a small waiting room next door. Two rows of chairs lined both sides of the wall. Like a lounge in a doctor's office, it was only a plain room with no decoration.

"After a dirge that lasts two minutes or so, the master of ceremonies will announce that the ceremony is to begin," the office worker continued. "You both enter the room and stand to the front. The master of ceremonies will say a few words and then all the attendees stand in silent tribute. Afterwards, you just follow the master of ceremonies' prompt and walk around the glass platform to view the body one last time. The guests will follow you."

As the office worker described the steps, Mr. Liang showed me how to walk to the glass platform.

"In a family with more than one child, the oldest one will hold the bereaved parent's arm," Mr. Liang said, demonstrating as if he were my father. He put my hand around his arm and said, "You, as the only child, will support your father like this and walk slowly to your mother's dead body."

I felt as if I were a poised bride walking with Mr. Liang down the aisle. Father and the office worker watched us aside.

"When you come here," Mr. Liang said. By then, we were standing in the midway around the glass platform. "You linger for a

271

moment. Face your mother and bow. The guests will follow you when they get to this spot."

Mr. Liang paused and allowed his words to sink in. He pointed to my mother's black-and-white portrait that faced squarely to the glass platform. He pretended he lifted the picture frame and said, "You step ahead before your father and take your mother's portrait with you, holding it straight with both hands in your arms, face up. Now you're the lead.

"You walk slowly toward the door and exit the room," Mr. Liang said.

I followed his steps and came to the doorway.

"You stand here, by the door with your mother's picture before you," Mr. Liang said at a moderate speed for fear I could not follow him. "Your father will stand next to you. He'll light the big joss stick. Both of you will stand here until all guests exit from the room. You show your gratitude for the guests' presence at the funeral by looking down in grief."

"Should I say something?" I asked lest I would miss a detail.

"No," Mr. Liang said with confidence. "It's a *Bai-shi*, unlike at a wedding banquet where you see smiles and hear gratitude from the newly-weds. Your solemn silence is sufficient. In the old days, you were supposed to kneel and bow to the guests. You would be too overwhelmed with the tearful mourning to say anything."

"Sir, you explain better than I can," the office worker interjected. She and I marveled at Mr. Liang's knowledge about the traditional and modern formalities of a Chinese funeral.

"I've lived too long," Mr. Liang said in a relaxed voice.

"What's next?" I asked.

"After the funeral," Mr. Liang answered, "you and your father will embark on the hearse together with the mourners. You'll go home to mourn your mother."

What a lesson. No wonder Mother used to say to me, "After you grow up, you'll understand many things." I guessed among the "many things" that she avoided discussing with me, planning a funeral was one of them.

* * * * * *

It was near noon. The guests in their plain dark clothes were arriving. Strangely, I felt no pressure at all. Perhaps Mr. Liang's rehearsal had reduced my nervousness. On the contrary, as each second approached nearer to the funeral, Father looked more and more tense; sitting in the waiting room, he lowered his head, and said nothing. I did not want to bother him. I walked out of the waiting room to see how many guests had arrived. As I saw Uncle Sahm and his family, I walked to them to say hi. Because the corridor was so long, I smiled as I walked briskly to meet them. My baggy, black, cotton pants flapped against me, evidently giving Uncle Sahm the impression I was too carefree.

"I know you take it easy about your mother's death," Uncle Sahm said after his greeting. "But this is a serious occasion. You shall learn to behave properly. Don't wear your smiling face to your guests."

Embarrassed, I tightened my face instantly like a mimosa folding its leaves when touched. *Do I really look at ease?* I questioned myself. *How many nights have I struggled with my dreadful thoughts about today, deplorably and desolately? Does Uncle Sahm know? Does anyone in my family know what a massive responsibility an only child must bear?* A fit of anger rushed to my mind. I had an impulse to correct Uncle Sahm's improper reminder on the spot. But Mr. Liang's words resonated with me. I held my peace and looked down in grief.

As the dirge rose, Father's grief grew. Only two of us were left in the waiting room. I got down on my knee and held Father's hand. I finally saw his welled-up eyes.

"*Baba*," I said, "Please don't be overly sad. Do you remember what I told you this morning? I'm an extension of Mother's life. Her body is dead but her spirit is always with us. So please don't dwell on her departure but on her continuation of life in me. We can get through this."

Father pulled out a pack of tissues from his pocket. He wiped off the tears in his eyes and from his nose. He took a deep breath and said, "OK. Let's proceed."

I held Father's arm and entered the ceremony room. Our relatives and friends were standing in an orderly formation—the immediate family at the front and friends at the back. Mr. Liang was on the side towards the back. I had dozens of legitimate reasons to qualify him to stand in the front row for his full devotion in helping out my family. His favor had exceeded even what an immediate family member should do. Our gaze met. Mr. Liang threw me a look of encouragement.

As planned, Mother's dead body was elevated to the same level of the ceremony room. Under the orange floodlight, she looked like a shiny wax figure, reclining on her back in her serenity. Her hair was still dark and dense. Her makeup must have been modified. Her lips were redder. Her forehead seemed to look darker, disguising the mild lump, which had become a new feature to help me recognize Mother's face. The lump was also a flaw that my handy Father could not fix.

As we stood before Mother's dead body, I could feel Father trembling. He burst into tears. I held his arm tightly in the hope that I could give him some strength. We bowed and continued to move on. Along with the dirge playing in the background, I began to hear sobbing and sniffling behind me. I made no mistake, just doing what I rehearsed with Mr. Liang. Holding Mother's portrait before my chest, I stood at the entrance and waited for the guests to exit. My eyes were dry again, not even affected by the thick smoke coming from the big long joss stick in Father's hand.

Everyone came out with a mournful look. *Goo-ma* walked in the company of her daughter-in-law. She blotted her swollen eyes with tissues. I had never seen her so sad. She probably not only mourned for Mother's death but also sympathized for her brother's forlorn new life as a widower.

The last people that left the ceremony room were Buddhist monks. I did not know we had invited them. I could not see them from the front either. Dressed in yellow robes with prayer beads in hands, half a dozen monks chanted a prayer song that I could not understand. They formed a circle around Mother's dead body and murmured in an alien language. I assumed they were reciting a Buddhist prayer specialized for a departed believer. They retreated from the room in a single file.

"Did you send these monks here?" I asked Father in a low voice.

"No. It's your *Yee-ma*'s idea," Father said. "For the respect of your mother, I'll leave the whole shebang at the will of your *Yee-ma* and *Yee-jeong*. They're her family, too."

I sensed Father's compromising reluctance. That feeling continued when we returned home. It is customary that the bereaved family must cross a burning metal basin before they enter the house. It is supposed to expel evil spirits and bad luck. So *Yee-jeong* arrived before us and set up a burning basin at the doorway. Holding Mother's portrait with my hands, I strode over the basin awkwardly, followed by Father. There was no rehearsal for this part of the ritual. I was worried that I would misstep and have my feet burnt rather than the fire scaring off evil spirits, if there were any.

It was also *Yee-jeong*'s idea that I walked in the company of his daughter, Graceful Swallow. Since I have no siblings, I was escorted by a female relative. So I would not be alone to take Mother's spirit home. After we entered the house, I placed Mother's portrait on the makeshift altar and Father planted the smoldering big joss stick into the incense burner. It was half burnt.

Traditionally, after the mourners offer incense to the deceased in her house, the bereaved family shall burn the paper offerings as well as the funeral accessories. Like a chief commander, *Yee-jeong* asked Wai Syu to control the fire in the metal basin. We threw in all sorts of paper offerings into the flame. They were ghost money for Mother to spend in heaven. It would make sense to practice this ritual if we were living at No. 14. We could burn anything to our ancestors in the open air in front of the house. But now we were living in an apartment building. Confined in space, a great cloud of smoke billowed from the metal basin, permeating the stairwell. If there was a fire alarm in our apartment building, the thick smoke would have triggered it.

I was relieved that I did not need to go near the fire again. I took off the hairpin with an indigo ribbon and passed it to Father. He also tossed his black armband into the flame. Seven days later I would learn that the white table cloth on the makeshift altar and Mother's portrait would also be burnt into ashes as a closure of our mourning.

To my astonishment, fire played such an important role after one's death. No wonder gunpowder is one of the four great inventions of ancient China. Our ancestors surely had a rich experience of playing with fire. I thought since Father was a chain smoker, to some extent, fire was his intimate friend. But as soon as he saw the white smoke spread through the house, his look changed from being mournful to resentful.

"What a mess!" Father seethed, and opened all the windows in the house. "He thinks he can turn this place into a temple."

He did not specify who but I knew he was talking about *Yee-jeong*.

"Take it easy," I said. "It only happens once and it's also the last."

After the ritual, Father went out in the company of Wai Syu to have a haircut. I was told to wash my hair and shower as a sign of a new beginning from head to toe. The customs and traditional belief that *Yee-jeong* brought into our house began to tire me. I kept saying to myself, w*hy am I doing all these things? Whom am I doing it for?* I felt foreign to the dos and don'ts of the old practices. They were harder for me to understand than the English grammar rules. Was this how superstition was passed down through generations? What if I were like Father who did not believe and did not want to follow suit? What if I just wanted to mourn Mother in my own way, simply and quietly? I knew Father felt the same way. I sympathized with him.

In terms of making a choice for living, I am more fortunate. My parents' generation has spent its entire life in acceding, willingly or not, to China's Communist Party movement; while the Chinese Echo Boomers—the post-80s and post-90s generations—have invested our lifetime in our own feelings and needs. Under the one-child policy, we have no choice of growing up with siblings, just as we cannot decide who can be our parents. But we have clearly known individualism from the day we were born. Once considered only in the capitalistic lexicon, the term "individualism" is now a mantra among hundreds of thousands of young Chinese.

Father often encourages me to follow my heart to choose the best way that works for me. I am grateful for that freedom of being able to make a choice. Like many young people, we challenge old traditions. We question them, simplify them, and even abandon them. Instead of reuniting with family during Chinese New Year, which is a rooted tradition, more people take the long vacation to travel for leisure. Instead of having a reunion meal at home at festivals, most Cantonese eat out to save the trouble of cooking and cleaning. The evening radio air in Guangzhou is filled with programs and commercials about solutions of various sexual problems. People are more open about sex so that couples cohabitate and enjoy their sex life before marriage. Or else, abortion is a quick fix to a mistake. More and more married couples enjoy the life of DINK—Double Income No Kids. All these changes would not be acceptable or even possible two decades ago.

I imagine it must be as hard as moving a mountain for ordinary people, such as my parents in their youth, to choose between what they want and what the tradition allows. Mother and Mr. Liang both told me before that in Red China, whoever spoke one negative word about the political leadership would be denounced or executed. The Chinese phrase—the wall has an ear—is a vivid description of how fearful people were in those days of their speeches. Mother used the phrase a lot to stop the unpleasant noise in the house. It was when we lived at No.14, usually after my bawling for something as a kid or Father's loud criticism. The *ear* that she was paranoid about was our gossipy neighbor, The Bitchy Stuff.

* * * * * *

Mother's death allowed me to witness how cancer had destroyed a life. According to the World Health Organization, cancer is a leading cause of death worldwide and accounted for around thirteen percent of all deaths in 2008. Colorectal cancer itself is the second most common cancer in women worldwide, and one of the most prevalent cancers in China, besides lung, stomach, liver and esophageal cancer. Now when I know someone has cancer, even if it appears in a fictional tale or TV drama, I feel as if a heavy sack has been loaded on my heart. Cancer is not easy to joke about once you have experienced it in your own life.

It was about a year from the day we found out Mother had cancer to the day she left us for good. That last year and the many that followed have deepened my understanding of many things. Mother was right. After I grew up, I would understand more adult matters.

I have come to realize where Father's pessimism comes from, and how Mother's depression has affected her whole life. It is a tough trial when two people are thrown together who are not interested in one another. It is a tragedy that neither of them can find happiness. Bound by traditional ways of doing, Father stuck with what was acceptable in the society at the time. His denial is shown in his mantra: It's not necessary. His early life experience had warned him not to dare authority or his life would be in trouble. He would rather seclude himself to live with his unaccomplished dreams.

Mother's attitude to the rooted Chinese values was slightly different. She obeyed exactly as she was told and as the norm allowed at the time. She would rather give up her right to say no in order to make everyone happy. She dared not to challenge *Popo* even though she was wrong to brutally punish Mother. She pleased her sister and brother-in-law even though they took advantage of her. She swallowed her pain even though Father was mean to her. She might pretend not to know her cancer to reduce my concern. No wonder my parents were reticent all their life. That is probably the only way to save them from troubles.

I remembered on one occasion after Mother's funeral, my cousin, Graceful Swallow, said to me, "You mother lived a tough life. Her cancer is caused by her depression." Seeing my bewildered look, she continued, "Yeah. We all have proto-oncogenes in our bodies. On any given days, these genes might induce a tumor. You see, your mother was under depression, mostly resulting from your father's rudeness, she was more prone to diseases. Her hyperthyroidism in earlier life was an example. Now she died of cancer."

At hearing her words, my heart quickened. Was it really Mother's long-time depression that was the killer of her life? Or was it Father who indirectly caused her death? What a horrendous presumption it was. No, I did not want to continue these dreadful thoughts. Why do we often blame someone's faults after bad things have happened?

After Mother's death, I overheard discussions from our relatives and friends over how she got the cancer. Some said it was a hereditary family disease. Some said her negligence of her health. Some said she was too thrifty to eat well. Some said it was an accumulation of overwork in years, both in the timber factory and as a homemaker. Father believed Mother was misinformed by her side of the family. Aunt Fragrance blamed the polluted air in Guangzhou in the last decade.

I took all of their speculations with a grain of salt. Even though both of Mother's parents had similar abdominal diseases, with all due respect, how come *Yee-ma* did not have cancer? Mother did not neglect her health. She was aware of the abnormal changes in her body. She consulted her older friends. She turned to traditional Chinese medicine for a solution. But she might not be knowledgeable enough about the severity of her symptoms.

One night after her death when I was cleaning my bedroom, underneath the mattress I found an old folded ledger, bounded by a rubber band. Curiously, I opened it to see what was in it. I saw Mother's handwriting. After a few pages of her scribbles about daily expenses on food and her period dates, there came a few more blank pages. Then the mundane records continued. Just when I began to show disinterest, among lines of illegible handwriting, she wrote clearly, "March 20, 2004, blood in stool after the dinner outside."

I burst into tears. For too long, my eyes had been in drought. But now, the tears that I had withheld all flooded out, unreservedly. Mother probably had no idea then that she had marked down one of the early symptoms of colon cancer. That was two years before her acceptance of a formal body checkup, three years before her death. Had she told me or a gastrointestinal specialist in time, her life might not have ended so soon. Our attitude towards her therapy might be also have been different. Why on earth had she kept this secret from me? I bet Father was in the dark as well.

I did not tell Father about Mother's notes. Nor did I tell him my reaction to the discovery of a gold necklace. Father told me a while before that Mother spent nearly all her savings on a gold necklace. She wanted to give it to me on my wedding day as a dowry. She kept it safely and secretly in her closet. Father had no idea where she hid it. But that day when I was cleaning her closet, I found the necklace in an inside pocket of one of her unworn coats. It was in a ring box wrapped by several layers of brown paper and in a small plastic bag. Its gold sparkled under the white light in the bedroom. On the back of the heart-shaped pendant was engraved two Chinese characters—*Xing Fu*, happiness. A ripple of grief swept through me. Holding the necklace in my palm, I wailed as if I had never done it before. The sound of it thundered in my eardrum and tore my heart. I did not stop until my tears had blocked my nostrils and I had to gasp through my mouth. My face was flushed. My eyes were swollen and sore. Thank heaven. My ten-minute fit did not catch Father's attention. He was in his workshop, probably mourning in his own way.

In the following few days, I became a little fearful to touch Mother's effects. If I had a choice, I did not want to disclose Mother's secrets. She had her reasons to keep them from us. However, Father urged me a few times that we should dispose Mother's stuff so we could move on with our lives. I decided to keep most of her stuff in my bedroom, at least for the time being—Mother's comb, her sunglasses, her apron, her kitchen tools, her new handbag, and even the birthday card from me. She got it earlier in the year on her fifty-third birthday—her last one. I remembered she beamed in tears when she got the new handbag from Prof. Zeitlin—her first birthday gift from a foreigner and my card.

In it, I wrote, "Dearest Mom, I am indebted to your love all these years. On your 53rd birthday, I hope you enjoy this joyful place where I bring you. Wish you happy birthday and good health." The joyful place I mentioned was a wildlife zoo in the outskirts of Guangzhou. Touted to be the largest in South China, the zoo offered a spectacular circus at night. As the advertisement promised, Mother had "a blast."

Whenever I re-read the birthday card, I was transported to that day and relived those loving moments. The whole day Mother wore her adorable smile that always tantalized me to kiss her dimpled cheeks. When she felt better, she walked ahead of me. When she was tired, she sat and leaned against me. For a long while, she rested her head on my shoulder, feeling safe, as if we were sisters, as if we were lovers, as if the world remained only the two of us, as if we could leave our social baggage behind. There, time and space froze for us. Yet, birth, age, illness and death continue the circle of life. Seasons change. Flowers bloom and fade. Nothing do we bring with us at birth, nothing can we take with us when we die. But the departed ones will always be remembered. In Octobers since, I have carried that weight of that October with me.